RIDING THE WAVE

Riding the Wave
Sweden's Integration into the Imperialist World System
by Torkil Lauesen

ISBN 978-1-989701-12-6

Published in 2021 by Kersplebedeb

To order copies of the book:
Kersplebedeb
CP 63560, CCCP Van Horne
Montreal, Quebec
Canada
H3W 3H8

info@kersplebedeb.com
www.kersplebedeb.com
www.leftwingbooks.net

Printed in Canada

The cover image is a detail from an export painting of Hongs at Canton (circa 1820, artist unknown), depicting the Thirteen Factories at Guangzhou. In the original, the flags of Denmark, Spain, the U.S., Sweden, Britain, and the Netherlands are visible.

RIDING THE WAVE

SWEDEN'S INTEGRATION INTO THE IMPERIALIST WORLD SYSTEM

TORKIL LAUESEN

KER
SPL
EBE
DEB
2021

Contents

Tables and Figures

In common English usage, Finland, Iceland, the Faroe Islands, and several other smaller islands are often considered part of Scandinavia. For the purposes of this book, however, the term refers only to the countries of Denmark, Sweden, and Norway. These three countries emerged as kingdoms in the period between the 10th and 13th centuries, and then became one kingdom—the Kalmar Union—in 1387, under Queen Margaret I of Denmark. Sweden was part of the union until 1523, when it became independent. Up until 1808 Finland was a province of Sweden. Norway was part of Denmark until 1814, when it entered a "personal union" with Sweden, with a common foreign policy and king. Norway became fully independent in 1905.

Over 10 million people live in Sweden today (compared to 5.3 million in Norway and 5.8 million in Denmark), and the three largest Swedish cities are Stockholm, Gothenburg, and Malmö. Today one in five inhabitants were born outside of the country.

The gross household income in International PPP$ in Sweden is the third highest in the world (behind Luxembourg and Norway) at $50,514 ($18,632 per capita), as compared to $43,585 ($15,480 per capita) in the United States—or $1,080 per capita in South Sudan and $1,320 in Liberia, countries which (as we shall see) are not as distant from Sweden as one might assume.

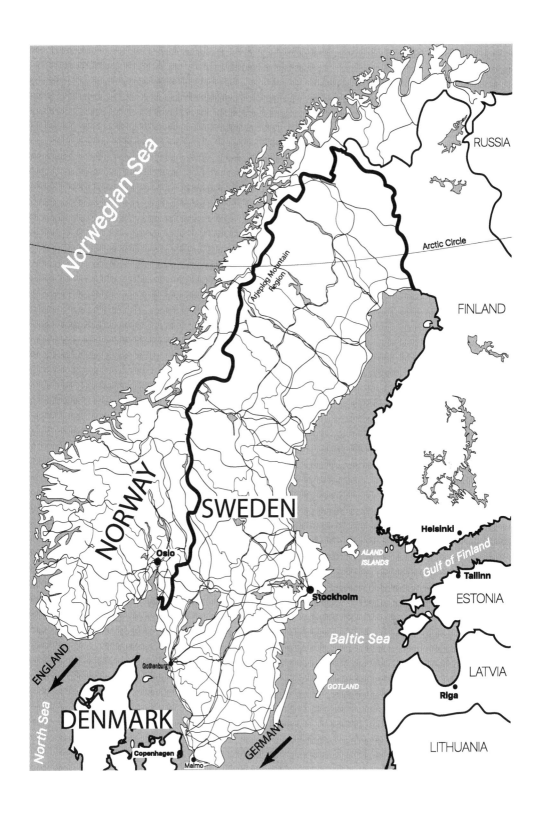

Introduction

This book is about Sweden's integration and role within global capitalism. It covers the period from 16th-century colonialism to the present day of transnational production chains. Sweden's economic and political system cannot be understood without this long and global perspective.[1] The development of global capitalism has significantly influenced the national contradictions that have come to define capitalism's special "Swedish model."

Globalization is not a new phenomenon. Capitalism has always been a world system. The breakthrough of industrial capitalism was closely linked to the Portuguese and Spanish looting of gold and silver from Latin America in the 16th century and Dutch, English, and French colonialism in the 17th and 18th centuries. The creation of the world system was at the same time a polarization of the world between a Northwest European core and the rest of the world, a colonial periphery. This process also shaped the birth and development of capitalism in Sweden.

The inter-imperialist contradictions of the late 19th century and the first half of the 20th century, between England, France, the USA, and Germany, were of great importance to the economic and political development of Sweden. Up until the Second World War, Sweden was economically and politically tied to Germany. The German defeat in the Second World War, however, changed and broadened Sweden's pattern of alliances in the direction of the USA and the rest of Europe. Simultaneous with the further development of the social democratic welfare state—the "people's home" (*folkhem*)—Sweden expanded its global economic and political influence in the 1950s and 60s. In the mid-1970s, the neoliberal counteroffensive hit Sweden's model welfare state hard, putting an end to 44 years

---

1. Torkil Lauesen, *The Global Perspective: Reflections on Imperialism and Resistance* (Montreal: Kersplebedeb, 2018).

of continuous social democratic rule. Outsourcing of industry, global finance, and migration flows have changed Swedish
society. One cannot understand Sweden without an analysis
of how national contradictions interact with capitalism's principal global contradictions. This may sound familiar, obvious,
and trivial. However, most studies of Sweden's economy and
politics start from a national perspective, with the global perspective merely presented as background information.

In this book, I will use examples from history, from
early colonialism to the present day, to trace the development of "the Swedish model." The "folkhem" is, according
to the Swedish self-perception, a special progressive form of
capitalism with social features. "Capitalism with a human
face." The Scandinavian capitalist welfare states are often
regarded as semi-socialist societies, by both left-wing politicians in the United States—like Bernie Sanders—as well as
politicians in many Third World countries. For the latter, the
Scandinavian countries' progressive image is bolstered by the
fact that they were not significant colonial powers and, even
moreso, because Sweden supported many Third World liberation struggles in the 1970s. Even on the more radical left, I
have come across the view that the social democratic welfare
state is a step towards socialism and that, "we can go with
the Social Democrats halfway to our goal." Such views are
manifestations of a lack of a global perspective. The global
perspective is not only important for analyzing the world; it is
equally important for strategies to change the world. In order
to develop effective anti-capitalist strategies, it is necessary to
start from the global contradictions. First of all, because they
have a decisive influence on the outcome of national contradictions, but even moreseo because we, as socialists, must be
internationalists, not only in words but also in deeds. We are
not struggling for the specific benefit of the citizens of privileged nations like Sweden, but for the proletariat regardless of
national or ethnic background. Finally, the global perspective
is necessary because capitalism can only be defeated through a

coordinated struggle. Internationalism is necessary if we want another, more equal and democratic, world order.

In what follows, I will describe how Sweden became part of the imperialist core—how it tried to be a significant European colonial power but was outmaneuvered by the great colonial powers. Instead, Sweden had to ride on the coattails of colonialism, especially that of Germany and Belgium. I describe the interaction between the breakthrough of industrial capitalism, the rise of social democracy, and the development of the Swedish welfare state, in the context of an increasingly globalized capitalism. Finally, I describe how neoliberalism has brought about economic change and altered the pattern of politics in Sweden, and provide an overview of the current economic and political situation.

Although the Scandinavian countries may seem more progressive than the leading imperialist powers, we will see that when you scratch the surface they are no different in their practice or ideology. For working-class people, they are certainly more comfortable than most countries, whether in the Global North or South—their exploits, however, are just as unscrupulous as those of the "hard-core" imperialist powers. While I focus on Sweden in the following pages, it is not because Norway or Denmark, my home country, are better or worse. It is because Sweden is the most important in economic terms; "the Swedish model" is the ideal type of capitalist welfare state and social democracy there is most advanced.

Louis Proyect's 2015–2016 series about Sweden in his blog "The Unrepentant Marxist" served as an inspiration to write this book, as did many other sources. I attempt to take this material and show how it fits within an overarching process of imperialist polarization and shifting global contradictions. Of course, these conclusions are mine alone. I would like to thank everyone who has read drafts of this book and provided me with useful comments. In addition, I would like to thank Karl Kersplebedeb for assuming the task of editing the book, both in terms of language and content.

SWEDEN:
NATIONAL AND
HISTORICAL CONTEXT

Early colonialism and the slave trade

The rise of capitalism in Europe and colonialism are two inseparable phenomena. It was the conquest of the Americas and the looting of Africa and Asia that boosted the development of capitalism in Europe. The Spanish colonies in Latin America provided the silver and gold that Europe needed so desperately for its growing trade. The European kings, nobility, and Church were insatiable in their lust for luxury; following in their footsteps, the growing bourgeoisie and members of the state apparatus also became consumers of more and new kinds of goods. Gold and silver coins were the necessary medium for the growing trade. The limited amount of these two metals hampered the circulation of goods. That is why the thirst for gold and silver from the "New World" was so great. Precious metals were looted—or mined by slave labor—in Mexico and Peru and were then transported in huge quantities, mainly to Spain. From there, they spread throughout Europe and quenched the budding capitalism's thirst for a means of exchange.[1] Between 1500 and 1800, approximately 100 million kg of silver were transported from South America to Europe.[2] The silver coins developed European manufacturing and paid for the import of goods from Asia—at the time, Europe had nothing of interest to Asia except gold and silver.

---

1. "The discovery of America was due to the thirst for gold which had previously driven the Portuguese to Africa, because the enormously extended European industry of the fourteenth and fifteenth centuries and the trade corresponding to it demanded more means of exchange than Germany, the great silver country from 1450 to 1550, could provide. The conquest of India by the Portuguese, Dutch and English between 1500 and 1800 had *imports from* India as its object— nobody dreamt of exporting anything there. And yet what a colossal reaction these discoveries and conquests, solely conditioned by the interests of trade, had upon industry: they first created the need for *exports to* these countries and developed large-scale industry." Frederick Engels, "Letter to Schmidt, C. London, October 27, 1890." In *Marx and Engels Correspondence* (Moscow: International Publishers, 1968).

2. Bill Warren, "Myths of Underdevelopment: Imperialism and Capitalist Industrialization," *New Left Review* 81 (September–October, 1973): 41.

Slavery was expanded and systematized in the colonies in South America and the Caribbean. The Spaniards and Portuguese initially used Latin America's Indigenous population as slaves in the mines and plantations. The Incan, Aztec, and Mayan peoples had developed societies that organized collective irrigation, production, and the distribution of food. The violent colonization broke down the structures of these Indigenous societies and famine ensued. In addition, Europeans brought epidemic diseases, such as smallpox, which killed millions of people. The colonization process brought the population to the brink of extinction in parts of South America, falling from an estimated 50 million in 1492 to 4 million in the late 1600s.[3] Because of a lack of labor, the Spaniards and Portuguese began a slave hunt in Africa, transporting their prey to their colonies in America. This business was so lucrative that England, France, the Netherlands, and Denmark soon got involved. Approximately 15 million captive Africans were thus transported across the Atlantic between 1700 and 1850.

Sweden attempted to become a colonial power but was not very successful. Around 1650, Sweden established a number of forts in present-day Ghana on the West Coast of Africa, intending them to be a staging area for looting, slave-hunting, and trade. The Swedish merchants did not manage to undertake more than fifty slave transports, however, before the forts were conquered by Denmark in 1663. Sweden also established a trading colony on the southern tip of South Africa in 1649, but it was conquered by the Netherlands in 1663. In 1784, King Gustav III purchased the Caribbean island of Saint-Barthélemy from France, but he was cheated: the island was small, had no drinking water, poor quality soil, and few inhabitants—and so could not be used to produce the sought after products: sugar and tobacco. It did serve as a free port until the 1870s, however, generating a modest revenue. Subsequently,

3. Leften Stavros Stavrianos, *Global Rift: The Third World Come of Age* (New York: William Morrow & Co., 1981), 80.

the island became less important and was sold back to France in 1878. Sweden also tried to establish colonies in India, but England and France prevented this.

As a curiosum, I will mention that Sweden attempted, under King Karl XII (1682–1718), to establish a colony on Madagascar in the Indian Ocean. The idea was that it should serve as a trade post and a pit stop for ships from the Swedish East Asian Company, on the important trade route between Europe and China. Madagascar was, at the time, an important base for pirates, mainly of Indian origin. In 1718, the pirates offered Karl XII the island of Sainte Marie near the coast and an area on the mainland in exchange for being protected by Sweden and "legalized" as Swedish citizens.

The pirates with their twenty-five ships and their fortune were to have the right to obtain land and settle in Sweden. Karl XII accepted the offer and a contract was drawn up; however, the king died before he could sign it. His daughter and successor, Queen Ulrike Eleonora, equipped an expedition in 1721 to realize the plan, but a lack of funds left the ships stranded in Cadiz in Spain, and the project came apart.[4]

In terms of acquiring colonies, Denmark was more successful than Sweden. It established 30 forts and trade posts along the West African coast. Between 1626 and 1825, Danish vessels carried approximately 100,000 captive Africans from West Africa to the Caribbean. Some of the slaves were sold in the Danish colonies in the Caribbean—St. Thomas (1672), St. John (1718), and St. Croix (1733)—where they mainly produced sugar and tobacco. The Danish East India Company also established trade posts in Tamil Nadu (Sri Lanka), in the Nicobar Islands, and in India in Tranquebar (1620) and Serampore (1755). In the North Atlantic, Greenland was re-colonized by Denmark in 1721, joining Iceland and the Faroe

---

4. Mikkelä Lundahl, "Symboliserar Göteborg verkligen det vi vill?" In Kärnfelt Johan (ed.), *I skuggan av samtiden: En vänbok till Sven-Eric Liedman och Amanda Peralta* (Göteborg: Forlaget Arachne, 2006), 319.

Islands as part of the Danish kingdom. Denmark sold its possessions in India to England in the mid-1800s, and the Danish West Indies—now called the Virgin Islands—to the United States for 25 million dollars in 1917. As Lenin commented:

> Who says that in our day there is no trade in human beings? There is quite a brisk trade. Denmark is selling to America for so many millions (not yet agreed upon) three islands, all populated, of course.[5]

Sweden did not manage to become a major slave trader, and yet the chains and bars on the Danish ships were made of Swedish iron. Sweden was the leading European iron exporter in the 17th century. Iron was involved in the colonial triangular trade between Africa, America, and Europe in several ways. It was used as a trading currency to buy slaves in Africa, for the production of chains and bars to keep the slaves locked up, and for tools for farming in the colonies. Denmark—and also England and Germany—bought large quantities of Swedish iron for these purposes.[6] Besides iron, Sweden exported timber and salted herring to feed the slaves who labored on the Caribbean plantations, and imported sugar, tobacco, and cotton.[7]

One possible reason for the lack of tenacity in Swedish attempts to acquire overseas colonies may be that there were prospects closer to home. In 1634, Peder Olofsson found a smooth and shiny black stone at Nasafjäll in the Arjeplog mountain region, in the north near the border with Norway. Upon closer examination, the stone was found to contain silver and lead. A "silver rush" broke out. Senator Karl Bonde expressed hopes that the discovery might solve Sweden's economic troubles. "With God's help, this will become the Swedish

5. V. I. Lenin [1916], "Ten 'Socialist' Ministers!" In *Lenin Collected Works*, vol. 23 (Moscow: Progress Publishers, 1964), 134–36.

6. Leos Müller and Göran Rydén, "Nationell, transnationell eller global historia," *Historisk Tidsskrift* 129, no. 4 (2009): 663–66.

7. Pierre Strandberg, *Sill och Slaveri, C-uppsats*, VT 2020, Historia och kulturarvsstudier: 21.

West Indies." Swedish Chancellor Axel Oxenstierna added: "In Norrland we have an 'India' within our borders, if only we realize we should be taking advantage of it."[8] The northern part of today's Sweden was at the time a very unpromising terrain, inhabited only by Sami and their herds of reindeer. National borders in the Scandinavian far north were not precisely established before 1700 and the Sami were to some extent an independent nation; therefore, the silver mining project was in fact a colonial venture.

The Sami were forcibly recruited to transport the silver ore to the south. However, it turned out that the ore was not as rich in silver as hoped, and production was abandoned after a few years. Still, the venture was the first industrial project in the region and as such signaled the beginning of the colonization of Sami territory, with the construction of roads and harbors to be used to service future iron and copper mines. At that point, the Sami were again used as cheap labor for the transport of ore to the harbors, from where it would be shipped further south in Sweden.

Sweden also colonized areas in the Baltic region in the 17th century. The country developed a strong militarized state machinery based on the landed aristocracy, which needed new territories to supplement its limited income from the lean farmlands in Sweden, which could barely sustain the peasantry.[9] Finland was a Swedish province until 1808, when Russia conquered it during the Napoleonic Wars. Over the centuries, many Finns immigrated to Sweden, where they served as cheap labor, especially in the forestry and mining industries.

8. Janrik Bromé, *Nasafjäll, ett norrländskt silververks historia* (Stockholm: A-B Nordiska Bokhandeln, 1923).

9. Immanuel Wallerstein, *The Modern World-System: Capitalist Agriculture and the Origins of the European World-Economy in the Sixteenth Century* (New York: Academic Press, 1974), 312.

Imperialism without colonies

In the first part of the 19th century, before the breakthrough of industrial capitalism, mercantile capital was dominant. Throughout the 18th century, European and North American naval power had enabled their mercantile capital to acquire a dominant position in world trade. Trade in Europe and North America flourished because of cheap commodities based on the exploitation of slave labor in the colonies.

Meanwhile, in Denmark and Sweden, a mercantile bourgeoisie based in shipping was gaining power. In the latter part of the 18th century, big merchants dominated economic life in Copenhagen, Gothenburg, and Stockholm. At first, they participated in the various trading and colonial companies controlled by the absolute monarchy. Later, they established independent trading companies, which challenged the power of the monarchy. The Scandinavian mercantile bourgeoisie blossomed from around 1750, in part due to the many wars at the time between the competing nations of England, France, Germany, the Netherlands, and the United States. The Scandinavian countries managed to remain neutral in most of these conflicts, and their merchant fleet could therefore provide the warring countries and their colonies with transport.

Founded in 1731, the Swedish East India Company (Svenska Ostindiska Companiet) made 132 expeditions to Asia, mainly to Guangzhou (Canton) in China. Between 1739 and 1767, a total of 16,533 tons of Bohea tea were imported by the company.[10] Cantonese tea was probably the fastest growing commodity in the 18th-century global economy. In England and Holland, drinking tea with lots of sugar became a part of

---

10. Christian Koninckx, *The First and Second Charters of the Swedish East India Company (1731–1766): A contribution to the Maritime, Economic and Social History of North-Western Europe in its Relationship with the Far East* (Kortrijk, Belgium: Van Ghemmert Publishing Company, 1980), 211. In Juan Martínez-Alier, *Ecological Economics: Energy, Environment and Society* (Oxford: Basil Blackwell, 1987), 211.

everyday life, even for the lower classes, as early as the 1730s.

The Swedish East India Company accounted for about 10–20 percent of European tea imports from 1730 to 1784. Together with the Danish Asiatic Company, the two enterprises accounted for a third of all Guangzhou's trade in tea.[11] Only 2–3 percent of the tea was consumed in Scandinavia, the rest being sold to independent dealers who smuggled it into Great Britain, the major tea-drinking nation in Europe, much to the chagrin of the mighty English East India Company.[12]

Metals in the form of semi-finished or finished products constituted the bulk of the Swedish East India Company's exports, predominanty bar iron at the beginning of the eighteenth century.[13] However, it turns out that most, if not all, of the bar iron did not get all the way to China but only to Cádiz, in Spain, where it was sold to pay for chests of silver. Silver was practically the only thing the Swedes could sell in China: "the cargo of Spanish piasters was the sine qua non of the Company's trade."[14]

The lucrative tea imports came to an end in 1784 when the British parliament passed a law that reduced the sales duties on tea from 119 percent to 12.5 percent. As the British market for illegal teas more or less disappeared so did the profitability of the Swedish company.

The Scandinavian merchant fleets found other products and customers, however, and maintained a very strong position into the next century.[15] As a result of the political union

11. Leos Müller, "Svenska ostindiska kompaniet och den europeiska marknaden för te." In Bertil S. Olsson and Karl-Magnus Johansson, eds., *Sverige och svenskarna i den ostindiska handeln 2: Strategier, sammanhang och situationer* (Göteborg: Riksarkivet, 2019), 237–61.

12. Müller and Rydén (2009): 662.

13. Koninckx, 1980.

14. Ibid.

15. "In 1878, Norway was still the third largest nation globally in terms of shipping tonnage, behind only Great Britain and the United States." Kirsten Alsaker Kjerland and Bjørn Enge Bertelsen, *Navigating Colonial Orders, Norwegian Entrepreneurship in Africa and Oceania* (New York: Berghahn Books, 2014), 2.

between Sweden and Norway in 1814, the administration of Norway's merchant fleets ended up under the Ministry of Foreign Affairs in Stockholm. Between 1875 and 1905, the combined Swedish/Norwegian merchant fleets were the third or fourth most important in the world. The English merchant fleet was the largest, the American was number two, then came the Swedish/Norwegian fleet, which was the same size as the German but larger than the French, Dutch, and Italian fleets.[16] Without a colonial territory of its own, Sweden had to set up a network of trade envoys in the service of this fleet. By the end of the 19th century, Sweden possessed more than one hundred consulates in different port cities around the globe.[17] The Norwegian and Danish merchant fleets are still of great importance; for instance, the Danish A. P. Møller-Maersk Line is one of the largest container shipping companies in the world today.

Mercantile and industrial capital from all the imperialist powers of Europe and North America demanded access to the global market; however, it was not always necessary to exercise territorial control over colonies in order to make a profit. The main goal of capital was to integrate the resources and markets of the colonial territory into one's own economic sphere. For a country like Sweden, whether this was possible depended on relations with the ruler of the colonial territory. Sweden could make special arrangements or, with luck, the colonial power might advocate free trade, as England did in the late 19th century.

In general, the Scandinavian countries did not have the nec-essary military power and administrative capacity to establish

---

16. Brian Redman Mitchell, "International Historical Statistics: Europe, 1750–2000," 571–73 and 710–20. Here from: Aryo Makko, "I imperialismens kölvatten? Ett maritimt perspektiv på stormaktsspel, kolonialism utan kolonier och den svensk-norska konsulsstaten, 1875–1905." *Historisk Tidskrift* 134, no. 3 (2014).

17. Kjell Emanuelsson, *Den svensk-norska utrikesförvaltningen 1870–1905. Dess organisations-och verksamhetsförändring* (Lund: CWK Gleerup, 1980).

and operate their own colonies. They had to ride the wave of the great colonial powers in order to enjoy the benefits offered by imperialism.

There was no difference, however, between the Scandinavian countries and the great colonial powers regarding their attitude towards colonialism. European colonialism can be seen as a unified whole in which large and small countries played different roles. Some managed territories and opened up markets, others provided capital, built infrastructure, or transported goods to and from the colonies. The Scandinavian countries earned large sums by navigating in the wake of the major colonial powers. The Frederiksstaden district of Copenhagen is full of mansions built with the profits made from the trade in slaves and colonial goods.

From emigrants to settlers

There is another way in which Swedes played a significant role in colonialism: as settler-colonists. This began as early as 1638, when Sweden established "New Sweden," financed by Swedish, Dutch, and German shareholders. New Sweden was located along the Delaware River, in present-day Pennsylvania, an area in which Swedish tobacco planters and fur traders had settled since 1610. New Sweden did not last long; it was conquered by the Netherlands in 1655 and became part of the New Holland colony. The Dutch governor Stuyvesant allowed the Swedish settlers to retain their land and continue as a "Swedish nation," governed by their own legal system and with their own militia. All able-bodied adult male settlers were part of the militia, whose primary task was to keep the Indigenous people in check and to gain access to land and other natural resources.

The semi-sovereign "Swedish nation" was maintained until 1681, when England conquered the area. Throughout the 18th century, Swedes continued to settle in New Jersey, Delaware, and Pennsylvania, though it was not until the 19th century that emigration from Sweden really took off. At which point, settlerism became more than just a strategy for a trading company to acquire goods—the new wave of emigration was partly a consequence of the poverty and distress that resulted from the rise of industrial capitalism in Europe, partly a result of the possibilities created by colonialism and the new means of transport, which enabled millions of Europeans to settle in the "New World."

In the early 19th century, Europeans experienced few political restrictions on the movement of labor across national borders. Passports were rarely used and immigrants gained relatively easy access to new homelands. Approximately 70 million people emigrated from Europe throughout the 19th century. They were often "surplus" labor in the countryside who could not find work in the cities. Poverty, even famine as in Ireland, drove the emigrants across the globe: 36 million to the United States, 6.6 million to Canada, 5.7 million to Argentina, 5.6 million to Brazil, and others to Australia, New Zealand, Rhodesia, South Africa, and Algeria. A significant number of the emigrants settled—claimed land—often displacing and dispossessing the original population in bloody conflicts. Overall, the proportion of emigrants accounted for more than 17 percent of the 408 million people living in Europe in 1900. By acquiring land or work in the New World, emigrants helped to reduce "reserve army of labor" in their old homelands, thus securing the remaining workers a better starting point in the struggle for higher wages. Emigration was a safety valve alleviating social unrest in Europe. The businessman, politician, and later Prime Minister of the Cape Colony in South Africa, Cecil Rhodes, described the situation well:

> I was in the East End of London (a working-class quarter) yesterday and attended a meeting of the unemployed. I listened to the wild speeches, which were just a cry for

'bread! bread!' and on my way home I wondered over the scene and I became more than ever convinced of the importance of imperialism. ... My cherished idea is a solution for the social problem, i.e., in order to save the 40,000,000 inhabitants of the United Kingdom from a bloody civil war, we colonial statesmen must acquire new lands to settle the surplus population, to provide new markets for the goods produced in the factories and mines. The Empire, as I have always said, is a bread and butter question. If you want to avoid civil war, you must become imperialists.[18]

Throughout the 19th and early 20th centuries, 1.2 million people emigrated from Sweden—about 25 percent of the population at the time, a proportion which is surpassed only by Ireland. By comparison, only 300,000 emigrated from Denmark, corresponding to 10 percent of the population. Approximately one million Swedes settled in North America, the rest went to other destinations, including Denmark, referred to as "the poor person's America" because the trip there was so much more affordable. Wages in Denmark were higher than in Sweden, in both agriculture and the growing industrial sector, and Swedish labor was sought after, considered diligent and cheap. Swedes found work in Danish quarries, railroad construction, shipyards, and especially in agriculture, which had prospered due to growing exports of grain, butter, and meat to the English market.[19]

Sweden was a poor country in the early 19th century. The high standard of living and level of equality that would come later had no precedent in Swedish peasant society. Poverty in the Swedish countryside gave way to regular famines in the

18. V. I. Lenin [1917], *Imperialism, the Highest Stage of Capitalism.* In: *Lenin Collected Works*, vol. 22 (Moscow: Progress Publishers, 1972), 256–57.

19. Rich Willerslev, "Svenske gæstearbejdere i København 1850–1914," *Fortid og Nutid*, no. 86 (1981): 224.

years 1867–69, when first cold weather and then drought made the crops fail.[20] A simultaneous economic boom in the United States accelerated emigration. The message home from the settlers was that life in the United States was so much easier. By 1910, approximately 665,000 Swedes had settled in the United States; in addition, approximately 700,000 second-generation Swedes lived there.[21] In 1900, just over 100,000 Swedes lived in Chicago, making it the second-largest "Swedish" city in the world.[22]

In the United States, impoverished European workers and peasants turned into settlers, in a nation that was on the verge of replacing England as the leading global power. The success of the settler state was based on the dispossession of the Indigenous population and the exploitation of African slaves. Land speculation and slavery generated the capital for the fast-growing US economy. The wealth of the first president of the United States, George Washington, came from speculating in land from which the Indigenous population had been displaced; 317 slaves labored to maintain his household and plantation.[23]

This racist hierarchy, embedded in the foundations of the American state, positioned immigrants from Northwestern Europe as an upper part of the working class. Between 1830 and 1860, 4.5 million immigrants from Europe arrived in the United States. These new Irish, German, Scandinavian, Italian, and Polish workers supplemented the former generations of European immigrants, Blacks, Latin Americans, and Asians, in the rapidly expanding agricultural and industrial sectors. Indians and Chinese were imported on what were

20. Olle Lundsjo, *Fattigdomen på den svenska landsbygden under 1800-talet* (Stockholm: Stockholm Universitet, Ekonomisk-historiska institutet, 1975), 134–40.

21. Sten Carlsson and Jerker Rosén (eds.), *Den svenska historien, band 13: Emigrationen och det industriella genombrottet* (Stockholm: Bonniers, 1992), 31–38.

22. Rasmus Lundgren, "100 000 svenskar i Chicago," *i Säkthistoria*, no. 8 (2018): 25.

23. Mount Vernon, "Ten Fact about Washington & Slavery."

known as "coolie contracts." Together with slaves and the remaining Indigenous population, the Asians were given the hardest work at the lowest wages. They built railroads and worked in mines and on plantations. The original settlers, the first generations of Anglo-Saxon origin, retained their privileged positions in skilled jobs or as foremen in charge of teams of workers. At the time, they received the highest wages of any worker in in the world, approximately double the wages in Britain. The Swedish immigrants were ranked just below the workers of Anglo-Saxon origin.

The result being that, by 1900, the American working class was divided by national origin into three main groups: At the top, the Euro-American labor aristocracy, a privileged layer of "born in the USA" workers who constituted approximately 25 percent of the industrial working class. They got the best-paid skilled jobs, protected by the American Federation of Labor (AFL). Below them was a layer of workers made up of the new immigrants from Europe, which comprised between 50 and 75 percent of the industrialized working class in the northern states. They were mostly unorganized and were systematically excluded from the AFL, and thus from the better-paid jobs. However, their wage levels were significantly above salaries in Northwestern Europe at the time.

At the bottom was the "colonial proletariat" of African, Latin American, and Asian origin. They did the hardest work for the lowest wages, on the railways and in construction, in mining, as well as on the plantations of the southern states. Cotton production, mainly carried out by labor of African origin, remained important to the economy. Between 1870 and 1910, cotton production tripled, accounting for 25 percent of total US exports. Blacks also worked in Alabama's coal mines and steel plants. Likewise, Mexicans, Asians, and the Indigenous population constituted an intensively exploited proletariat in the southwestern states, as field workers, on cattle and sheep ranches, in the mines, in railroad construction, and in the urban service industry. The salary of these proletarians was about $4 a week. The industrial proletariat in the northern states from Eastern and Southern Europe earned $6–$10 a week, while the skilled labor aristocracy received $15–$20 a week.[24]

Gerald Horne describes how Europeans settlers could climb up "the class ladder with sugar stalks and Africans as the rungs," by acquiring a share of the profits from land privatization and speculation and the benefits from slavery. A racist ideology of white supremacy was gradually shaped as a "pan-Europeanism: an invented solidarity between Europeans that transcended class, ethnic, and religious lines."[25] Through the journey across the Atlantic and the confrontation with the Indigenous population as well as slavery, an identification of belonging to the white race was strengthened.

Racism against Indigenous people, Blacks, Latin Americans, Indian and Chinese immigrants, combined with an identity as Anglo-Saxon Protestants of Northwest European origin, lent a particular quality to American nationalism. The United States was God's own land ruled by the white man. Racism and nationalism blocked the development of solidarity based on class consciousness. The trade unions and socialist and communist movements never succeeded in establishing as strong a foothold as they did in Europe. Not even social democracy developed in the United States. But racism and, as a consequence, the anti-racist struggle have been prominent recurring features of US history, and the ideology of white supremacy has characterized US domestic and foreign policy right up to the present day.

As mentioned above, emigration to the US helped alleviate pressures that might have led to social upheaval in North-

---

24. J. Sakai, *Settlers: The Mythology of the White Proletariat from Mayflower to Modern* (Montreal & Oakland, CA: Kersplebedeb and PM Press, 2014), 126–27.

25. Gerald Horne, *The Apocalypse of Settler Colonialism: The Roots of Slavery, White Supremacy, and Capitalism in Seventeenth-Century North America and the Caribbean* (New York: Monthly Review Press, 2018), 91.

western Europe. It significantly reduced the "reserve army of labor," which led to more favorable conditions for the wage struggles of those workers who remained behind.[26] An analysis of Swedish emigration shows that it led to increased membership in trade unions and the Social Democratic Workers' Party. Furthermore, the tendency to strike and to vote for left-wing parties in parliamentary elections increased.[27]

It was not only poor workers and peasants who immigrated to the colonies seeking lands of opportunity; British imperialism also provided an opening for Scandinavian entrepreneurs to participate in colonial exploitation. Take, for example, the case of Joseph Stephens, born in Stockholm in 1841 of two British parents. Like so many other sons from the middle classes, Stephens hoped to make his fortune through a career in the colonies. When he was just 19 years old, his father took out a loan to finance the journey from Sweden, and he arrived in India in December 1859. Stephens became an apprentice in civil engineering, and after completing his apprenticeship became a railway contractor with the Great India Peninsular Railway Company, which built railways and infrastructure in the Bombay region, the cotton belt of India. The American Civil War had disrupted the supply of cotton produced by slaves and this increased the demand for Indian cotton to feed the booming textile industry in England. Stephens's firm organized the construction of railway stations and fencing for the railway company and storage houses and ginning factories for the cotton industrialists. By 1865, Stephens employed thousands of workers; his archive provides a detailed account of the contracts with carpenters, masons, stone workers, and headmen. If a worker failed to provide services in the agreed upon time and manner, they were liable to be fined and jailed.

26. Jonas Ljungberg, "The Impact of the Great Emigration on the Swedish Economy," *Scandinavian Economic History Review* 45, no. 2 (1997): 159–89.

27. Karadja Mounir and Erik Prawitz, "Emigrationen till Amerika och den svenska arbetarrörelsen," *Ekonomisk Debatt* 46, no. 8 (2018): 19.

By 1867, after only seven years, Stephens's colonial activities had made him a fortune. Now 26 years old, he wrote to his father explaining that he had two options: to be a construction manager in England and live as a member of the bourgeoisie or to buy an estate with a manor house in Sweden and live like landed gentry. He chose the latter, purchasing a 600-acre forest and industrial estate in Huseby, in Småland in southern Sweden. He married a woman of "class" and sat in the Swedish parliament.

In the following years, Joseph Stephens turned his estate into an ironworks and timber lot. His colonial experience informed his business regime in Sweden, as he pursued new connections in imperial England and attempted to sell his timber to the Indian railways. He also managed workers and artisans on his estate through contractual relationships, as he had done in India.

Stephens's life story recently came to light when his personal archive was discovered at his old manor house, the Huseby Bruk.[28] Discussing the discovery of the archive, Arun Kumar wrote:

> The Stephens' archive weave together India (the colony), England (the coloniser), and Sweden (a Western nation state) in one thread which, otherwise, may appear totally disconnected in the mid-nineteenth century. Stephens' life history forces us to rethink our understanding of India's railway development, the wider distribution of colonial wealth in the Western world, and the transnational nature of British imperialism.[29]

---

28. Materials from the archive are kept at Linnaeus University and at the Huseby Estate.

29. Arun Kumar, "A Scandinavian 'Nabob' of the British Empire: The Discovery of a New Colonial Archive," *The Wire*, January 2, 2021.

German Imperialism and the "Congo Conference" in Berlin

In the 1890s, Sweden underwent rapid industrialization, which led to a rise in wages in the mining, iron, and timber industries, forestry, and agriculture. The industrial breakthrough in Sweden was linked to the development of capitalism, specifically in Germany.

In the early 19th century, present-day Germany was regarded as a relatively backward part of Europe. In the second half of the century, however, Germany moved from a semi-peripheral position to the core of the capitalist world system. The development of the English colonial empire gave way to an expansion of the core which encompassed the northwestern part of continental Europe.[30] Between 1840 and 1870, British foreign trade increased by 500 percent, part of which included imported agricultural products from Germany and Scandinavia.[31]

The German industrial revolution occurred between 1850 and 1875, under the Prussian military regime of Otto von Bismarck. The German rural nobility, known as "Junkers," had made their fortunes by supplying food to the expanding English market; they would become a cornerstone of the emerging industrial and financial bourgeoisie, together with the new industrial capitalists. Both the industrialists and the Junkers wanted the Prussian state to build a strong navy and to pursue an active military colonial policy in order to secure access to commodities such as copper, rubber, cotton, and vegetable and mineral oils.

Raw materials were considered necessary if Germany was to compete with England, France, and the new ascendant power—the United States. As the general and future president Paul Von Hindenburg stated:

---

30. Zak Cope, "German Imperialism and Social Imperialism 1871-1933." In Immanuel Ness and Zak Cope (eds.), *The Palgrave Encyclopedia of Imperialism and Anti-imperialism*, vol. 1, (New York: Palgrave Macmillan, 2017), 652.

31. Eric J. Hobsbawm, *Industry and Empire* (New York: Penguin Books, 1968), 139.

Without colonies, no security regarding the acquisition of raw materials, without raw materials, no industry, without industry, no adequate standard of living and wealth. Therefore Germans, do we need colonies.[32]

Like Cecil Rhodes in England, in the 1890s the German Junker and colonialist Ernst von Weber argued that a colonial empire would save Germany from recurring crises of overproduction and unemployment. According to Weber, Germany needed a "mass export of revolutionary tinder" in order to avoid a bloody social revolution.[33]

Germany, like the other European powers and the United States, regarded the rest of the world as a resource to be used and exploited at will. The problem was how to divide up the world, as imperialist rivalry was becoming a principal contradiction in the world system. For that reason, in 1884 a conference was held in Berlin to agree upon how to divide up Africa between twelve countries and thereby avoid "unnecessary" expenditures on warfare.

In this power game, smaller states such as Sweden sought to secure their interests. The problem was explained by Swedish diplomat Carl R. A. Georgsson Fleetwood, immediately before the conference:

It is a well-established fact that European politics is hardly European any more, but Asian or African—it is in these remote parts of the world that the fate of Europe is being decided. Are we at the beginning of a new era in colonial politics? In which case, will we second- or third-rank state powers become even more insignificant than before—or might commercial interests possibly give us increased influence—or might we possibly act as

---

32. Maria Mies, *Patriarchy and Accumulation on a World Scale: Women in the International Division of Labour* (London: Zed Books, 1986), 98.

33. John Phillip Short, *Magic Lantern Empire: Colonialism and Society in Germany* (New York: Cornell University Press, 2012), 68.

colonizers on a smaller scale, so as to benefit in some way from the drain caused by the growing emigration?[34]

Sweden's top representative at the Berlin conference was Gillis Bildt, who a few years later briefly served as the country's prime minister (1888–1889). Sweden did not manage to acquire any colonies at the conference but did endorse the division of Africa adopted by the major colonial powers.[35] Sweden's strategy was to try to secure its trade interests by obtaining special agreements from the major colonial powers. For example, Sweden managed to be "particularly favored" by Belgian King Leopold's International Congo Association. As a result, Swedish soldiers, sailors, businessmen, and missionaries would eagerly participate in the colonization of the Congo.[36] King Leopold welcomed Sweden's participation in the "civilizing" mission; in a letter to Swedish King Oskar II, he wrote that Sweden already had "authorised several outstanding officers from her splendid army to enter into the service of the International Congo Association. Important stations, central nodes for vast areas in the middle of Africa, are today managed by Swedes."[37]

King Leopold's International Congo Association is today known to have been one of the most brutal colonial regimes, as reflected in the drastic decline in the Congo's population from 20–30 million in 1884 to only 8.5 million in 1911.[38]

34. Gwendolyn Fleetwood and Wilhelm Odelberg (eds.), *Carl Georgsson Fleetwood: Från studieår och diplomattjänst. Dagböcker, brev och skrifter 1879–1892*, vol. 1, 1879–1887 (Stockholm: P. A. Norstedt & söner, 1968), 560.

35. David Nilsson, *Sweden-Norway at the Berlin Conference 1884–85: History, National Identity-Making and Sweden's Relations with Africa*. Current African Issues 53 (Uppsala: Nordiska Afrikainstitutet, 2013), 5. Here from Louis Proyect, "Swedish imperialism in Africa." Louis Proyect, The Unrepentant Marxist (blog), July 9, 2015.

36. Ibid., 30–35.

37. Ibid., 51.

38. Georges Nzongola-Ntalaja, *The Congo: From Leopold to Kabila: A People's History* (London: Zed Books, 2002), 22.

Sweden's main strategy, however, was to strengthen its ties with Germany by supporting its positions at the conference. On December 7, 1884, as negotiations were coming to an end, King Oskar II wrote to Bildt:

> I have followed the ongoing Congo conference with interest; however, *one question* above all others has been on my mind. Are Germany's new and, in some cases, surprisingly active colonial policies, the main goal (if a goal it can still be said to be?) or is this really just a means of luring its western neighbor *even further* along the same road and thus, for a long time, weakening its power and diverting its attention from Alsace Lorraine? [emphasis in the original][39]

Bildt answered the king, stating that, in terms of European power politics, the goal of Germany's colonial ambitions was partly to neutralize France's desire for revenge for its defeat in 1871 and partly to exacerbate tensions between France and England, but that the main purpose was to obtain resources and open markets as well as to bolster Germany's national prestige.[40]

In the 1890s, Germany built a sizeable merchant and navy fleet and established naval bases as far away as the South Coast of China. The German Navy was very active in the Mediterranean, north of the African coast and east of Turkey, in fierce competition with England and France. Within a few years, Germany built up a colonial empire. By 1906, East Africa (Tanzania), South West Africa (Namibia), Cameroon, New Guinea, Togo, the Caroline, Paula, and Marianne Islands,

39. Oscar II, *I Gillis Bildts arkiv*, vol.1: *Brevväxling kungliga personer*. Avskrift av brev—utdrag. Från Oscar II till Gillis Bildt. Stockholm, 7. Dec. 1884. "King Oscar II letter to Gillis Bildt." Here from: Nilsson (2013), 50. The Imperial Territory of Alsace-Lorraine was a territory created by the German Empire in 1871, after it annexed most of Alsace and the Moselle department of Lorraine following its victory in the Franco-Prussian War.
40. Gillis Bildts, "Letter from Bildt to Oscar December 17, 1884." *RA: Gillis Bildts arkiv*, Vol. 1. Here from: Nilsson (2013), 33.

the Marshall Islands, Samoa, and Kiauchau were German colonies, with a combined land mass the size of India. Besides which, German economically dominated Bulgaria, Romania, and Turkey.[41]

It was in this colonial context that the idea of the German *Herrenvolk*, or master race, developed. The basic elements of Nazi race theory were developed during this period and practiced in South West Africa, present-day Namibia. However, it would be a mistake to label German colonialism as especially brutal—English, French, Dutch, and Belgian colonialism were no less so. The racism, national chauvinism, and brutality of Nazism were later condemned by the other European powers, but as poet and politician Aimé Césaire wrote:

> Yes, it would be worthwhile to study clinically, in detail, the steps taken by Hitler and Hitlerism and to reveal to the very distinguished, very humanistic, very Christian bourgeois of the twentieth century that without his being aware of it, he has a Hitler inside him, that Hitler inhabits him, that Hitler is his demon, that if he rails against him, he is being inconsistent and that, at bottom, what he cannot forgive Hitler for is not crime in itself, the crime against man, it is not the humiliation of man as such, it is the crime against the white man, the humiliation of the white man, and the fact that he applied to Europe colonialist procedures which until then had been reserved exclusively for the Arabs of Algeria, the coolies of India, and the niggers of Africa.[42]

In parallel with the expansion of the colonial empires, there developed the idea of Europe as the historical cradle and center of civilization. The myth imagined a thousand-year continuity, from ancient Greece's philosophy and culture to the liberal values of Western capitalism. In actual fact, however,

---

41. Richard Krooth, *Arms and Empire: Imperial Patterns before World War II* (California: Santa Barbara Harvest Press, 1980), 35–36.

42. Aimé Césaire, *Discourse on Colonialism* (New York: Monthly Review Press, 2000), 164.

it was not until the Renaissance and the dawn of capitalism that Europe began to cultivate the idea of Greek antiquity as its origin. The problem with this idea is that the Renaissance is separated from classical Greece by centuries, during which neither the European economy nor its philosophy or culture were by any means the center of world civilization. Christianity was also an element of this construction, supposedly a central element of specifically European values. Yet Christianity was not founded in Paris, Rome, or Berlin, but in the Middle East. The "Holy Family" and the Egyptian and Syrian Church Fathers had to be Europeanized and Jesus portrayed as a blond Northern European to fit the myth.

Along with colonialism, it was the breakthrough of industrial capitalism in England that made Europe rich and powerful. Science and culture fused with rationality and technical efficiency. Values of democracy and social justice developed within the framework of Europe and North America while the same states killed, enslaved, and exploited people throughout the world.

European ideas of a racial and ethnic hierarchy were bestowed a scientific legitimacy. Colonial practice was translated into the social and biological sciences, as theories about the superiority of the Aryan race and its birthright and duty to rule over the "primitive races." Eugenics was widely accepted, in Scandinavia as elsewhere. Racism was popularized with the concept of "the white man's burden" and in literature. In zoos and fairs all over Europe, Africans, Asians, Indigenous peoples of North America, Bedouins, and Inuit were exhibited like animals.

European racism reflects the hierarchical division of humanity that colonialism created. Colonialism is a shared European responsibility. The racism and national chauvinism that characterize modern-day right-wing populism—including in Sweden—have their origins in the ideas of colonialism. The dehumanization of the peoples of the colonies was a prerequisite for the idea of Europe and the West as the center of civilization.

How industrial capitalism came to Denmark

Industrial capitalism had its breakthrough in England in the first decades of the 19th century, followed by France, Germany, the Netherlands, and Belgium in the middle of the century. In Scandinavia, the breakthrough occurred first in Denmark in the 1870s and then in Sweden in the late 1880s.

The development of capitalism in Denmark is the story of a special kind of bourgeoisie. This bourgeoisie was not a "classic" industrial bourgeoisie as in England—the conditions for that were simply not present. Denmark had no raw materials for the development of heavy industry, no large domestic market to provide the basis for large-scale industry, and when against these odds small industries did nonetheless take form, they encountered crushing competition from England and others. When industrial development finally took off in the last quarter of the 19th century, it was based on the processing of agricultural products for export and the production of agricultural machinery. It was all about agriculture in Denmark.

An important prerequisite for Denmark's integration into the imperialist core was the export of agricultural goods to feed the rapidly growing working class in England. In September 1910, Lenin was participating in the 8th International Socialist Congress, which was being held in Copenhagen; while there, he went frequently to the King's Library to research Danish agricultural development. As he would later note:

> In addition, a specific feature of Danish imperialism is the superprofits it obtains from its monopolistically advantageous position in the meat and dairy produce market: using cheap maritime transport, she supplies the world's biggest market, London. As a result, the Danish bourgeoisie and the rich Danish peasants (bourgeois of the purest type, in spite of the fables of the Russian Narodniks) have become "prosperous" satellites of the

British imperialist bourgeoisie, sharing their particularly easy and particularly fat profits.[43]

From 1820 to 1880, grain exports from Denmark to England doubled, as did their prices. Later, when a duty on live cattle and meat was abolished in England, the export pattern shifted towards animal products and Danish meat prices nearly tripled. In the 1870s, when wage levels in England began to rise, this led to an increased demand for meat and animal products including butter, eggs, and bacon from Denmark. In this period, 80–90 percent of Danish exports were agricultural goods, and by far the largest market was England.[44] Thus, the Danish bourgeoisie acted as an intermediary between family-run farms and the growing English market, in the form of agricultural processing industries, the manufacture of agricultural and dairy machinery, not to mention transport and logistics in connection with exports across the North Sea. New roads, railways, and harbors, with steamship routes connecting the agricultural producers to European markets, all added to the infrastructure.

As early as 1846, the liberal bourgeoisie entered into an alliance with the farmers, in the form of the Society of the Friends of Peasants (*Bondevennernes Selskab*). In the following period, a peasant class, mainly consisting of mid-size farmers, established itself as a petty bourgeois faction closely linked to the emerging industrial bourgeoisie. The Danish bourgeoisie was thus a peculiar mix of rural and urban bourgeoisie, represented by the (liberal) Left Party and opposed to the (conservtaive) Right.

With the development of industrialization, the contradiction between the bourgeoisie and a growing working class was deepening. The first trade unions were founded in 1869. Louis Pio, a clerk in the postal service, founded the Danish Social

---

43. V. I. Lenin [1916], 134–36.

44. Erling Olsen, *Danmarks økonomiske historie siden 1750* (København: Gads forlag, 1962), 48–49.

Democratic Party in 1871 as part of Marx's First International. Despite this fact, the Marxist influence was marginal. *The Communist Manifesto* was mentioned for the first time in 1883 in an obituary of Marx, which was not very laudatory and displayed ignorance as to his ideas. Early Danish social democracy was influenced by Ferdinand Lassalle's ideas and focused on how the existing state could address the problems of unemployment and social needs in general. In Copenhagen, specifically, the miserable conditions in the new working-class districts proved fertile ground for socialist ideas. From the start, the party had strong ties to the trade unions. Besides support for the trade union struggle for higher wages and better working conditions, the strategy was always to acquire legislative power by getting representatives into parliament. There was no talk or plans of revolution, only political reform within the existing society. Still, the bourgeoisie and state power were terrified by even those moderate socialist ideas.

The reason why, despite its moderation, Danish social democracy in this early period had a revolutionary flavour was because of what became known as the Battle of the Common. The incident occurred in the context of a bricklayers' strike in 1872. Acting on behalf of the Danish section of the International Working Men's Association, Louis Pio convened a support meeting at a central park in Copenhagen. Even though the demands were not radical, on May 4, 1872, the night before the meeting, the leadership—Louis Pio, Harald Brix, and Paul Geleff—were arrested and imprisoned. This resulted in a confrontation between workers and police at the Common, a park in the working-class neighborhood of Nørrebro in Copenhagen. Pio was sentenced to six years in prison, Geleff to five, and Brix to four, for crimes against the state constitution.[45]

---

45. Pio, Brix, and Geleff served their sentences in Vridsløselille State Prison. Built in 1859, this was the same prison I ended up in, in 1991. Through their memoirs, I was able to learn which cells they had been held in. I suggested a plaque be placed on the doors in question to commemorate that it was here that the founders of Denmark's Social Democratic Party had been imprisoned, but neither the Social Democrats not the prison authorities showed much interest.

As a consequence of these verdicts, the Minister of Justice issued a ban on the International Working Men's Association. This was serious blow to the movement. When the leadership was released, they were marked by their years in isolation in prison. Pio and Geleff were paid by the police to emigrate to the United States and internal divisions in the party encouraged reformism.[46] In 1889, the leaders of the party's left-wing faction were purged.

(As a fitting postscript to this sorry state of affairs, once in the United States Pio became active in the Danish immigrant community, moving first to Chicago and then helping to found an ill-fated "socialist colony" in Kansas, while publishing various works including a Danish cookbook and a Scandinavian-English dictionary and guide for young people. At the World's Fair in Chicago in 1893, Pio managed to get himself hired as a kind of PR agent for the state of Florida. He managed to secure funding to found a new city in Florida on the banks of the St. Locie River, to be known as "White City." While the official story was that this name was in hommage to Chicago—known as the "White City" because of its white buildings—in a letter to a close friend, the "socialist" Pio explained that "The colony has started ... [If] the absent Madams and legitimate kids are counted in, the city will amount to c. 500 souls, all white as snow. Chinese, Negroes and other Coloreds are expressly excluded from Access.")[47]

At the turn of the century, the Danish bourgeoisie continued to profit from growing exports of refined agricultural goods to England, which made it possible to provide significant wage increases and better working conditions to the labor force. In the period from 1870 to 1913, real wages doubled.[48] This also led to a reduction in the level of class conflict. In 1899, after four months of strikes and lock outs, the trade union movement

---

46. Olsen (1962), 187–88.

47. Børge Schmidt, *80 Louis Pio breve og en bibliografi* (København: Fremad, 1950).

48. Olsen (1962), 191.

and the employers' union entered into what was known as the September settlement. The trade union movement recognized the right of employers to manage and allocate work and employers recognized the trade union movement. Furthermore, the settlement stated that all disputes should be decided by negotiation and mediation. If this failed, the case should be brought before a Labor Court to resolve the conflict. Class struggle was to be settled in a fixed institutional framework, to put an end to strikes and labor unrest. Reforms were introduced in 1901, establishing parliamentary rules and extending voting rights. Prior to then, only 15 percent of the population had had the right to vote; women, so-called "imbeciles," and the poor were excluded. It was 1915 before women and domestic servants received the right to vote in general elections. The September settlement and the consolidation of the parliamentary system meant that trade unions and the Social Democrats were recognised as legitimate political movements. Social Democrats were elected to parliament and in 1916 they entered a coalition government with two ministers. Lenin wrote about this in his article "Ten 'Socialist' Ministers!":

> Huysmans, the Secretary of the International Social-Chauvinist Bureau, has sent a telegram of greetings to Danish Minister without portfolio Stauning, the leader of the Danish quasi-"Social-Democratic" Party. The telegram reads: "I learn from the newspapers that you have been appointed Minister. My heartiest congratulations. And so, we now have ten socialist Cabinet Ministers in the world. Things are moving. Best wishes.[49]

Lenin was not impressed:

> The Danish "Social-Democratic" Party completely succumbed to this international situation, and staunchly

---

49. Lenin [1916]. "Ten 'Socialist' Ministers!" In *Lenin Collected Works*, vol. 23 (Moscow: Progress Publishers, 1964), 134–36.

supported and supports the Right wing, the opportunists in the German Social-Democratic Party. The Danish Social-Democrats voted credits for the bourgeois-monarchist government to "preserve neutrality"—that was the euphemistic formula. At the Congress of September 30, 1916, there was a nine tenths' majority in favour of joining the Cabinet, in favour of a deal with the government! The correspondent of the Berne socialist paper reports that the opposition to ministerialism in Denmark was represented by Gerson Trier and the editor J. P. Sundbo. Trier defended revolutionary Marxist views in a splendid speech, and when the party decided to go into the government, he resigned from the Central Committee and from the party, declaring that he would not be a member of a *bourgeois* party. In the past few years the Danish "Social-Democratic" Party has in no way differed from the bourgeois radicals.

Greetings to Comrade G. Trier! "Things are moving," Huysmans is right—moving towards a precise, clear, politically honest, socialistically necessary division between the revolutionary Marxists, the representatives of the *masses* of the revolutionary proletariat, and the Plekhanov-Potresov Huysmans allies and agents of the imperialist bourgeoisie, who have the majority of the "*leaders*," but who represent the interests, not of the oppressed masses, but of the minority of privileged workers, who are deserting to the side of the bourgeoisie.

The social history of 19th-century Denmark is relatively peaceful. There was no showdown with the nobility as in the French Revolution of 1789 or as in the violent bourgeois revolutions that swept across Europe in 1848; certainly nothing like the communist Paris Commune of 1871. This relatively peaceful quality to Danish history persisted into the 20th century.

The Social Democrats' chief ideologue in Denmark, Gustav Bang, laid out the strategy in 1904:

There are two ways to get to a new society. One is to knock over the game—overturn the pieces; the other is to move the pieces, one by one. Our opponents want nothing better than that we opt for the first, but we are going the other way—we move the red pieces of the Social Democrats further and further forward, until we finally put the enemy in checkmate.[50]

As the game unfolded, however, the Social Democrats were drawn into the system—finally in fact becoming the system.

How industrial capitalism came to Sweden

Due to natural preconditions, the structure of the economy, and the character of the bourgeoisie, the industrialization of Sweden occurred very differently from in Denmark.

As early as the first half of the 17th century, Sweden had been an important iron exporter, largely to the Netherlands, the hegemonic power in Europe at the time. Wars had deprived the Dutch of their sources of iron in Spain and Germany. At the same time, the demand for iron to produce armaments was on the rise, thanks to what was to become known as the Thirty Years' War.

Dutch capital, entrepreneurs, and technicians were attracted by Sweden's plentiful iron ore, easily accessible charcoal, and waterpower. The Dutch entrepreneur Louis de Geer organized the immigration of Walloons as skilled workers and introduced the Walloon iron refining process in Sweden. A cannon factory was established using ore from the Dannemora mine, 100 miles north of Stockholm and less than 30 miles from the Baltic Sea. Later, the Dutch established factories at Ullfors,

---

50. Gustav Bang (1904). Here from: Lisa Togeby, *Var de så røde?* (København: Fremads Fokusbøger, 1968), 2.

Wessland, Hillebola, and Strömsberg, causing Swedish iron production to increase from 6,650 tons in 1620 to more than 17,300 in 1650.[51]

The first industrial factories in Sweden were established in the early 19th century. As in England, it was the textile industry that pioneered the use of spinning and weaving machines operated by wage-workers. The raw cotton was produced by slave labor in the plantations of the southern states of the United States and the technology was imported from England, but the emergence of the Swedish textile industry was primarily based on the domestic market: at first, finer fabrics for the upper class; later came cotton linen for the working class and peasantry.[52]

By the 1860s, Sweden's industrialization was based on the processing of raw materials such as iron ore, copper, and timber, and benefited from access to cheap energy in the form of hydropower.

One example of an early Swedish industrial enterprise is Bofors Bruk. Bofors had refined iron and manufactured weapons since 1646. In the 1870s, the craft manufacturing methods were replaced by industrial production, and Bofors become one of Europe's leading steelmakers. In 1883, it took up the production of cannons again. In 1894, Bofors was purchased by Alfred Nobel, who modernized arms production and expanded it to include various types of explosives, especially his invention dynamite—and yes, he also established the Nobel Prize in 1895.

While Denmark is characterized by small-scale industry, the exception being its shipyards, Swedish industry is dominated by larger companies. While Denmark was primarily tied to English imperialism, Sweden navigated in the wake of

---

51. B. Boëthius, "Swedish Iron and Steel 1600–1955," *Scandinavian Economic History Review* 6, no. 2 (1958): 150.

52. Sven Beckerts, *Empire of Cotton: A New History of Global Capitalism* (New York: Vintage, 2015). L. Schön, "British Competition and Domestic Change: Textiles in Sweden 1820–1870," *Economy and History* 23, no. 1 (1980): 61–76.

Germany, not least through the export of iron for manufacturing and timber for the construction of housing for the rapidly expanding urban German working class.

Symbolizing the importance of iron and steel exports for the Swedish economy, a fountain was erected in the port city of Gothenburg in 1927, on the Järntorget (the Iron Square).[53] It was at this square that iron produced in Swedish ironworks was measured before being loaded and shipped to the rest of the world. The official name of the fountain is *The Five Continents*. In the five corners of the fountain are statues of naked women who, by their ethnicity, are meant to symbolize the five continents of the world. From the center of the fountain, water springs from a bowl towards the women, just as Swedish iron flows out to the whole world, which responds gratefully by sending gifts back from the five continents, symbolized by water spraying back towards the center of the fountain. A symbol of Sweden's integration into the imperialist world system.

credit: Máté Sall Vesselaényi

53. It was Magnus Berg who first showed me this fountain, which he has described in: *Förlåta men inte glömma. Röster om rasism, nationalism och det mångkulturella samhället i Namibia och i Sverige* (Stockholm: Carlsson, 2004), 4–6.

A revolutionary beginning and a breakthrough for reformism

The 1890s were in many ways a turning point in Sweden's history. The breakthrough of industrial capitalism created many new jobs, massive emigration removed much of the reserve army of labor, and, consequently, wages doubled over the course of the decade. The Swedish Social Democratic Party was established and the foundations of the welfare state were laid.

All this had a revolutionary prelude, however. The history of Swedish socialism dates back to 1847, when Per Götrek, a Stockholm bookseller, published *On the proletariat and its emancipation through true communism*, inspired by the writings of the French utopian socialist Etienne Cabet.[54] Götrek was religious—for him, communism was synonymous with the original ideals of Christianity. Marx's ideas about religion being the "opium of the people" had apparently not reached or convinced him. In addition, Götrek was what today would be called "straight edge and sober living": he did not use alcohol or other drugs and he was a vegetarian. Götrek was also engaged in the struggle for equal rights for women, something unusual amongst socialists at the time, and agitated for women's political education:

> through this, she will learn to realize her position, realize that she is missing out on everything that a sensible human being has the right to demand from society, namely education, the right to work and to choose her work, the right to make decisions concerning her person and her actions, the right to participate in establishing the laws she must obey.[55]

---

54. Per Götrek [1847], *Om proletariatet och dess befrielse genom den sanna kommunismen: Jämte bihang: Om kommunisternas beslutade stora emigration till Icarien.* Reprinted in: *Frilansens urkundsamling* 5 (1944).

55. Herman Lindqvist, "Kungens order: Skjut på demonstranterna," *Aftonbladet*, October 4, 2008.

Götrek brought together a group of people, mainly artisans who had picked up new ideas while traveling and working in France, some typesetters, and Johan Ellmin, a doctor who worked among the poor in Stockholm. The group met regularly in an apartment in the center of Stockholm. In February 1848, *The Communist Manifesto* was published in German. Two weeks later, it was for sale in Götrek's bookstore, and he immediately began translating it into Swedish. Before he could finish, however, riots broke out in Paris and other European cities; on March 2, 1848, news of the unrest reached Stockholm. The uprising was a bourgeois revolution against absolutism and for civil liberties, universal suffrage, and parliamentarianism. Stockholm's revolutionary communists saw 1848 as a dress rehearsal for the socialist revolution.

Götrek's group participated in disseminating leaflets and posters to mobilize for a "banquet" on Saturday, March 18. The "banquet" took place in the afternoon at De la Croix's large hall at Brunkeberg Square in Stockholm. It was organized by the Society of Friends of Reform, an association of liberals and radicals. The *men* in the main hall were members of parliament, intellectuals, teachers, and shopkeepers. An elite, certainly, and yet many of them did not have the right to vote for the political assembly because they did not belong to any of the "venerable" traditional four estates: nobles, clergy, large landowners, and upper bourgeoisie.

This left-leaning political elite now made fiery speeches calling for an uprising—a common tactic at the time for revolutionaries trying to spark rebellions in the streets. Outside at Brunkeberg Square, an excited crowd quickly gathered. They demanded the removal of the king and the introduction of a republic. The authorities intervened, cleared the street, and arrested the most active protesters, but the demonstration just moved to the area between the royal castle and the great cathedral. On the way, the demonstrators passed by the house of August von Hartmansdorff, the president of the high court, who was very unpopular because of his suppression of freedom of the press; all twelve windows of his third-floor apartment were smashed. King Oscar I, who was returning to the palace from the opera, met the demonstrators at the square in front of the cathedral. He promised the crowd that the arrested protesters would be released. Some hailed the king as he left the scene, believing that the danger was over, but the demonstration marched on to Gustav Adolf's square. Stones were thrown at the houses of Archbishop Wingård, Governor C. F. Horns, and Minister of War Peyron—and also at some houses belonging to Jewish businessmen. Doors and windows were smashed, and the king's guard intervened to put an end to the unrest. There was street fighting and the guard shot into the crowd.

The next day, Sunday March 19, the unrest continued. The regular army was deployed against the protesters in the center of the city, where barricades had gone up. The troops were met with a volley of stones. The king gave the order to fire on the protesters—twenty were killed and approximately two hundred were seriously injured in the fighting. In the following days there were army patrols in the streets around the clock. And so the March 1848 revolt in Stockholm came to an end.

These events had consequences, however. The police kept a close watch on Götrek's activities. It became difficult for him to find a print shop willing to print the *Manifesto*. Nevertheless, he finally managed to find a printer and, in December 1848, Götrek published *The Voice of Communism*, as his version of the *Manifesto* was called.[56] In order to not further provoke the state, he modified Marx and Engels's text—where they wrote "a violent overthrow of the present social order," Götrek's translation read "a radical reorganization of the present social order." Marx and Engels would not be satisfied with Götrek's translation of the slogan "Proletarians of all countries, unite!"—which he turned into "The voice of the people is the voice of God."[57]

---

56. Karl Marx and Friedrich Engels [1848], *Kommunismens röst: förklaring af det kommunistiska partiet,* translated by Götrek Per. Reprinted by Pogo Press (Solna, 1976).

57. Knut Bäckström, *Götrek och Manifestet* (Stockholm: Gidlund, 1972).

But Götrek's modifications did him no good: in early 1849 he and members of his group were brought to justice and the organization was dissolved by the court.

There was a broad and severe crackdown on the left in the years that followed. Sweden became one of the most reactionary and undemocratic political regimes in Europe.[58] All women and 80 percent of men were denied the right to vote in late 19th-century Sweden. The state and the bourgeoisie feared the "dangerous classes." The French Revolution of 1789 was still fresh in their memories and the revolutionary uprisings in many European cities in 1848 had reached Stockholm. At this point in history, the bourgeoisie could not afford the "luxury" of introducing parliamentary democracy or the right to form trade unions, as this would have threatened the system's very existence. As Marx and Engels wrote: "A spectre is haunting Europe—the spectre of communism."[59]

It remained a spectre, however. Gradually, the European state powers changed their tactics based on the motto: better reform than revolution. In 1871, the English parliament recognized the right of workers to organize themselves in trade unions. In France, Napoleon III introduced the *Loi Ollivier* in 1864, which gave workers the right to organize, issued a decree regulating the treatment of apprentices, and limited working hours. By including "the dangerous classes" in the political process and thereby turning them into citizens of the state, the ruling class hoped that social conflict would take a more controlled course. Suffrage was expanded to include working-class men and the first public social and health insurance policies were introduced in Northwestern Europe in the last quarter of the 19th century.

The struggle of the proletariat for better living conditions

---

58. Mats Parner, *Tusentals stenkast från Storkyrkobrinken*. Erik Gamby, *Per Götrek och 1800-talets svenska arbetarrörelse* (Stockholm: Tiden, 1978).

59. Karl Marx and Frederick Engels [1848], "The Communist Manifesto." In *Marx and Engels Selected Works*, vol. 1 (Moscow: Progress Publishers, 1969), 98–137.

and political rights combined with European colonialism and became the driving force in a new dynamic of capitalist accumulation on a global scale. Colonialism was a centrifugal force that propelled capitalism across the globe, at the same time as it was a polarizing force that divided the world into a core and a periphery. A periphery drained of value, which maintained the profit levels and a growing consumer market in the core. This dynamic solved capitalism's inherent contradiction between the need to expand production and the lack of sufficient consumption power to realize a profit. In the second half of the 19th century, the proletariat's living conditions began to improve in England. For the first time in the history of capitalism, capitalists had to pay a wage above subsistence level. This development spread from England to Germany and the rest of Northwestern Europe, including Sweden.[60]

Initially, the rising wages affected only a small fraction of the working class, being limited to the skilled and best-organized industrial workers. However, compared to living standards in the first half of the century—and compared to the workers and slaves in the colonies—there were definite improvements in wages and working conditions for the working class as a whole. By the turn of the century, widespread hunger—as we still see today in the Third World—had disappeared from Western Europe.

This trend changed the character of the class struggle. The economic improvements and political concessions that the capitalist class was neither able nor willing to provide to the working class in the core in the first half of the 19th century became possible towards its end. The concessions were not given voluntarily, nor were they a cunning bribe.

In Sweden, less than 25 percent of men and no women had the right to vote for parliament; this exclusion of the larger

60. Johan Söderberg, "Long-term Trends in Real Wages of Laborers." In Rodney Edvinsson, Tor Jacobson, and Daniel Waldenström (eds.), *Exchange Rates, Prices, and Wages, 1277–2008* (Stockholm: Ekerlids Förlag, 2010), 464.

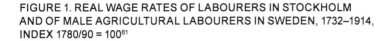

FIGURE 1. REAL WAGE RATES OF LABOURERS IN STOCKHOLM
AND OF MALE AGRICULTURAL LABOURERS IN SWEDEN, 1732–1914,
INDEX 1780/90 = 100[61]

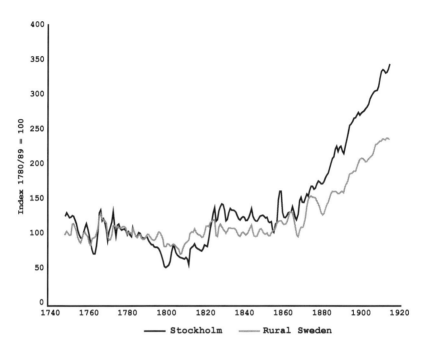

part of the population from political influence led to the emergence of a particularly broad coalition for democratic rights, which took the form of a Liberal–Social Democratic alliance. This laid the basis for the social reformism that came to characterize 20th-century Sweden.[62]

In Europe and the United States, the working class fought for the improvements to their economic and political conditions. Rising wages, better working conditions, and expanded political rights, however, lent credence to the possibility of winning reforms within the system, which in turn made it less risky for the capitalists to grant the working class additional political rights. These compromises made the class struggle less hostile. The revolutionary part of the labor movement weakened as

---

61. Based on a chart in Ibid., 464.

62. Erik Bengtsson, *Värdens Jämligste land?* (Stockholm: Arkiv, 2020).

reformism grew stronger. The Paris Commune was defeated and the International disintegrated in 1871, while trade union and political struggles for reforms met with success. Reformist Social Democratic parties were gaining popularity everywhere in Northwestern Europe.

These reforms and compromises between capital and the working class gradually expressed themselves on the institutional level in the form of state administration. The state began to act on behalf of capitalist society as a whole. As the "dangerous classes" were transformed into citizens, the state began to pay attention to the welfare of its population, their health, personal safety, level of education, and so on. The wellbeing of citizens of the state was increasingly seen as a source of national prosperity and strength. This led to a host of new scientific methods and practical policies for the development of welfare, or what the philosopher Michel Foucault called "biopolitics" or "biopower"—the governance of the power of life.[63] Ruling class concern for people's wellbeing was something new. The rulers of medieval and early modern Europe governed the population with brutality. Subjects were to make their bodies and lives available to the rulers at all times, to maximize the extraction of wealth. This was accomplished by physical punishment and the threat of death. In contrast to this, the new forms of biopolitics sought to control and promote the health and general wellbeing of the population, in order to strengthen the power of the state. A healthy population was considered the prerequisite for a well-functioning economy and a peaceful and orderly society.

However, this transformation had a negative consequence. Biopolitics created unity between the citizens and nation-states of Northwestern Europe and North America—*against* the populations of their colonial empires. The interests of the nation-state became the interests of the working class. As it was in the interest of the nation to acquire colonies, it was in

---

63. Michel Foucault, *Security, Territory, Population* (London: Palgrave Macmillan, 2008).

the interest of the working class to support the colonial empire. Biopolitics meant that the welfare of the citizens of one nation spelled death and misery for those of another. This is what Mark G. E. Kelly calls biopolitical imperialism:

> One might imagine that biopolitical imperialism would mean a flow of biopolitics itself outward into the periphery. I ... argue that, though some movement in this direction does exist, it is not the main way in which biopolitical imperialism operates. Imperialism is a form of power that by and large does not care about the lives of its victims. Imperialism, therefore, is primarily thanatopolitical, a politics of death, contrasting with the biopolitics of the population found in the imperial metropole. There is, I ... contend, a direct relation between the two things, in which death is figuratively exported and life imported back, in a systematic degradation of the possibilities for biopolitics in the periphery, arising out of the operation of biopolitics in the center.[64]

Kelly cites the historian Mike Davis for a number of specific examples of biopolitical imperialism. In case studies of India, China, and Brazil, Davis shows how the imperialist powers, through direct government intervention and economic policies, destroyed the health and welfare of these countries' populations in order to accommodate their own citizens. One example was the massive export of food that took place from India to Britain, even while the people of India were starving:

> Between 1875–1900—a period that included the worst famines in Indian history—annual grain exports increased from 3 to 10 million tons, equivalent to the annual nutrition of 25 million people. Indeed, by the turn of the century, India was supplying nearly a fifth of Britain's wheat consumption at the cost of its own food

---

64. Mark G. E. Kelly, *Biopolitical Imperialism* (Winchester: Zero Books, 2015), 18.

security ... . During the famine of 1899–1900, when 143,000 Beraris died directly from starvation, the province exported not only thousands of bales of cotton but an incredible 747,000 bushels of grain. [Equivalent to 20,330 tons of corn —TL][65]

The "power of life" in Northwestern Europe was premised on the "power of death" in the colonies.

The birth of the welfare state

The idea of a capitalist state providing welfare for its working class did not originate in Sweden but in Germany, in the state capitalist regime of Otto von Bismarck. The Prussian Duke Bismarck represented the interests of the conservative landowners, the Junkers, against the liberal bourgeoisie and republicans. Bismarck, an ardent supporter of the monarchy and Reich Chancellor from 1871 to 1890, was an important architect of the German Empire, which was based on a strong central state with the emperor (or Kaiser) as unifying figure at the top. To secure his strong central state, Bismarck chose to forge an alliance with the working class against the liberal bourgeoisie's desire for less state regulations and expenditures. Thus, in 1881, Bismarck first attempted to introduce an accident insurance law to compensate workers for workplace injuries, to be paid for by employers. The purpose was twofold: to isolate the working class from the influence of more radical forces, and to gain its support in opposing the liberal bourgeoisie's demand for a new constitution, which would have weakened the Kaiser's power. In 1883, a broader Health Insurance Law was passed, with workers contributing one-third of the cost and employers the rest. In 1884, an accident insurance

65. Mike Davis, "The Origin of the Third World," *Antipode* 32, no. 1 (2000): 59, 66.

law was finally passed, completely financed by employers. In 1889, a pension plan and disability insurance for workers were adopted. Bismarck also introduced other forms of government intervention in the economy, including a state monopoly on tobacco imports and sales and the nationalization of the railway system.[66]

Thus, the German state developed legislation against the immediate interests of capital. But make no mistake—Bismarck was no socialist. At the same time as these social reforms were being implemented, a number of repressive laws were adopted to restrict the ability of the more radical wing of the socialist movement to organize. This combination of policies split the German Social Democrats into a reformist and a revolutionary wing, laying the groundwork for social democracy's capitulation to imperialism in the form of support for armaments and nationalism, which contributed to the outbreak of World War I.

The goal of Bismarck's policy was to make Germany a world power on a par with Britain and France. The social reforms were intended to ensure internal unity and class peace while the state pursued an aggressive foreign policy with demands for colonies and increased access to foreign markets—a policy that was also expected to compensate capital for the costs of the social reforms.

As in England, the establishment of the German colonial empire contributed favorably to domestic economic development. From 1886 to 1911, wages in Germany grew significantly. Following this increased economic and political influence, the center of gravity of the socialist movement moved from England and France towards Germany. The German socialist movement grew rapidly, taking organizational form in trade unions and political parties, but at the same time a division arose between revolutionary communists and reformist socialists.

---

66. Cope (2016), 656–57.

The German Social Democratic Party (SPD) came to play a prominent role in the development of reformism in Europe. The SPD found strong support among the upper strata of the German working class. Wilhelm Liebknecht, founder of the German Social Democrats, stated at the 1892 party congress:

> You who sit here are also, most of you, aristocrats to a certain extent, among the workers—I mean in so far as income is concerned. The laboring population in the mining regions of Saxony and the weavers of Silesia would regard such earnings as yours as the income of a veritable Croesus.[67]

The leading ideologue of the German social democrats, Eduard Bernstein, believed that Marx had been proved wrong on several points. Writing in 1889, Bernstein explained that Marx's thesis of capitalism's polarization between poverty and wealth was wrong, pointing to how the standard of living of the German working class was actually rising.[68] Furthermore, Bernstein criticized Marx's statement in *The Communist Manifesto* that "The working men have no country." Bernstein conceded that this may have been the case in 1848, when the *Manifesto* was written, but insisted that by the end of 19th century it was no longer true. According to Bernstein, the working class had gained political and social rights by virtue of social democratic political struggle, and in that process they had become citizens of the nation-state. Social democratic political struggle was therefore from that point on fundamentally national, their task being to reconcile the interests of the working class and the nation. Following this logic, social democrats supported German colonialism. In "On the Military Question, Foreign Policy and the Colonial Question,"

---

67. K. Prandy, A. Stewart, and R. M. Blackburn, *White Collar Unionism* (London: Macmillan, 1983), 54.

68. Eduard Bernstein (1889), *Die Voraussetzungen des Sozialismus and die Aufgaben der Sozialdemokratie* (Hamburg: Rowoht, 1969).

Bernstein argued that Germany had every right to conquer new colonies in order to be able to produce industrial products from tropical raw materials.[69] He concluded that it was possible for the working class to achieve improvements in wages and living standards and to win more and more political rights, all within the framework of capitalism. By means of parliamentary struggle, the working class—which, after all, constituted the majority of the population—could acquire state power and introduce socialism, nice and quietly, with no need for revolution. Bernstein's revision of Marx became the DNA of social democrats, which, at future critical historical junctures, repeatedly caused them to take the side of capital and the nation-state against socialism and international solidarity. The split between social democrats and communists in Germany had severe consequences. A Social Democratic government under the leadership of Friedrich Ebert and Defense Minister Gustav Noske used the army and paramilitary forces to bloodily suppress the socialist/communist uprisings of 1919.

Colonialist and racist attitudes spread fast within the SPD. In 1900, the party supported German participation in the Eight-Nation Alliance, a multinational military coalition set up in response to the Boxer Rebellion in Imperial China. The forces consisted of 45,000 troops from the German Empire, Japan, Russia, Britain, France, the United States, Italy, and Austria-Hungary. At the German Social Democratic Congress in Mainz later that year, Rosa Luxemburg was the only member to condemn this imperialist aggression. At the same time, the SPD opposed Chinese (so-called "coolie") immigration to Germany. Chinese workers were viewed as competing with the European working class and had to be excluded from the labor market in Europe.[70]

---

69. Ibid., 177.

70. Otto Bauer (1907), "Proletarische Wanderungen," *Die neue Zeit: Wochenschrift der deutschen Sozialdemokratie* 1907, no. 41: 489.

The Social Democrats' position on colonialism was also reflected in meetings of the Second International. In the first years of the Second International, there was a consensus on a clear position against colonialism. However, at its 7th Congress, in Stuttgart in 1907, the anti-colonial line was challenged by the German Social Democrats. There, just three years after the German army and settlers had committed genocide against the people of South West Africa, SPD president Eduard Bernstein—agreeing with party founder Ferdinand Lasalle—stated that:

> People who do not develop may be justifiably subjugated by people who have achieved civilisation ... . Socialists too should acknowledge the need for civilized peoples to act like the guardians of the uncivilized ... our economies are based in large measure on the extraction from the colonies of products that the native peoples have no idea how to use.[71]

Another leading Social Democrat, Eduard David, put it bluntly: "Europe needs colonies; it does not have enough of them. Without them, we would be economically like China."[72] (May I add: Exactly!)

The German Social Democrats' nationalist strategy was successful in terms of attracting voters. With Karl Kautsky at the forefront, it became Europe's strongest and most influential social democratic party. In the 1912 German elections, the party won the most seats in the Reichstag, with 34.8 percent of the votes. Like the other social democratic parties in Europe, the SPD voted for war credits in 1914, thereby aligning itself with capital in Germany's conflicts with France and England over the imperialist division of the world.

---

71. H. Tudor and J. M. Tudor, *Marxism and Social Democracy: The Revisionist Debate, 1896–1898* (Cambridge: University Press, 1988), 52.

72. John Riddell (ed.), *Lenin's Struggle for a Revolutionary International* (New York: Pathfinder, 1984), 6.

The first Swedish socialist party program was written in 1882 by August Palm, a tailor. He had returned to Malmö in 1881 after working and traveling in Germany and Denmark. It is therefore no wonder that it was largely a translation of the Danish Social Democrats' program from 1876, which in turn was more or less a copy of the German Social Democrats' Gotha Program of 1875.[73] Marx had these harsh words to say about the Gotha Program, regarding its split from internationalism:

> Lassalle, in opposition to the *Communist Manifesto* and to all earlier socialism, conceived the workers' movement from the narrowest national standpoint ...

> Not a word, therefore, about the international functions of the German working class! And it is thus that it is to challenge its own bourgeoisie—which is already linked up in brotherhood against it with the bourgeois of all other countries—and Herr Bismarck's international policy of conspiracy ... . Bismarck's *Norddeutsche* was absolutely right when it announced, to the satisfaction of its master, that the German Workers' party had sworn off internationalism in the new program.[74]

In April 1889, the Swedish Social Democratic Party (officially the Social Democratic Workers' Party of Sweden, the *Sveriges Socialdemokratiska Arbetareparti,* or SAP) was formed with the support of the trade union movement. In 1896, Hjalmar Branting was elected to the Riksdag—the parliament—as Sweden's first Social Democratic member of parliament. In 1897, the SAP released its first official party program—written by Axel Danielsson and based on the German Social

---

73. E. Wiinblad and Alsing Andersen, *Det danske socialdemokratis historie fra 1871 til 1921* (København: Forlaget Fremad, 1921), 8.

74. Karl Marx and Frederick Engels (1875), "Critique of the Gotha Programme." In *Marx and Engels Selected Works,* vol. 3 (Moscow: Progress Publishers, 1970), 13–30. *Norddeutsche* was a daily newspaper and the official organ of Bismarck's government.

Democrats' Erfurt Program—in which nationalism and reformism were taken even further.

It was not only the Social Democrats who were inspired by political ideologies from Germany. The Swedish conservative social scientist and politician Rudolf Kjellén (1864–1922) developed the idea of the Swedish *folkhemmet*—the "people's home"—inspired by Bismarck's German state. *Folkhemmet* would become a core concept in the ideology of the Swedish Social Democrats. Kjellén was a member of parliament from 1905 to 1917 and an acclaimed professor at Gothenburg University, known today as "the father of geopolitics." In his book *Introduction to the Geography of Sweden*, published in 1900, he described the Swedish people as having Germanic origins and the state as a living organism in need of "lebensraum"— living space. Kjellén hoped to reconcile conservatism with an anti-Marxist form of socialism that eschewed class struggle in favor of nationalism: the state was to provide the basis for a national community, a unified national people, without any division of citizens into separate economic classes.[75] He wrote in 1915:

> One thing is certain: only on its own soil can Sweden build up the happy "folkhem" [people's home], which it is meant to be. Nationalism provides the only salvation from the voices of our age who, in the name of a misunderstood internationalism, wish to lure wide sections of the people into relinquishing their providential living conditions—i.e. their own innermost personality.[76]

As the two countries were meant to share a common destiny, Kjellén was a keen advocate of Swedish participation in the First World War, on Germany's side. According to Kjellén,

---

75. Hans Dahlqvist, "Folkhemsbegreppet: Rudolf Kjellén vs Per Albin Hansson," *Historisk Tidsskrift* 122, no. 3 (2002): 452.

76. Rudolf Kjellén (1915), "Nationalism och socialism," *Nationell samling*, 56. Here from: Ibid.: 454.

war had an educational and healing effect on the character of the nation. In 1910 he wrote that war "is like a bath for the renewal of nationalism. Nothing teaches us so tangibly as war that we are our own nation, that we belong to a common homeland."[77]

With Germany's defeat in the First World War, Kjellén—himself a member of parliament—became opposed to parliamentary democracy. In one article he stated that "parliamentary democracy is not an idea suited for 1914." In a lecture delivered in Uppsala in 1921, he envisaged the collapse of democracy in Germany, predicting that a leader would emerge from the broad strata of the people to create a new society.

There is much disagreement as to the extent to which Sweden's Social Democrats were influenced by Kjellén in the development of their version of *folkhemmet*, but it is certainly clear that there are some similarities. The chairperson of the Social Democrats at the turn of the century, Hjalmar Branting, hoped to forge a socialism based on cross-class alliances: "The goal ... is through struggle to achieve a solidarity that ... extends across the nation and through this ... to include all people."[78]

In 1925, Swedish Prime Minister Per Albin Hansson (1865–1946) used the term in a speech, emphasizing that the social democratic "folkhem"—unlike Kjellén's—should be built on a firm foundation of equality and democracy.[79] The Social Democrats, however, were in fact moving away from class politics by adopting this concept. In one article in the social democratic journal *Ny Tid* (autumn 1929), Hansson evoked the *folkhem* in a polemic against the communists:

That is where ... the class concept seems self-limiting and isolating, whereas the concept of the people instead

77. Rudolf Kjellén (1910) "Fredens fariséer," 42. Here from Hans Dahlqvist (2002): 455.

78. Sheri Berman, *The Primacy of Politics: Social Democracy and the Making of Europe's Twentieth Century* (Cambridge: Cambridge University Press, 2006), 157.

79. Dahlqvist (2002): 459.

opens the path to cooperation ... . There is hardly any doubt that the concept of the people is much more unifying than the class concept and thus also in terms of agitation the former gives better results than the latter.[80]

The *folkhem* was to be managed by a political party representing the people of the nation, not special class interests. The "home" should provide security for everyone. In Hansson's *folkhem* one is a "fellow citizen." Economic class disparities were to be leveled out, class power replaced by parliamentary democracy. In *folkhemmet*, the emphasis was on reducing differences in income rather than changing the relations of property ownership. Although Kjellén's Bismarckian national conservatism differed from social democracy, the two shared a common ground of nation-based state capitalism.

Getting rid of Lenin

Sweden was not unaffected by the split between social democrats and communists that developed in the years before the First World War. The crises of the Second International and the formation of factions such as the Zimmerwald Movement divided the social democrats and led to the emergence of a left-wing opposition. One of the points of disagreement concerned the possibility of revolution in Russia. The German Social Democratic leaders Bernstein and Kautsky were of the opinion that socialist revolution could only take place in the most developed parts of Europe, not in backwards Russia. Lenin, on the other hand, saw the possibility of a socialist revolution in the weakest link of European capitalism and hoped that such an event might trigger revolutions in the more developed

---

80. Per Albin Hansson (1929), "Klasskampsbegreppet," *i Från Fram till folkhemmet*, 186. Here from Dahlqvist (2002): 461.

European countries.

In the spring of 1917, this possibility began to materialize. The German government allowed Lenin to travel home in a sealed train from his exile in Switzerland, hoping that his presence in Russia would help to end the war. Lenin left Germany at the Sassnitz seaport on April 12, traveling by ferry to Trelleborg in Sweden. He planned to pass through Sweden to Finland and from there to Russia. It is not known whether the Swedish government was informed about this journey by the German authorities; however, the Social Democrats were well aware of the arrival of the Russian revolutionary. Erik Palmstierna (1877–1959), an aristocrat and naval officer—and a leading Social Democrat—sprang into action; as he would recall in his memoirs:

> When Lenin passed through Stockholm at that time, I heard about it and called Branting [the leader of the Social Democratic Party and later Prime Minister] with the words: "You know Kerensky. Tell him that Lenin will arrive on the next train and must be shot down or imprisoned when he crosses the border. Send him a telegram." Branting just laughed and said, "You're really crazy; one does not do that," but I interrupted him and replied on the phone: "You are an old-fashioned liberal and you think like it was the 1880s. What we need now are men who dare to act!"[81]

Six months later, in October 1917, Palmstierna became Minister of Naval Affairs in the Liberal–Social Democratic government and later, in 1920, Minister of Foreign Affairs in the first Social Democratic government, led by Branting. He never made any secret of his wish to see Lenin dead. In his memoirs, he also recounted a meeting with the Russian Tsar's minister-in-exile, in Stockholm in 1918:

---

81. Erik Palmstierna, *Orostid: politiska dagboksanteckningar*, vol. 2 (Stockholm: Tidens förlag, 1952), 163.

Gulkevitj, the Russian minister, who attended one of
my wife's "Tuesdays for the diplomatic corps," had many
interesting things to say about the situation in Russia.
I told Gulkevitj that when Lenin had passed through
Stockholm, I found out about it and phoned Branting ... [82]

Gulkevitj was disappointed that Branting had not taken the
suggestion to kill Lenin seriously. Palmstierna recalled his
reaction:

Gulkevitj understood the situation and said with tears in
his eyes: "Mon cher baron, vous aviez le sort de la Russie
entre mains." [My dear Baron, you held Russia's fate in
your hands.] Just think if Branting had listened to my
advice. [83]

Things did not turn out that way; instead, Lenin crossed the
Torne River at Haparanda, out of Swedish territory and into
the center of world history.

The civil war in Finland

The inter-imperialist rivalry of the First World War opened
a window of opportunity for revolutionary change in Europe.
Lenin's Bolsheviks succeeded in Russia and that inspired
a more or less spontaneous uprising in Germany from
November 1918 to January 1919, which was crushed by right-
wing militias supported by the Social Democratic government.
On March 21, 1919, the Hungarian Soviet Republic was proclaimed—it was not long-lived, however: on August 1, 133
days later, the revolution was brought to a close by the entry

---

82. Ibid.

83. Ibid. Palmstierna, who was from an aristocratic family, called himself the "red baron" after the
famous First World War German fighter pilot.

of the White Romanian army into Budapest. The Russian Revolution also affected Finland, Sweden neighbor. Between January and May 1918, Finland experienced a bitter civil war. On one side stood the "reds," socialists and communists, consisting primarily of urban and rural workers living in the south of the country. On the other side stood the "whites," made up of the Swedish-speaking middle and upper classes and the farmers who dominated the north. The whites received military support from Germany, which was concerned by the spread of revolutionary socialism in the East. The attitude of the Swedish Social Democrats toward the revolutionary movement in Finland was not much different from that of the German Social Democrats.

The Swedish Social Democrats, who at the time were participating in a government coalition alongside the Liberal Party, were worried about the possibility of a "red" victory and its potential to generate radical left-wing political activity in Sweden. In his diary, Palmstierna disclosed how the leader of the white forces, General Mannerheim, had asked the Swedish government for permission to transport arms through Sweden and to send a contingent of Swedish soldiers and officers to assist the white army. The Swedish government could not do so openly, however. Palmstierna explained:

> Overall, is impossible for us to act as a party, as the situation has developed along pure class lines. On one side the Socialist Party, workers and small farmers, on the other side state power, ruled by the Swedish upper class—who have our sympathies. It is not possible to openly take sides. Doing so would immediately trigger serious struggles here at home.[84]

The government secretly favored the whites but was under domestic and foreign pressure. Officially, the Swedish king

---

84. Ibid. Here from: Rainer Andersson, *Vad gjorde du i Finland, far? Svenska frivilliga i finska inbördeskriget 1918* (Stockholm: Sahlgrens förlag, 1999), 38.

and the Liberal–Social Democratic government declared that Sweden was neutral in the civil war. Many Swedish socialists opposed supporting the whites, as did the allied powers of England and France, wary of their ties with the German Empire.

This formal neutrality, however, did not prevent the Swedish government from extending covert support. General Mannerheim had eighty-four Swedish volunteer officers on his staff. What's more, a Swedish brigade of approximately one thousand soldiers, under the command of Hjalmar Frisell, participated in the fighting against red forces in and around Tampere. The government secretly authorized the export of 2,000 rifles, 100,000 cartridges, 10 machine guns, and 50,000 hand grenades to the white army. In addition, Swedish volunteers were allowed to carry large quantities of arms. The total quantity of arms and supplies smuggled across the border remains unknown, but it was not uncommon for fully loaded train carriages to cross bringing weapons to the white side. In February 1918, the Swedish government also supplied naval escorts, aircraft patrols, and icebreakers to the German cargo ships that sailed from Germany, heavily laden with arms and one thousand white Finnish elite soldiers who had received special military training in Germany.

The Swedish government, and Minister of Naval Affairs Palmstierna himself, had their own agenda, in addition to opposing the reds: to take advantage of the civil war to acquire the Åland Islands from Finland. The islands were strategically located in the middle of the Gulf of Bothnia in the Baltic Sea. The Swedish government sent a military expedition to the islands in February 1918. Swedish propaganda justified this on humanitarian grounds, but the actual motive was to strengthen Sweden's geopolitical standing in the Baltic Sea.[85]

---

85. Anthony F. Upton, *The Finnish Revolution 1917–1918* (Minnesota: University of Minnesota Press, 1980), 90–120

After the white victory in May 1918, suspected reds were hunted down and interned in concentration camps where thousands were executed or died due to malnutrition and illness. A total of 37,000 people perished in connection with the civil war in Finland.[86]

Swedish capitalism in the interwar period

Sweden experienced a period of industrial expansion in the interwar years. Sweden's wood, paper, metal, and machine industries bolstered its international position throughout the 1920s. The Electrolux Group was founded in 1910; its first product was a vacuum cleaner, but soon many other home appliances and electrical machines for use in professional kitchens and laundries were being produced. Electrolux is today the world's second-largest manufacturer of household appliances. Founded in 1927, Volvo established itself as a manufacturer of safe, reliable, good-quality personal cars and trucks. Saab, which stands for Svenska Aeroplan Aktiebolaget, was founded in 1937, specializing in the production of weapons systems, airplanes, and electronics. In 1947, it expanded to producing cars. Husqvarna dates back to 1689; up until the 1870s, it mainly manufactured firearms. It later began producing motorcycles, mopeds, and bicycles, different kinds of tools, and sewing machines. Arms production continued with the popular Husqvarna submachine gun, among other weaponry.

Another important Swedish enterprise in the early 20th century was the Kreuger Group. In 1915, Ivar Kreuger consolidated ten match companies under the name United Swedish Match Factories, the flagship company within the group being a match company he had founded in 1910. The

---

86. Pekka Hämäläinen "Revolution, Civil War, and Ethnic Relations: The Case of Finland," *Journal of Baltic Studies* 5, no. 2 (1974): 117–25.

First World War complicated Swedish access to phosphorus and calcium carbonate, vital components in the production of matches. Nevertheless, Kreuger managed to secure better supplies than any other factory and acquired his main competitor, Jönköping-Vulcan Match, the two companies merging into Svenska Tändsticks AB. The Kreuger Group was formally established in 1917 and grew rapidly through the acquisition of leading match companies in Europe, the United States, and South America. Kreuger set up a holding company, International Match Corporation, which had its headquarters in New York.

Today, matches are considered an insignificant product, but at the time, they were a tremendously important commodity: everybody bought matches, every day. In the 1920s, Kreuger was one of the most prominent and powerful business executives in Europe. His company became a symbol of monopoly capital: the Kreuger Group accounted for two thirds of the world's production of matches and controlled more than two hundred match factories in thirty-five countries. It had an official monopoly on the sale of matches in fifteen countries and dominated the market in another ten.

There are many colorful examples of the tricks and methods Kreuger used to maintain its monopoly position. In Peru, where Kreuger had an official monopoly on the sale of matches, the company hired "provocateurs" who would approach people, preferably foreigners, asking them for a light. If the victim used matches that did not come from a Kreuger company, or a lighter, it triggered a heavy fine, half of which went into the pocket of the provocateur.[87]

In Belgium, Kreuger paid an agent, Sven Huldt, to persuade local match makers to be part of a joint company to resist Kreuger's own company. As soon as the deal was in place, Huldt sold out to Kreuger. In countries such as Turkey, Yugoslavia, Guatemala, Ecuador, and Peru, Kreuger obtained

87. John Train, *Berømte finansfiaskoer* (Oslo: Forlaget Periscopus, 1993), 73.

his official monopoly by financing loans to the government. Kreuger also received France's highest award after lending 75 million francs to the French state.[88]

Throughout the 1920s, Kreuger established a broad network of financial and industrial enterprises, in parallel with the match companies. The Swedish companies he controlled were concentrated in the paper, machine, telecommunications, and mining industries. In 1930, the Kreuger Group accounted for 64 percent of activity on the Stockholm Stock Exchange.[89]

Like today's transnational corporations, Kreuger used a web of shell companies. In the 1920s, he had more than 400 companies registered in Liechtenstein and similar places where there were minimal regulations and no taxes. Not even the companies' directors or accountants were fully informed of Kreuger's many transactions, and even his personal assistant, Kristor Littorin, was kept in the dark. Kreuger was self-reliant and made all major decisions on his own. He was a great admirer of Napoleon Bonaparte; as Kreuger put it, he "did not hold war councils because one first-class brain is enough for an entire army."[90]

The world economic crisis that followed the New York stock market crash in 1929 caused huge problems for the Kreuger Group. Initially, however, Kreuger managed to keep everything going through a series of daring cons. President Herbert Hoover received him regularly at the White House to discuss the global economic situation and ask his advice. When Lee, Higginson & Co. of Boston, a huge investor in Kreuger's business, suspected something fishy they sent a director, Donald Durant, to Stockholm to investigate the matter. Kreuger organized a large party, attended by prominent figures and diplomats, to impress Durant. It worked, and Durant went home confident that Kreuger's financial situation

88. Bill Wilson, "Kreuger: The Original Bernard Madoff?" *BBC News*, March 13, 2009.

89. Stig Algott, *Stockholms fondbörs 100 år* (Stockholm: Nordiska bokhandeln, 1963).

90. Train (1993), 77.

was sound. It later turned out that many of the guests had been paid to attend the party. One of the directors of International Match, Percy Rockefeller, also suspected mismanagement, and asked for a personal meeting with Kreuger. During the interview, Kreuger appeared to receive telephone calls from English Prime Minister Stanley Baldwin, Stalin, and Henri Poincaré, one of the leading scientists of the time. Rockefeller was impressed and subsequently reassured his colleagues, "We are lucky to be associated with Ivar Kreuger." Only later was it revealed that Kreuger had simply spoken into a silent phone. Kreuger became increasingly desperate, forging Italian bonds for $143 million and using them as collateral to take out a number of loans.[91]

Eventually, it became impossible to hide that something was seriously wrong in the company. The price of Kreuger shares fell on the New York Stock Exchange from its highest listing of over $46 in March 1929 to $4.50 near the end of 1931. When the banks began to demand Kreuger repay its loans in the autumn of 1931, the company's liquidity crisis became acute. Kreuger sought to raise capital by selling a large stake of shares in LM Ericsson, a major telephone company. The US company ITT was initially willing to pay $11 million for the shares but then withdrew. That was the end for Ivar Kreuger, who shot himself in his Paris apartment. An audit subsequently revealed that Kreuger was bankrupt; claims against the estate totaled over a billion dollars—an amount which at the time was more than Sweden's total public debt.[92] The so-called Kreuger Crash resulted in a wave of bankruptcies and suicides among Swedish CEOs and the resignation of the prime minister.[93]

---

91. Ibid., 78–79.
92. Ibid., 79.
93. The Economist, "The Match King," December 19, 2007.

The Stockholm School of Economics

The capitalist world crisis of the 1930s got rid of smaller and less profitable companies, thereby leading to a greater concentration of capital. At the same time, banking and financial capital in Sweden strengthened its hold on the productive industrial sector. As the Kreuger Group fell apart, the financier Knut Wallenberg picked up the pieces, strengthening his position as the leading capitalist in Sweden.

On the political front, one consequence of the Kreuger Group's collapse was that political parties associated with big capital were weakened. Several prominent Liberal politicians were personally involved in the Kreuger scandal. Liberal and business-friendly economic politics, which had been prevalent in the 1920s, had no solutions for the problems that had arisen in the wake of the world economic crisis. This paved the way for a social democratic economic policy that would attempt to regulate capitalism to avoid future crises.

The Swedish social democratic capitalist welfare state developed its own economic theory and practice based on ideas from the Stockholm School of Economics. Paradoxically, the aforementioned financier Knut Wallenberg was the main financial sponsor of the institution. Founded in 1909, its original purpose was to educate economists in order to be able to modernize Sweden's economy and develop international trade. The connection between the capitalist Wallenberg and the development of social democratic economic policy can be traced to a common German inspiration.

The Swedish Social Democrats were, as previously mentioned, inspired by the German Social Democrats' Gotha Program, which—besides being nationalistic and focused on reforms within the capitalist framework—also disputed Marx's theory of labor being the source of value creation.

The American Marxist Louis Proyect has explained the conection between the German Social Democrats and the

Stockholm School of Economics.[94] At the time, the German Social Democrats supported Eugen Böhm von Bawerk's theory of value; Bohm-Bawerk is considered the father of the Austrian School of Economics, which included economists such as Ludwig von Mises and Friedrich Hayek, the theoretical architects of neoliberalism. Someone else who was inspired by Böhm-Bawerk and shared his criticisms of Marx's theory of value was Knut Wicksell (1851–1926), the first and founding professor of the Stockholm School of Economics. But if Wicksell was inspired by Bohm-Bawerk and if the Stockholm School of Economics later developed economic policies associated with John Maynard Keynes, how does one explain this strange mixture of neoliberal and social-liberal economic thinking? The answer lies in Wicksell's economic theories.

Knut Wicksell was a very eclectic person. He was partly inspired by the classical ideas of David Ricardo and the Austrian School of Economics, both very liberal sources, but also by Keynes's early writings, which recommended that the state should regulate capitalism. No wonder Wicksell has been called the "economist of economists." Despite his liberal roots, he concluded that a capitalist economy left to its own devices would produce recurrent devastating crises and make the rich richer and the poor poorer. To counter this, state-regulated interest rates and monetary policy were necessary. Wicksell's theoretical specialty was interest rates, prices, and monetary policy, and he was a strong advocate of using interest rates to maintain price stability. In addition, he advocated progressive taxation to promote a more equal distribution of wealth.

Wicksell was also influenced by the classical economist Thomas Malthus and his theories about overpopulation. He was deeply worried that technological development, productivity, and the volume of production would not be able to keep pace with population growth. He sought to determine the

94. Louis Proyect, "The economic theory and policies of Swedish social democracy," Louis Proyect: The Unrepentant Marxist (blog), September 25, 2015.

"optimal population size" and, as a result, was a strong advocate of birth control.

Wicksell was a controversial figure who was outspoken on many social issues. He was strongly opposed to alcohol and prostitution; he questioned social hierarchy, the institution of marriage, the Church, monarchy, and the military. His wife, Anna Bugge, was a prominent feminist. At a lecture in 1908, he poked fun at the idea of Jesus's "virgin birth," which led to his conviction for blasphemy and two months' imprisonment. Wicksell saw himself as more than just an economist; he wanted to be a social reformer.[95]

Notwithstanding all this, in 1916 Wicksell became a government advisor on finance and banking matters. He died in 1926, but his Stockholm School of Economics was to be further developed by esteemed economists such as Bertil Ohlin, Gunnar Myrdal, and Erik Lindahl. Dag Hammarskjöld, the later Social Democratic minister and Secretary-General of the United Nations, was also a pupil of Wicksell's.[96] (We will return to Hammarskjöld later.)

In 1937, Bertil Ohlin published an article entitled "Some Notes on the Stockholm Theory of Savings and Investment," in the influential *Economic Journal*. The article was published in response to Keynes's book *The General Theory of Employment, Interest and Money*, which had appeared the year prior. The purpose of the article was to draw international attention to the Stockholm School of Economics, which according to Ohlin had anticipated Keynes's findings. Gunnar Myrdal, who was also a supporter of Keynes's ideas, maintained that he and the School of Economics had first suggested adjusting national budgets to slow down or speed up a national economy.

---

95. Mats Lundahl, *Knut Wicksell on Poverty: No Place is Too Exalted for the Preaching of these Doctrines* (London: Routledge, 2005), 96.

96. Benny Carlson and Lars Jonung, "Knut Wicksell, Gustav Cassel, Eli Heckscher, Bertil Ohlin and Gunnar Myrdal on the Role of the Economist in Public Debate," *Econ Journal Watch* 3, no. 3 (September 2006).

Of greater importance to immediate political concerns, Wicksell and his pupils influenced Ernst Wigforss (1881–1977), who was the Social Democratic Finance Minister for most of the period from 1924 to 1949, as well as being a special advisor to the trade union movement. Wigforss was a knowledgeable economist in his own right and a Keynesian before Keynes, so to speak. Like Keynes, Wigforss believed that left unregulated, capitalism would run off track. There was an inherent imbalance in capitalism between the growing supply of goods and the limited purchasing power created by wages and profits from the same production. This contradiction would lead to crises of overproduction/underconsumption and then to unemployment. The state had to regulate capitalism, partly through interest rates and monetary and fiscal policies to stimulate employment, partly through state-initiated projects, such as new infrastructure and social housing, to promote employment and thereby increase purchasing power. During the economic slump of the 1930s, the Social Democratic government implemented Wicksell and Wigforss's ideas about interest rates and monetary and price policy, to get the wheels of the economy spinning again.[97] Wigforss is also regarded as the mastermind behind the high and progressive income tax in Sweden, used to finance social welfare measures and redistribute income in society.

In the post–World War II Cold War, with its two rival political blocs around the United States and the Soviet Union, the Stockholm School of Economics enjoyed international appeal for promising a "third way" between a liberal capitalist economy and a socialist planned economy. The supposed accomplishment of this third way was to have achieved a high level of social equality and welfare without undermining the "efficiency" of the capitalist market economy. In order to succeed, however, such an economic strategy requires that some political and class-related preconditions be met.

---

97. Lars Jonung, "Knut Wicksell's Norm of Price Stabilization and Swedish Monetary Policy in the 1930s," *Journal of Monetary Economics* 5 (1979): 459–96.

The division of power

Despite almost half a century of continuous Social Democratic governments, capitalism has never been challenged in Sweden. The economy is firmly based on the accumulation of capital, a market economy, and private ownership of the means of production. Sweden is a capitalist state based on the rule of law, freedom of expression, and the right to organize. However, it is a special form of capitalist state. The Swedish state has been characterized by a division of power between the working class and the bourgeoisie via parliamentary mechanisms. This division of power does not mean that class struggle has ended. It is an expression of it.

The Swedish capitalist welfare state does not solely represent the interests of capital or the working class. The state is an organization that class society establishes in order to maintain social peace and uphold the optimal conditions for its mode of production. The prime minister of the welfare state is not the representative of narrow capitalist interests or of working-class interests but is simply the representative of the current mode of production. Power accrues to the government best suited to serve, preserve, and develop the existing mode of production, based on the informal social contract between capital and labor. This is how a capitalist welfare state comes to exercise hegemony. As Gramsci explained: "Obviously, the fact of hegemony presupposes that the interests and tendencies of those groups over whom hegemony is exercised have been taken into account and a certain equilibrium is established."[98]

There is nothing new, special, or controversial about the division of state power between classes. In a series of articles from 1848–50, collected under the title *The Class Struggles in France*, Marx described how the constitution of the bourgeois state grants political rights to the classes it exploits:

---

98. Antonio Gramsci [1929–35], *Prison Notebooks*, vol. 2, Notebook 4 (New York: Columbia University Press, 1996), 183.

The comprehensive contradiction of this constitution, however, consists in the following: The classes whose social slavery the constitution is to perpetuate— proletariat, peasantry, petty bourgeoisie—it puts in possession of political power through universal suffrage (sic). And from the class whose old social power it sanctions, the bourgeoisie, it withdraws the political guarantees of this power. It forces the political rule of the bourgeoisie into democratic conditions, which at every moment help the hostile classes to victory and jeopardize the very foundations of bourgeois society. From the first group it demands that they should not go forward from political to social emancipation; from the others that they should not go back from social to political restoration.[99]

Sweden's constitution and parliamentary system serve the same purpose. They guarantee the economic predominance of capital while at the same time providing political rights to all citizens. With this power-sharing arrangement, class struggle is limited to dividing up the benefits from the accumulation of capital. Throughout the last century, this state form became increasingly important for the management of capitalism in the core. What's more, this state form became the owner of infrastructure, institutions, and even means of production, and the capitalist welfare state developed a significant public sector employing many people (a fact that would help to secure its existence).

It is important to remember, however, that the emergence of this power-sharing arrangement and the subsequent construction of the welfare state were tied closely to the development of imperialism—a fact that is denied or dismissed by social democrats and many on the left, who tend to view class struggle

---

99. Karl Marx [1850], "The Class Struggles in France, 1848 to 1850, Part II. From June 1848 to June 13, 1849." In *Marx and Engels Selected Works*, vol. 1 (Moscow: Progress Publishers, 1969).

from a strictly national perspective. Seen from such a perspective, reformism waged a very successful struggle.

Imperialism and the split in socialism

It was this combination of nationalism and reformism that Lenin fought against so fiercely in the Second International, in the years around the First World War. He rhetorically asked the question:

> Is there any connection between imperialism and the monstrous and disgusting victory opportunism (in the form of social-chauvinism) has gained over the labour movement in Europe? This is the fundamental question of modern socialism.[100]

Lenin's answer was affirmative. Imperialism promoted extraordinary profits and national chauvinism, which laid the basis for what Lenin called a "labor aristocracy" and for the success of its political representatives, the Social Democrats. Lenin described the phenomenon in his pamphlet *Imperialism, the Highest Stage of Capitalism*:

> As this pamphlet shows, capitalism has now singled out a handful (less than one-tenth of the inhabitants of the globe; less than one-fifth at a most "generous" and liberal calculation) of exceptionally rich and powerful states which plunder the whole world simply by "clipping coupons." Capital exports yield an income of eight to ten thousand million francs per annum, at pre-war prices and according to pre-war bourgeois statistics. Now, of course, they yield much more.

---

100. V. I. Lenin [1916], "Imperialism and the Split in Socialism." In *Lenin Collected Works*, vol. 23 (Moscow: Progress Publishers, 1964), 105–120.

Obviously, out of such enormous superprofits (since they are obtained over and above the profits which capitalists squeeze out of the workers of their "own" country) it is possible to bribe the labour leaders and the upper stratum of the labour aristocracy. And that is just what the capitalists of the "advanced" countries are doing: they are bribing them in a thousand different ways, direct and indirect, overt and covert.

This stratum of workers-turned-bourgeois, or the labour aristocracy, who are quite philistine in their mode of life, in the size of their earnings and in their entire outlook, is the principal prop of the Second International, and in our days, the principal social (not military) prop of the bourgeoisie. For they are the real agents of the bourgeoisie in the working-class movement, the labour lieutenants of the capitalist class, real vehicles of reformism and chauvinism. In the civil war between the proletariat and the bourgeoisie they inevitably, and in no small numbers, take the side of the bourgeoisie, the "Versaillais" against the "Communards."

Unless the economic roots of this phenomenon are understood and its political and social significance is appreciated, not a step can be taken toward the solution of the practical problems of the communist movement and of the impending social revolution.[101]

The concept of "Social Imperialism," meaning social democratic politics at home and imperialism abroad, was widely used by Lenin.

---

101. V. I. Lenin [1917], "Imperialism, the Highest Stage of Capitalism." In *Lenin Collected Works*, vol. 22 (Moscow: Progress Publishers, 1972), 193–94.

The split in Sweden

The Social Democrats in Denmark and Sweden did not start out revolutionary and then become reformist. Under the tute-lage of the German Social Democrats, these parties were born reformist. Nonetheless, they each had minority radical fac-tions. As a result of Lenin's ideological struggle in the Second International, there was in Sweden — as in the rest of Europe — a split between the vast majority of Social Democrats and the minority of Communists, who in Sweden organized as the *Socialdemokratiska Vänsterparti* (Social Democratic Left Party). In 1919 they joined the newly formed Third International (the Comintern), and in 1921 they changed their name to the *Sveriges Kommunistiska Parti* (Communist Party of Sweden).[102]

This split created distrust between the two wings of the Swedish labor movement. The Social Democrats regarded the Communists as traitors to their nation because of their wholehearted defense of "socialism in one country"—the Soviet Union. The Communists, in turn, considered the Social Democrats to be class traitors because they cooperated with capital.

There is no doubt that the organizational split strengthened the position of the Social Democrats in parliament. First, it sent a signal that the Social Democrats were unequivocally committed to reforms within a capitalist framework. Second, the fear of radical forms of socialism helped convince the bour-geoisie to accept the existence of Social Democratic govern-ments, as the lesser of two evils. Following their parting with the radical left, the Social Democrats would play a leading role in Swedish politics: with the exception of four years (1928–32), they would control the government from 1921 to 1976. Karen

---

102. In 1929 the Swedish Communist Party split. One faction remained in the Comintern, the other left and changed its name to the Socialist Party. In 1967 it changed its name again, to *Vänsterpartiet Kommunisterna* (VPK) (Left Party Communists). In 1990 it changed once again, to simply *Vänsterpartiet* (Left Party).

Anderson and Steven Snow have described the role of Sweden's Social Democrats in government:

> The Social Democrats were historically linked to the unions, from which they derived much political support, but as a party often in government, it felt obliged to reduce the economic losses from labor conflicts. In the 1920s the SAP "repeatedly advocated general interests over and above the struggle of individual groups of workers for better working conditions." Throughout this period, in fact, the SAP often stood with employers on the issue of wage rates. When the employers said that a wage reduction was unavoidable, the Social Democratic representatives in the unions often supported them. In 1920, for example, in response to a recession and in the face of unions' appeals, the Social Democratic Minister of Finance declared "The demand for increased wages must cease." The party was also willing to criticize outbreaks of violence in clashes between workers and police. In several labor disputes, even though the police apparently used excessive force, the SAP proved willing to denounce the tactics of striking workers. "Offenses against existing law must always be condemned," the SAP Prime Minister argued.[103]

The world economic crisis in the 1930s provided the opening for the Social Democratic movement's big breakthrough. Social Democrats put forth an economic policy that was able to pull capitalism out of its crisis, not only in Sweden but also throughout Northwestern Europe as well as the United States, where such policies took the form of President Roosevelt's New Deal. Through social welfare programs, infrastructure construction projects, and social housing, jobs were created

---

103. Karen Anderson and Steven Snow, "Forestalling the Business Veto: Investment Confidence and the Rise of Swedish Social Democracy," *Social Science Quarterly* 84, no. 1 (March 2003). Here from Proyect, "The economic theory and policies of Swedish social democracy."

and this in turn increased purchasing power and got the wheels of capitalism turning again. The social democrats were managing capitalism better than the liberals and conservatives. At the same time, social democratic policies defused the threat of social unrest in response to the crisis.

Another reason for the parliamentary success of the Social Democratic Party was its transformation from a working-class party into a "people's party." The Social Democrats were able to form coalitions, not only with capital but also with farmers. In 1933, the Social Democratic government drafted an agreement with the *Bondeforbundet* (Farmers' Federation—the predecessor of the Center Party). The Farmers' Federation agreed to support the Social Democratic government's labor market policy in exchange for subsidies for agricultural commodities. The opposition denounced the settlement as shameless horse-trading, but regardless, it signaled the start of a long-term collaboration.

As previously noted, social democratic economic policy is based on the idea of a "third way." Not naked capitalism and the dictatorship of the bourgeoisie but also not communism and the dictatorship of the proletariat. Instead, a political system where the working class and capital must work together to avoid mutually destructive confrontations and must try to achieve a high employment rate and maximum productivity. To achieve these goals, conflict between labor and capital must be resolved peacefully in a fixed institutional framework.

Following a major strike in 1909, the Swedish labor market had been characterized by many unregulated conflicts and wildcat strikes. These reached a high point in 1930–32 (see table below). In 1931, the Communist Party (*Vänstrepartiet Kommunisterne*) led a general strike to protest against the deaths of five workers who had been shot by soldiers deployed to protect scabs at a strike at a paper mill in Ådalen.[104] The general strike led to calls for a general election, which returned the

---

104. There is a beautiful film by Bo Widerberg from 1969 about the incident, *Ådalen 31*.

Social Democrats to power. They immediately began negotiations with the trade unions and the Employers' Association to establish lasting peace in the labor market.

After long and difficult negotiations, in 1938 the trade union movement and Employers' Association entered the so-called *Saltsjöbadsavtalet* (the Saltsjöbaden Agreements, named after the seaside community where the accords were finalized). The main principle of this agreement was that all conflicts must be resolved by negotiations and mediation. The Swedish Trade Union Confederation (*Landsorganisationen*, LO) was to seek peaceful solutions and cut off all political and financial support to member unions that refused to accept a settlement proposed by the national union. The LO could also prohibit a strike if it included more than 3 percent of the members of a member union. Not all unions were enthusiastic about the *Saltsjöbadsavtalet*—as the Swedish Transport Workers' Association's put it, "For fear of death, one commits suicide."[105]

TABLE 1. INDUSTRIAL DISPUTES IN SWEDEN, 1932–1936[106]

Year	Disputes	Workers	Days Lost
1929	180	13,000	667
1930	261	21,000	1,021
1931	193	41,000	2,627
1932	182	50,000	3,095
1933	140	32,000	3,434
1934	103	14,000	760
1935	98	17,000	788
1936	60	4,000	438

105. Svenska Transportarbetareförbundet (2009), *Dags för ett nytt Saltsjöbadsavtal?*

106. B. R. Mitchell (ed.), *European Historical Statistics, 1750–1970* (London: Macmillan, 1975), 177–78. Here from Louis Proyect, "The economic theory and policies of Swedish social democracy," Louis Proyect, The Unrepentant Marxist (blog), September 25, 2015. Note that in the original, the "Disuputes" and "Workers" columns of this table indicate that the figures are in thousands, which appears to be an error, and for that reason has not been repeated here.

Sweden and Nazi Germany

From the mid-1930s, the world economic crisis began to abate and inter-imperialist rivalry once again took precedence as the principal contradiction in the development of the capitalist world system. Once again, Germany sought to translate its economic strength into increased global power. It was Germany's ambition to become the dominant power in continental Europe, subjugate the Soviet Union, and conquer territory in Asia and Africa from the old colonial powers. At the beginning of the Second World War, the United States hoped that Germany and the Soviet Union would destroy each other, leaving the global field open. After the Japanese attack on Pearl Harbor in December 1941, however, the US entered the war on the Allied side in a tactical alliance with the Soviet Union.

From December 1941 until May 1945, the contradiction between the Axis Powers (Germany, Japan, and Italy) and the Allies (the United States, England, and the Soviet Union) was the principal contradiction. It had a decisive impact on all other contradictions in the world—and thus also on developments in Sweden.

Although Sweden (like Denmark) remained neutral during World War I, Swedish capital (like Danish capital) profited handsomely from exports to Germany. Sweden's special relationship with Germany continued through the 1930s, and Swedish iron, steel, and machinery, especially ball bearings, were of particular importance to German industry, not least for the manufacture of military armaments. In the late 1930s, 75 percent of Sweden's iron exports went to Germany (see table on the next page.)[107] In 1934, Hitler stated that without

107. Christian Leitz, *Sympathy for the Devil: Neutral Europe and Nazi Germany in World War II* (Manchester: Manchester University Press, 2000), 65. Here from: Louis Proyect, "When the Swedish Social Democrats partnered with Nazi Germany in the name of neutrality." Louis Proyect, The Unrepentant Marxist (blog), August 5, 2015.

Swedish iron ore Germany would not be able to wage war. In turn, Sweden imported German coke and coal, which were an essential energy source. Germany's payments for Swedish iron during the war were made partly with gold stolen from Belgium, the Netherlands, and Jews in occupied Europe, all melted down to avoid detection.[108]

TABLE 2. GERMAN IMPORTS OF SWEDISH IRON ORE, 1933–43[109]

Year	Tons (Millions)
1933	2.3
1937	9.1
1942	9.0
1943	10.1

In December 1939, Social Democratic Prime Minister Per Albin Hansson formed a national unity government of all parties in the Riksdag, except the Communists. In 1940, the Social Democrats' new program declared that the party was now "One with the Swedish nation."

Denmark and Norway were occupied by Germany in April 1940. The Danish Social Democratic government under Vilhelm Buhl chose to cooperate with the occupying power, both politically and economically. The government announced that any resistance was illegal. Sabotage was terrorism. In August 1941, parliament unanimously approved a law making communist organizations illegal. Roughly 300 communists, including three members of parliament, were arrested by Danish police and sent to a prison camp in Denmark; 150 were later transferred to Stutthof concentration camp in Poland, where 22 died. Parliamentary elections were held in

108. Proyect, "When the Swedish Social Democrats partnered with Nazi Germany in the name of neutrality."

109. Leitz (2000). Here from Proyect, "When the Swedish Social Democrats partnered with Nazi Germany in the name of neutrality."

March 1943, with an all-time high participation of 89.5 per-cent—there was massive support for the policy of cooperation. In August 1943, however, the Social Democratic government broke off relations with Nazi Germany after public unrest and strikes in many major cities in Denmark. The fortunes of war had shifted and it was now time to change horses. Norway was the only Nordic country to make a clean break with Nazi Germany when it was occupied: the Norwegian army resisted the occupation and the government and King Håkon went into exile in England.

In his article on Sweden and Nazi Germany, Louis Proyect recounts how in July 1940 an agreement was concluded allow-ing German troops to transit through Sweden. Every month, approximately 30,000 Nazi soldiers traveled by Swedish rail to Norway and the eastern front, along with 1,500 freight wagons loaded with arms and other supplies. When Germany launched Operation Barbarossa against the Soviet Union in November 1940, Swedish trains transported 75,000 tons of German military equipment to the front and wounded soldiers from the front to hospitals in Norway. Sweden also sold and leased trucks to Germany for use within Sweden. The Swedish authorities established camps in Sweden for German troops transitting through and provided supplies of oil, food, etc., just as Swedish airspace was made available for German military aircraft on their way to the Soviet Union.[110]

In 1940, when Torgny Segerstedt, editor of the *Göteborgs Handels- och Sjöfartstidning*, criticized these Swedish policies, the government confiscated three issues of the newspaper. When Segerstedt subsequently criticized the fact that the Swedish army commander Olof Thörnell had received the Grand Cross of the Order of the German Eagle along with a letter from Hitler and Ribbentrop, the newspaper was once again con-fiscated and Segerstedt was called before King Gustav V to

110. Ibid.

receive a reprimand.[111] In *Sympathy for the Devil: Neutral Europe and Nazi Germany in World War II*, Christian Leitz describes the Social Democratic Hansson government as follows:

> In view of continued Swedish supplies to the Third Reich it is not surprising that relations between Sweden and the Allies "remained characterized for the rest of the war by suspicion and anger on the part of the Allies and nervousness over post-war trade prospects among the Swedes." Although, by 1944, Germany was evidently losing the war, Sweden continued to make a vital contribution to the German war effort. In September 1944 Churchill brought the attitude of the Swedes to a point when he accused them of "calculated selfishness, which has distinguished them in both wars against Germany." Why did the Swedish government not respond more readily to the growing Allied pressure? One important reason was that, even during the second half of the war, the Swedish government and an overwhelmingly pro-Allied Swedish public accepted trade with Germany as a national right under international law. ... Essentially, Hansson seems to have wanted to sit out the war without having to make any radical changes in the course of Sweden's policy of neutrality. In this undertaking Hansson was very willingly supported by his foreign minister, Gunther ... . Gunther's policies were quite pro-German even in the later stages of the war.[112]

Despite increasing pressure from the Allies to stop trading with Germany, Sweden continued to export iron and ball bearings to the Nazis until January 1945.[113]

---

111. Erik Lindorm, *Ny svensk historia, Gustaf V och hans tid 1938-1947.* Side 355. (Stockholm: Wahlström & Widstrand, 1979).

112. Leitz (2000). Here from Proyect, "When the Swedish Social Democrats partnered with Nazi Germany in the name of neutrality."

113. Ibid.

The Swedish far right

Sweden's relationship with Germany was not just a matter of business dealings. Political developments in Germany also affected Sweden. The far right has generally played a greater role in Sweden than in Norway and Denmark, both before and after the Second World War. Apart from the inspiration from Germany, the Swedish far right had its own ideologues, such as the previously mentioned Rudolf Kjellén. The far right enjoyed support in academia, amongst the bourgeoisie, as well as in military and police circles.

Per Engdahl (1909–1994) was a particularly central figure on the organizational level. As a young man, in the late 1920s he joined the *Sveriges Fascistiska Kamporganisation* (Fascist Struggle Organization of Sweden). In the 1930s, Engdahl was a leading member of various fascist groups. In 1941, he joined the *Riksförbundet Sverige-Germany* (National Sweden-Germany Federation) and, at the same time, formed the *Svensk Motstan* (Swedish Opposition), later known as the *Nysvenska Rörelsen* (New Swedish Movement). In July 1941, he wrote an open letter to the Prime Minister, in which he suggested that Sweden become a vassal state of Germany, arguing that "Sweden cannot assert its interests politically or economically except in accord and cooperation with the dominant power on the European continent."[114]

In 1941, Engdahl published the book *Det kämpande Tyskland* (The Struggling Germany), a tribute to Hitler with a preface by Sven Hedin, a pro-Nazi explorer and academic, highly decorated in both Germany and Sweden, and a member of the Swedish Academy.[115] The book included articles by a variety of prominent figures: Fredrik Böök, professor of literary history at Lund University; Rütger Essén, professor of philosophy

---

114. Per Hans Engdahl, "Majestät Konungen och pressen," *Arbetartidningen*, October 20, 1949: 2.

115. Per Hans Engdahl, *Det kämpande Tyskland* (Malmö: Dagens Böcker, 1941).

and a diplomat; Sigrid Gillner, a Social Democrat member of parliament who turned Nazi; the poet Irma Nordvang; the journalist Christer Jäderlund; Olympic sports shooter Axel Gyllenkrok; and Gustaf Jacobson, a professor of philosophy and history. Sympathy for Nazi Germany was widespread in Sweden in 1941.

Engdahl was undeterred by the German defeat. In the summer of 1945, demonstrations were organized by Engdahl's New Swedish Movement in Malmö, in the South of Sweden, against the "Allies' aggression and the emptiness of their ideology." During this period, Engdahl was also involved in helping Nazis to escape from Denmark, Norway, and Sweden to safety in West Germany, Spain, and Latin America.[116] In 1951, Engdahl and the New Swedish Movement organized a congress in Malmö, which founded the *Malmörörelsen* (Malmo Movement), also known as the European Social Movement. The remnants of European Nazism and fascism in Sweden, Italy, Britain, Spain, France, Portugal, Belgium, and the Netherlands were all represented at this conference. It is noteworthy that the first postwar attempt to reorganize the international fascist movement chose Malmö as its base.[117]

In his autobiography, *Fribytare i folkhemmet* (Pirates of the People's Home), published in 1979, Engdahl focused his attention on immigration.[118] In 1983, inspired by this book, Sven Davidsson—a friend of Engdahl's from the New Swedish Movement—founded the Keep Sweden Swedish organization. This organization merged with the *Framstegspartiets* (Progressive

---

116. Heléne Lööw, *Nazismen i Sverige 1924-1979: pionjärerna, partierna, propagandan* (Stockholm: Ordfront Förlag, 2004), 51. See also: Christian Holtet, *Dobbeltmordet i Køge bugt* (København: Forlaget Solidaritet, 2014), 245. In his memoirs, Engdahl describes in detail how this was accomplished. Per Engdahl, *Fribytare i folkhemmet* (Stockholm: Cavenfors, 1979).

117. Oliver Schröm and Andrea Röpke, *Stille Hilfe für braune Kameraden—Das geheime Netzwerk der Alt- und Neonazis* (Berlin: Christoph Links Verlag, 2001), 58–59. See also: Anders Widfeldt, "A Fourth Phase of the Extreme Right? Nordic Immigration-critical Parties in a Comparative Context," *NORDEUROPAforum*, no. 1-2 (2010).

118. Per Engdahl (1979).

Party) to form the *Sverigepartiet* (Sweden Party), Davidson being its vice president. The new party only existed for a short time, since in 1988 it became part of the *Sverigedemokraterna* (Swedish Democrats), in which Davidson remains a leading force, sitting on its board.[119] As such, there is an unbroken line of individuals and organizations connecting the fascism of the 1930s and the Swedish Democrats. The Swedish Democrats are today the leading right-wing party in Sweden; they received 17.6 percent of the vote in the September 2018 parliamentary elections, coming in third after the Social Democrats (28.4 percent) and the Liberal Party (19 percent).

Engdahl was also friends with Ingvar Feodor Kamprad (1926–2018), the founder of IKEA. Kamprad's grandparents were related to the Field Marshal and later German President Paul von Hindenburg. His parents became big landowners in Småland, the southeastern part of Sweden. In 1942, Kamprad joined Engdahl's New Swedish Movement and the two men became close friends. The relationship continued after the war, and Engdahl was one of the few people from outside the family to attend Kamprad's wedding in 1950. Kamprad only left the New Swedish Movement in the 1950s—perhaps to avoid compromising his company IKEA. Kamprad's membership became public knowledge in 1994, when some of Engdahl's personal letters were published in connection with his death. Kamprad publicly regretted his membership in the New Swedish Movement; in an interview on Swedish television in August 2010, however, he insisted that "Per Engdahl was a great person; I will maintain that position as long as I live."[120]

The far right in Sweden is therefore different from in Denmark, where the movement was marginalized after World War II and never really recovered. Today's populist right-wing Danish People's Party is rooted in a mix of ultra-liberalism

119. Sven Ove Hanson, "Från Engdahl till Åkesson," *Tiden Magasin*, February 6, 2013.

120. Karl-Johan Byttner, "Världens rikaste svensk fyller 90—Ingvar Kamprads karriär kantas av mysterier," *Veckans affärer*, March 24, 2016.

and Islamophobia. In recent decades, however, it has adopted more social democratic positions on issues like eldercare while maintaining its strong opposition to immigration from the Global South. This does not make the Danish People's Party less unpleasant or dangerous than the Swedish Democrats. On the contrary: it has managed to become mainstream, an acceptable partner for both the Liberals and the Social Democrats in the Danish Parliament.

I will come back to the position of the Swedish populist right wing; for the moment, however, lets return to the development of the *folkhemmet* following the Second World War.

Sweden in the American World Order

Sweden's most important trading partner Germany lost the war. Huge areas of Europe and Japan lay in ruins, while the productive forces of the United States had grown and had been modernized during the war. The imperialist rivalry that had dominated world politics since the turn of the century was resolved. The United States succeeded the British Empire as the new global hegemon.

Western Europe was rebuilt on American terms, via the Marshall Plan. The idea was to develop Europe as a united market for US investments, commodities, and culture. Monopoly capital became increasingly multinational. A large number of international agreements were concluded and various economic, political, and military international institutions were established to administer a more global capitalism under the leadership of the United States. At first, the United Nations with its Security Council consisted of the victorious Allied nations (China excluded); its sub-organizations dealt with everything from development and culture to health and the labor market. International financial and banking systems were reorganized under the Bretton Woods agreement, which enshrined the dominant position of the United States in the world, symbolized by the US dollar serving as the global currency. The US established an extensive network of approximately 800 military naval and air bases in 177 countries, allowing it to quickly intervene anywhere in the world. At the end of the war, the US demonstrated the effects of its new weapon, the atomic bomb, on Hiroshima and Nagasaki. As such, throughout the 1950s, the United States was the undisputed leader of an increasingly globalized capitalism, with Canada, Western Europe, Australia, and Japan being junior partners obliged to submit to US interests.

The United States wanted "free trade" and put pressure on the old European colonial powers to decolonize in order to open up Asia and Africa for US capital and exports, while Latin America was to remain America's very own private backyard. India was the first major colony to become independent in 1947, because the USA wanted it to. This was not out of any sympathy for colonized people. The USA was no friend of decolonization at any price. Decolonization was only welcome when the newly independent countries were to be ruled by regimes that guaranteed US access to their raw materials, cheap labor, and markets. The American position on decolonization was characterized by two things: (1) Demanding decolonization in the context of the contradiction between the USA and the old colonial powers; (2) Making sure that the governments of the newly independent countries fit in with the USA's economic, strategic, and political plans in the context of the contradiction between the USA and the socialist bloc.

The British led a barbaric colonial war against Malaya and benefited from full US support because the Malayan liberation movement was led by communists. The same was true of the French fighting against anti-colonial movements in Indochina. On the other hand, the Netherlands were forced by the United States to grant Indonesia independence because Sukarno's vision for the country had become acceptable to US interests. The United States also made it clear to the French that the countries of Indochina should become independent once the communists were defeated. The USA got militarily involved in the Indochina conflict when the French seemed incapable of defeating the communists after the battle of Dien Bien Phu in 1954.

The principal contradiction in the first two decades following the war was the contradiction between the United States and the socialist bloc. It was not only America's position in the world system that was strengthened by the war, but the Soviet Union's too. Something must have gone right in the 1920s and 30s, despite the power struggle between Stalin and Trotsky, since the Soviet Union was able to defeat the German war machine and rebuild the country after the war. In addition, communists seized state power in parts of Eastern Europe. Communist parties were also popular in many Western European countries, due to the role they had played in the struggle against the Nazi occupation. In China, the Communist Party proclaimed the People's Republic in 1949. One third of the world system was part of a socialist bloc detached from the reach of western capital. To counter this threat to US hegemony, NATO was established and "cold" and "hot" wars were launched to keep the socialist bloc in check. All these contradictions were critically important to Sweden's postwar development.

Sweden benefited from having an intact production apparatus and access to a large export market in Europe. Companies such as Volvo, Saab, Electrolux, Husqvarna, and LM Ericsson were expanding rapidly. Sweden quickly adapted to the new world order, taking part in the US Marshall Plan for the reconstruction of Europe and becoming a member of the OECD. At least officially, however, it maintained its military neutrality and, unlike Denmark and Norway, did not join NATO. Covertly, however, Sweden supplied NATO with military intelligence on Soviet movements in the Baltic region.

In the postwar period the Social Democrats were firmly in power in Sweden, with majority governments and enjoying good relations with the trade unions and capital alike.

Supplementing the Saltsjöbaden Agreement between the trade unions and Employers' Association, the Social Democrats introduced the Harpsund Democracy, named after a manor house that serves as the prime minister's recreational residence. In the 1950s and 60s, the manor became the venue for numerous informal meetings between the government, the Employers' Association, and trade unions, where political guidelines were laid down to ensure a peaceful labor market.

Social Democratic governments under Prime Minister Tage Erlander in the 1950s and Olof Palme in the 1960s and 1970s took Per Albin Hansson's idea of the *folkhem* and developed it further into the capitalist welfare state, which was to include practically the entire population.

Swedish neocolonialism

The US demand for free trade after the Second World War forced Europe's colonial powers to decolonize, thus opening Asia and Africa up to US capital and exports. The old form of colonialism had lost its legitimacy and utility. Direct administrative and military rule over the colonies increasingly came to represent a financial burden for the European powers. Imperialism changed character, switching from the directly violent exploitation of colonialism to the more market-driven exploitation of neocolonialism in the form of unequal exchange. The Third World exported mainly raw materials and agricultural products produced by low-wage labor and imported industrial goods produced by relatively high-wage labor in the US and Europe.

In the colonial period, Sweden had been forced to operate in the wake of the great colonial powers, especially Germany; neocolonialism, however, provided new opportunities to acquire direct economic and political influence in Asia and Africa. One example of this was LAMCO, the Liberian

American-Swedish Minerals Company.

In 1955, LAMCO discovered one of the world's largest and cleanest deposits of iron ore in Mount Nimba in Liberia, in West Africa. The ore was easily accessible, just below ground level; no underground mineshaft or tunnels were necessary, all that was required was to scrape the surface and start digging. LAMCO consisted of Marcus Wallenberg's Stockholm Enskilda Bank, Skånska Cement, Sentab, Atlas Copco, Nordström Linbanor, and Grängesberg. The Swedish investors owned 75 percent of LAMCO, the American Bethlehem Steel Corporation the remaining 25 percent.[121] The Grängesberg firm, which had experience dealing with iron ore in the northern part of Sweden, also received a contract with LAMCO concerning maritime transport and sale of the ore.

Exports began in 1963 after LAMCO built a 270km railway from the mine to the coastal town of Buchanan, where LAMCO established a new port, drawing on experience with the ports of Narvik, Svartön, and Oxelösund in Sweden. A total of $250 million was invested in the project, and in the investment phase 11,600 people were employed in the construction work. The mine made Liberia the world's largest iron ore supplier in the 1970s.

According to contemporary media accounts, a "little *folkhem*" was established in Liberia in connection with the mining site, complete with safe roads, modern homes, schools, hospitals, supermarkets, recreation facilities, and even a police station and courthouse. Locals worked at the mine, but the managers, skilled workers, and technicians were recruited in Sweden, attracted by the high wages and low taxes.[122]

During the production phase, around 15,000 people worked at LAMCO in Liberia. In Sweden, it was presented as a successful example of a "development project" in a poor African

---

121. Ylva Mannerheim and Johan Mannerheim, *Lamco:s Liberia* (Stockholm: Unga filosofer, 1968), 24.

122. Eva Ersson Åbom, "Ett folkhem i Liberia," *Företagshistoria*, no. 4 (2013).

country. The progressive image cracked in 1966, however, when Swedish television aired the documentary *Svart vecka i Nimba* ("Black Week in Nimba"). The film tells the story of a strike at LAMCO and the Swedes are portrayed as racist neocolonialists.[123] The following year another strike broke out. The Liberian government deployed the army to protect LAMCO's property and the Swedish management. President Tubman declared the strike illegal and workers identified as strike leaders were arrested and later fired.

Siahyonkron Nyanseor, one of the workers, recounted his experience at LAMCO:

> I was taught mechanical technology, welding, electricity, Iron Ore Handling Plant Operations, and many other technical skills. After the nine-month intensive train-ing, we graduated, and were assigned to LAMCO. Our group was part of the "Liberianization scheme." We were supposed to replace the European/American expatriate employees. However, when the all Liberians crew took over the operations of the Control Room, amenities such as the drinking water cooler, icebox (refrigerator), toilet facility (portable toilet), etc. were removed from the sta-tion. We had to call for relieve, to get a drink of water and use the toilet.

> When I left LAMCO in December 1968 to come to the United States, I was earning 40 cents per hour, whereas the expatriates that we replaced were making some-where in the neighborhood of $2,500.00 to $3,000.00 US dollars per month. In addition, their benefits package included one-month paid vacation; free housing in the company's residential area, healthcare benefits, the use of the company supermarket, private school for their chil-dren, mess hall, recreational privileges, etc. The benefits

---

123. Roland Hjelte, Ingrid Dahlberg, and Lars Hjelm, *Svart vecka i Nimba : Kring en svensk industri i ett u-land, Lamco i Liberia*. Dokumnetarfilm. STV (1966).

provided for Liberian workers were substandard, at best, inferior.[124]

Throughout the 1960s and early 1970s, LAMCO was making big money, as the high-quality Liberian ore was much in demand on the world market. In the mid-1970s, however, the oil crisis hit the world economy and, as a result, a period of protracted stagnation set in. The steel industry was particularly hard hit and LAMCO had to reduce production as company profits decreased. When there is less food on people's plates they start fighting over the crumbs. LAMCO and the Liberian government were increasingly at odds over the operation of the mine and how to split the profits. At the same time, Liberia was increasingly politically unstable, and in April 1980 President Tubman was assassinated in a bloody military coup. LAMCO finally abandoned its operations in Liberia in 1983. LAMCO's activities still had consequences for Liberia, however, as former LAMCO employee Nyanseor explained:

> Whatever arrangement or agreement LAMCO and the Liberian government had unfortunately did not include the protection of the Atlantic Ocean and the environment, nor even the safety and health of the people. LAMCO was given "carte blanche" to dump the waste from the iron ore into the ocean.

> Over the years, several individuals who once worked in the LAMCO environment contracted lungs-related illnesses and eventually died. I suspect some of these deaths could be attributed to the poor environmental conditions they worked in.[125]

---

124. Siahyonkron Nyanseor, "My LAMCO-Buchanan Experience" (2015).

125. Ibid.

Patrice Lumumba and Dag Hammarskjöld

Colonialism and neocolonialism in Africa led to resistance and demands for political freedom and economic development to benefit the people. This struggle interacted with the principal contradiction at the time, between the USA and the Soviet Union. One Swede in particular came to play a significant role in the decolonization of Africa — Dag Hammarskjöld (1905–61).

The Hammarskjöld family were aristocrats; Dag's father, Hjalmar Hammarskjöld, was prime minister from 1914–17 for the Conservative Party. As mentioned previously, Dag Hammarskjöld studied under Knut Wicksell and received a degree at the Stockholm School of Economics. He quickly rose through the ranks of the civil service and from 1951–53 was Minister of Foreign Trade in Tage Erlander's Social Democratic government. Then his career made a leap: in 1952, the United Nations was due to have a new Secretary-General after the departure of Trygve Lie. After lengthy and difficult negotiations between the United States and the Soviet Union, Hammarskjöld was chosen as a compromise candidate. Thus, in 1953, at only 47 years of age, Hammarskjöld was elected Secretary-General of the UN. In 1960, he became deeply involved in the crisis around the decolonization of the Congo. The Swedish Air Force also contributed nine Saab 29B "barrel" jet fighters and two reconnaissance aircraft to the UN force deployed in the Congo in 1960–64 to resolve the crisis.[126]

The Congo had become the personal property of Belgian King Leopold II at the Berlin Conference in 1884, with Sweden's support. Ever since it was colonized, it had been exploited and tortured. The Belgians enslaved workers to plunder the country, extracting rubber, ivory, timber, and minerals. The Belgians developed a brutal system of local militias

126. Sweden produces its own jet fighters. Bo Widfeldt, *The Saab J 29* (Surrey, UK: Profile Publications Ltd., 1966).

and mercenaries to protect the interests of their mining, banking, and trading companies.[127] Very little of Congo's wealth benefited the people. As Mauricio Brum has written:

> Ironically, Leopold II had an incomparably bigger power in Africa than in his own country; while in Belgium he was a symbolic figure in a parliamentary monarchy system, in Congo he had absolute powers, just like in the old days.
>
> In a short period of time, the king focused his economic interests in the export of latex, an abundant product in the region's forests, using troops of mercenaries to force the local population to cater to his interests. The extraction of ivory and mining also helped to fill Leopold's coffers.
>
> Imposing productivity quotas so high that they were rarely reached, the Congo Free State little by little acquired such infamy that it eventually was denounced by other colonial powers: the mutilation of the local population as a form of punishment for not fulfilling the quotas—and living conditions so precarious that they provoked a mortality rate comparable to a genocide. ...
>
> [I]t is estimated that up to 15 million people died during Leopold II's rule, either due to the repression or the terrible living conditions imposed on the local population, with widespread disease and malnourishment.[128]

The process of decolonization in some African countries was driven by radical liberation movements, which took advantage of the "window for change" opened by the inter-state rivalry between the US and the Soviet Union. In the Congo, Patrice

127. Adam Hochschild, *King Leopold's Ghost: A Story of Greed, Terror, and Heroism in Colonial Africa* (Boston: Houghton Mifflin Company, 1998), 278–79.

128. Mauricio Brum, "How Belgium cut off hands and arms, and killed over 15 million in Africa," *Gazeta do Povo*, February 12, 2019.

Lumumba (1925–1961) became a leading figure in the liberation movement in the late 1950s. Lumumba's parents were poor peasants, but he succeeded in getting an education as a clerk at the post office. In 1958, he was one of the founding members of the *Mouvement National Congolais* (MNC), which managed to unite the various ethnic groups in the country to demand independence from Belgium. Lumumba was inspired by Kwame Nkrumah, Ghana's first president after independence in 1957 and a prominent anti-colonial politician and theorist. He met Nkrumah at the Pan-African Conference in Ghana in 1958 and they became close friends, both political and personal.

In June 1960, Lumumba was elected as the first prime minister of the Democratic Republic of Congo, after his socialist-oriented party won a large majority in the elections with a mandate to form a post-independence government. On Independence Day, June 30, 1960, Belgian King Baudouin gave a speech in which he praised Belgian colonialism and the work of "the genius"—his predecessor, King Leopold II— for having "helped" the people of the Congo. King Baudouin ended his speech with these words:

> Don't compromise the future with hasty reforms, and don't replace the structures that Belgium hands over to you until you are sure you can do better. Don't be afraid to come to us. We will remain by your side, give you advice.[129]

In his reply, Lumumba reminded the audience that Congo's independence was not some gift from Belgium:

> ... For this independence of the Congo, although being proclaimed today by agreement with Belgium, an amicable country, with which we are on equal terms, no Congolese worthy of the name will ever be able to forget

---

129. Ludo De Witte, *The Assassination of Lumumba* (London: Verso, 2001), 1–3.

that it was by fighting that it has been won, a day-to-day fight, an ardent and idealistic fight, a fight in which we were spared neither privation nor suffering, and for which we gave our strength and our blood. We are proud of this struggle, of tears, of fire, and of blood, to the depths of our being, for it was a noble and just struggle, and indispensable to put an end to the humiliating slavery which was imposed upon us by force.[130]

Lumumba was determined to detach the Congo from Belgian neocolonialism, but he survived only seven months as president. A few weeks after independence, the copper-rich Katanga province, led by Moise Tshombe, declared its independence from Congo. Tshombe acted in coordination with Belgium, which sent 6,000 elite soldiers to support the secession. The aim was to ensure that Belgian mining companies could continue operating as they had under colonialism. The threat to the Congo's integrity caused Lumumba to ask the UN to send a peacekeeping force to the country, and this triggered a Belgian-backed military coup. Lumumba was arrested on December 1, 1961, with US and Belgian assistance; United Nations troops that were present on the scene did not intervene.[131] Lumumba was imprisoned in Camp Hardy military barracks, 150km from the capital city, Leopoldville; there, a conflict broke out between the soldiers, some of whom wanted Lumumba to be released and reinstated as president. On January 17, with the help of Belgian forces and coup backers, former Belgian Minister of African Affairs Harold d'Aspremont Lynden handed Lumumba and his closest advisors Maurice Mpolo and Joseph Okito over to Tshombe in Lubumbashi,

---

130. Patrice Lumumba, "Speech at the ceremony of the proclamation of Congo's independence, June 30 1960." In *The Truth about a Monstrous Crime of the Colonialists* (Moscow: Foreign Languages Publishing House, 1961), 44–47.

131. Georges Nzongola-Ntalaja (2002), *The Congo: From Leopold to Kabila: A People's History* (London: Zed Books, 2002), 110.

the capital of Katanga province.[132] Hammarskjöld's response, as Secretary-General of the United Nations, was simply to appeal to the coup makers to grant Lumumba "due process" (sic). A few hours after arriving in Katanga on January 17, Lumumba and his associates were brutally beaten and tortured by Katangan and Belgian officers.[133] Later that evening, Lumumba and his advisors were transported outside the city and executed in the presence of Tshombe and some of his companions. Lumumba's execution was carried out by a death squad under the command of a Belgian officer, Julien Gat. A Belgian police commissioner, Frans Verscheure, was in charge of the killings.[134] Lumumba and his comrades were quickly buried, but the next day Verscheure and another Belgian police commissioner, Gerard Soete, along with his brother and some soldiers, returned to the graves to move the bodies, as they feared the executions had been observed.[135] On January 21, the same team once again dug up the bodies, cut them into small pieces, and dissolved them in sulfuric acid in an attempt to erase any trace of the atrocity.[136]

The assassination of Lumumba was not some spontaneous act carried out by a small group of criminals in the pay of the mining companies. In 2000, the Belgian sociologist and writer Ludo De Witte discovered a memo from the Belgian government ordering the execution of Lumumba, as well as

---

132. Didier Gondola, *The History of Congo* (Westport: Greenwood Publishing Group, 2002), 126.

133. John Prados, *Safe for Democracy: The Secret Wars of the CIA* (Chicago: Rowman & Littlefield, 2006). In 2002, after a parliamentary commission issued a report on Belgium's role in the coup and the killing of Lumumba, the Belgian government officially apologized for its actions. See: Belgische Kamer van volksvertegenwoordigers (2001), Parliamentary Committee of enquiry in charge of determining the exact circumstances of the assassination of Patrice Lumumba and the possible involvement of Belgian politicians.

134. De Witte (2003).

135. In a 1999 interview on Belgian television about Lumumba's assassination, Soete displayed a bullet and two teeth that he claimed he had taken from Lumumba's body. Usnews.com, "Patrice Lumumba—Mysteries of History."

136. De Witte (2003), 140.

documents specifying the details of how it was done. In 2001, a Belgian government report described both Belgian and American plans to kill Lumumba, including a CIA plan to poison Lumumba, ordered by President Eisenhower.[137] A plot that was later confirmed by "declassified" CIA documents.[138] In 2013, the State Department itself confirmed that Eisenhower had authorized the liquidation of Lumumba.[139]

While rumors swirled, the Belgian puppet-regime of Katanga separatists waited a month before officially announcing Lumumba's death. It was February 13 when Katangan Radio first announced that "Lumumba has been killed by agitated villagers, three days after he fled from prison."[140]

As president, Lumumba had hoped for UN support to safeguard the decolonization process and the integrity of the Congo, but there was no help to be found from Hammarskjöld's UN. As Helen M. Hintjens and Serena Cruz have explained:

> King Leopold's conquests were based on violence on such a massive scale that the death rate was quite unprecedented. History matters, since the conflict that arose at independence between Patrice Lumumba and the Belgian authorities, a conflict that was transposed to one between Lumumba and Hammarksjöld, was a conflict about the meaning of history. Dag Hammarskjöld may not have appreciated the depths of Belgian self-deception over the bloody history of the Congo. East-West obsessions

---

137. Martin Kettle, "President 'Ordered Murder' of Congo Leader," *The Guardian*, August 10, 2000.

138. Stephen Weissman, "Opening the Secret Files on Lumumba's Murder," *Washington Post* July 21, 2002. See also: Madeleine G. Kalb, "The CIA and Lumumba," *The New York Times*, August 2, 1981.

139. Office of the Historian. *Foreign Relations of the United States, 1964-1968*, vol. 23, *Congo, 1960-1968*.

140. BBC, "Ex-Congo PM Declared Dead," February 13, 1961.

during the Cold War added another layer to the disputes over the legacy of the colonial past.[141]

Lumumba and Hammarskjöld were men of different personal backgrounds, ideologies, and objectives. Ludo de Witte has made the following assessment of these differences:

> Lumumba intended to jettison the deadweight of colonial heritage and combat any neo-colonial designs on the country, the aims of the United Nations Secretary General were with a liberal kind of peace, and with maintaining public order.[142]

Hammarskjöld's hostility towards Lumumba was no secret, as Lumumba challenged his interpretation of the UN mandate in the Congo. Lumumba wanted the UN to defend the elected government and the decolonization process and regarded the secession of the Katanga province as an act of blatant sabotage.[143] The Katanga separatist movement represented the interests of Belgian capital, white settlers, and their Congolese partners, and sought to ensure that the Congo's wealth remained in their hands. Hammarskjöld interpreted the situation differently; in his view, separatist movements were inevitable, given the ethnic diversity of the country. According to de Witte, Hammarskjöld went so far as to describe Tshombe's goal, an independent Katanga state, as "legitimate."[144]

---

141. Helen M. Hintjens and Serena Cruz, "Continuities of Violence in the Congo: the Legacies of Hammarskjöld and Lumumba." In Carsten Stahn and Henning Melber, *Peace Diplomacy, Global Justice and International Agency: Rethinking Human Security and Ethics in the Spirit of Dag Hammarskjöld* (Cambridge: Cambridge University Press, 2014).

142. De Witte (2003).

143. Mohamed Salih, "Poverty and Human Security in Africa: The Liberal Peace Debate." In David Francis (ed.), *Peace and Conflict in Africa* (London: Zed Press, 2009), 171–84. See also: Crawford Young, "Ralph Bunche and Patrice Lumumba. The Fatal Encounter." In Robert A. Hill and Edmond J. Keller (eds.), *Trustee for the Human Community. Ralph J. Bunche, the United Nations, and the Decolonization of Africa* (Ohio: Ohio University Press, 2010).

144. De Witte (2003), 14.

In the confrontation between American and Soviet interests at the UN, Hammarskjöld sided with the US. Hammarskjöld wanted to appear above politics, to be seen to be supporting peace and the rule of law. The UN should limit itself to what is now known as "humanitarian intervention"; defending an elected government and the integrity of the new state, not to mention changes in the colonial economy which went against imperialist interests, were not part of his job.

Unlike Lumumba, Hammarskjöld expected the Belgians to act reasonably towards a United Nations with a Swedish Secretary-General at its head. According to Hammarskjöld, "law and order" was the top priority for the UN—the kind of "law and order" that facilitates "business as usual," not the "law and order" that might secure the safety of an elected president. Lumumba was taken prisoner on December 1, 1961, in the village of Lodi on the left bank of the Sankuru River. He was denied UN protection by the Ghanaian contingent of UN soldiers stationed nearby who were aware of the situation.[145] The task of the UN troops was to protect the white settlers, not the elected prime minister, based on a position that the UN could not interfere in the Congo's internal affairs.[146]

Hammarskjöld and his right-hand man, the American Ralph Bunche, had apparently concluded that Lumumba posed a greater threat to peace and law and order than the separatists in Katanga did. When the killings of Lumumba and his advisors came to the attention of the UN Security Council, it asked Hammarskjöld to investigate what had happened. He initially refused, and the Security Council had to repeatedly insist that an investigation be conducted; when one finally was, it went nowhere. Nothing was clarified and no one was punished for the execution of Lumumba.[147]

---

145. Nzongola-Ntalaja (2002), 110.

146. De Witte (2003), 58.

147. Ibid., 154.

It would seem that Hammarskjöld did not recognize the contradiction between the "human face" of capitalism at home in Sweden and the brutality of imperialism in the Congo. The profit rates of Belgian investments in the Congo were two to three times higher than investments in Europe. Belgium's largest company, the Société Générale de Belgique financial group, received 40 percent of its profits from its investments in the Congo.[148] That is something Belgians did not want to have to give up.

Dag Hammarskjöld, the Swedish Social Democrat, chose to side with Belgian and American neocolonialism against the democratically elected socialist prime minister of the independent state of the Congo.

After the Belgians and Americans got rid of Lumumba, their interests began to come into conflict with one another. While the Belgians and their mercenaries were safeguarding the old colonial interests, the multinational companies linked to the United States were increasingly unhappy with how Belgium was trying to keep the whole cake for itself.[149]

When Hammarskjöld finally realized that it was Belgian interests that constituted the primary threat to Congo's peace and "free enterprise," he decided to intervene in Katanga, but it was too late. On his way to negotiations on September 18, 1961, his aircraft crashed; Hammarskjöld and the other fourteen persons on board were never found and the circumstances surrounding the crash were never resolved. Historian David Gibbs believes that Hammarskjold's death was not just some random accident but that there is "evidence that Belgian mining interests were responsible," although "the dirty work" would have been carried out by local accomplices. Gibbs explains that, "Much of the Belgians' animus was directed against

148. David N. Gibbs, "Dag Hammarskjold, the United Nations, and the Congo Crisis of 1960–1: A Reinterpretation," *The Journal of Modern African Studies* 31, no. 1 (March 1993): 165. Here from Proyect, "Swedish imperialism in Africa."
149. Ibid.: 170–73.

Hammarskjöld personally," even though he actually started out as being attentive to Belgian interests.[150] What may have sealed his fate, according to Gibbs, was that he had begun to cater to Swedish and American interests at the expense of the Belgians in Katanga:

> The facts are as follows. The Hammarskjold family was associated with the Liberian-American Swedish Minerals Company, known by the acronym LAMCO. This syndicate of six separate Swedish mining companies was closely connected with Boliden, another Swedish enterprise with interests in copper mining, and with the International African American Corporation. Several persons from the syndicate were involved in the UN force in the Congo, notably Sture Linner, the first head of civilian operations, who was, at the time of his hiring, a "managing director" of LAMCO. Two other Swedes employed by the UN mission as consultants also had connections with LAMCO: Sven Schwartz had been a director at a constituent company as well as chairman of the board at Boliden, and Borje Hjortzberg-Nordlund was listed as an "alternate director" at LAMCO. Both assisted the UN in evaluating the prospects for economic development, especially in the mining sector, and their interest in the Congo probably alarmed the Belgians, especially those affiliated with the Union miniere, which regarded the Swedes as interlopers in what had histori-cally been a special "preserve" for Belgian capital. Such suspicions were increased when it was discovered that Bo Hammarskjold, the brother of the Secretary-General, was on the board of directors of Grangesberg Oxelosund, the largest of LAMCO's constituent companies ... . The death of Hammarskjöld took place in the context of intense competition among Western mining companies

---

150. Ibid.: 169.

for access to Katanga, and had very little to do with the rivalry between East and West.[151]

Lumumba's death was the result of his efforts to free Congo from Belgian imperialism. When Hammarskjöld finally turned against Belgium's conduct in the Congo, he became almost as unpopular as Lumumba among the Belgian imperialists and settlers. The UN system's lack of interest or ability to confront the logic of imperialism left the Congo with the same economic structures sustained by brutal violence as had existed under colonialism. Belgium's "rubber terror" turned into "coltan terror." King Leopold's ghost continues to haunt the Congo.[152]

In Sweden, Hammarskjöld received a posthumous Nobel Peace Prize, and John F. Kennedy called him "the greatest statesman of our century." Lumumba did not even get a grave.

Neocolonialism presented itself to the Third World under the veil of development aid and liberal democracy, but exploitation and oppression continued. In a 1964 speech to the UN, Che Guevara denounced the imperialist exploitation of the Congo:

> I would like to refer specifically to the painful case of the Congo, unique in the history of the modern world, which shows how, with absolute impunity, with the most insolent cynicism, the rights of peoples can be flouted. The direct reason for all this is the enormous wealth of the Congo, which the imperialist countries want to keep under their control.[153]

Today, diamonds as well as minerals that are critical for the production of smartphones are extracted under the same conditions as in colonial Congo. Child labor and brutal militias

---

151. Ibid.: 163, 174.

152. Hochschild (1998), 159–62.

153. Che Guevara, "December 11, 1964, 19th General Assembly of the United Nations in New York." In *Che Reader* (New York: Ocean Press, 2005). Here from Louis Proyect, "21st Century Socialism." CounterPunch (website), January 31, 2020.

still secure high profits. Congo is also a source of the minerals required for the batteries that store energy produced by windmills and solar panels, and which will be in high demand for electric cars. It is estimated that lithium-ion batteries for electric vehicles alone will require up to 43 percent of the cobalt and 50 percent of the lithium produced globally. "Green" capitalism will be no better than fossil-fuel capitalism.[154]

Olof Palme

While these dramatic events were taking place in Africa, the capitalist welfare states in Northwestern Europe, Canada, the United States, Australia, and New Zealand continued to flourish. In Sweden, the Social Democrat Olof Palme's first government (1969–76) represented the pinnacle of the capitalist welfare state, testing the limits of the compromise between capital and the working class.

Olof Palme (1927–86) was from a bourgeois family; his father was a wealthy CEO and his mother an aristocrat who owned large landed estates. Olof, however, was not the first to break out of the family mold—his aunt Anna Palme had married Dr. Upendra Dutt, an Indian surgeon, and their son Rajani Palme Dutt (1886–1974) became the chief intellectual, and for a short period also chairman, of the Communist Party of Great Britain. While Palme Dutt was loyal to the Soviet Union and the Communist Party all his life, Olof Palme was strongly opposed to the Soviet Union. Many years after the fact, he would describe how the 1948 Communist seizure of power in Czechoslovakia, when he was just 21 years old, had had a decisive impact on his political views:

---

154. Proyect, "21st Century Socialism."

For many of my generation, the 1948 Prague coup was a crucial political experience. There were no mitigating circumstances to excuse the outrage. Czechoslovakia was a developed industrial nation with functioning democratic institutions. Yet Czech democracy was crushed overnight by military force, resulting in relentless persecution of dissent.[155]

Palme's hostility toward the Soviet Union had practical consequences. When he was in the United States studying economics and political science, the CIA attempted to recruit him. He was apparently not hostile to the idea, and after a student conference in Prague in 1949 he passed on information to the US Embassy in Stockholm about three Swedes who had been in attendance, members of the communist association *Clarté*: Gunnar Claesson, Gunnar Svantesson, and Hans Göran Franck, who would later be president of Amnesty International in Sweden.[156]

From the Second World War to the early 1960s, one pretty much had to be pro-Moscow if one was a communist. While there was the Trotskyist alternative, this remained confined to small groups without much influence. The need to defend socialism in one country and the Cold War made other positions difficult. The divisions within the Communist Parties that resulted from the Soviet interventions in Prague (1948) and Hungary (1956) led to the formation of new socialist parliamentary parties in Europe. It was not until the 1960s, however, that new revolutionary left oppositions emerged as a result of criticisms of the Communist Party of the Soviet Union.

155. Olof Palme, "En borgerlig regering—ett steg tillbaka," i *Fackföreningsrörelsen*, no. 17/18 (1968). An article based on a speech Palme delivered in Malmo on August 21, 1968, after the Soviet Union invaded Prague. Here from: Stellan Andersson, "Biografiska notiser 1948."
156. Thomas Pettersson and Ewa Stenberg, "CIA villa värve den unge Olof Palme," *Dagens Nyheter*, January 12, 2008.

Palme became a Social Democrat, and after graduating he began working in the state administration. In 1953, at only 26 years of age, he became the secretary of Prime Minister Tage Erlander. Like his mentor, Palme was an academic (indeed, the only Social Democratic prime minister to come from the working class was Per Albin Hansson in the 1930s). While it generally took years to rise through the Social Democratic party apparatus, Palme's career was on a fast track. He was described by the press as the gray eminence behind Erlander; as an example of the prime minister's great confidence in him, when Erlander came down with a severe cold during a state visit to the Soviet Union in April 1956, the 29-year-old Palme was sent to negotiate in his place with Khrushchev.[157]

In 1958, Palme was elected to the Riksdag, the Swedish parliament. He was minister without portfolio from 1963–65, Minister of Traffic and Transportation from 1965–67, Minister of Education from 1967–69, and in 1969 he became Prime Minister and Chairman of the Social Democratic party. Palme represented a political administrative class that had developed alongside the institutionalization of the division of power between capital and the working class. This layer does not cater to narrow class interests but seeks to fine-tune cooperation between capital and the trade union movement. The administrative class serves the interests of this particular form of the capitalist mode of production, working to ensure "the system" works smoothly. Members of the administrative class float in and out of top positions in national and international politics, state administration, financial foundations, large corporations, and academia.

There was another side to Olof Palme, however. He was a person who knew his own mind; just as he was critical towards the Soviets, he was also critical towards certain aspects of the USA. During his studies in the United States in the late 1940s,

157. Henrik Berggren, *Underbara dagar framför oss: en biografi över Olof Palme* (Stockholm: Norstedts Forlag, 2010), 234–35.

he had seen and was upset by the racism against Black people, and in the 1960s, like many other young people, he became outraged by the horrors of the Vietnam War. Palme led the Swedish government's criticism of US aggression in Vietnam. As early as 1965, he spoke out against the US war in Vietnam at a public meeting in the Swedish town of Gävle. In 1968, as the US war effort intensified, Palme attended a demonstration alongside the North Vietnamese ambassador to Moscow, who was visiting Stockholm at the time. Palme was a speaker at a subsequent protest meeting at Sergels Torg, in Central Stockholm: "… if you want to speak of democracy in Vietnam, it is obvious that it is represented to a much greater extent by the NLF than by the United States and its allied junta."[158]

In January 1969, Sweden became the first Western country to recognize North Vietnam. In his 1972 Christmas address, Palme compared the B-52 bombings of Hanoi to the atrocities of fascism:

> Guernica, Oradour, Babi Yar, Katyn, Lidice, Sharpeville, Treblinka. There, violence triumphed, and yet history's judgment has not spared those responsible. Now we add a new name to the list: Hanoi, Christmas 1972.[159]

The US government was naturally upset about the prime minister's statements. Nixon called Palme "a Swedish arsehole" and brought the US ambassador home for consultations. The situation was not so bad as to interfere with the covert military cooperation between Sweden and the US, however, which continued unperturbed. Officially, Sweden was neutral; however, as early as 1952 it had begun working with NATO. Sweden provided intelligence on Soviet activities in the Baltic and received US weapons technology in return. In 1960, the United States provided Sweden with a secret security guar-

---

158. Swedish Riksdag, *Fred och säkerhet - säkerhetspolitiska utredningen, SOU 2002:108, December 20, 2001* (Stockholm: Statens offentliga utredningar, Utrikesdepartementet, 2002), 248.

159. Henrik Arnstad, *Skyld* (Oslo: Forlaget Spartacus, 2010), 162.

antee: in the event of a Soviet attack, the United States would intervene on Sweden's side.[160] As part of this collaboration, US experts assisted the Swedish arms manufacturer Saab to develop the Viggen jet fighter, to improve the accuracy of Swedish Polaris missiles, and to partially subsidize anti-submarine weapons for the Swedish Navy.[161]

There is no doubt that Vietnam appreciated the Swedish government's support, which was unique in the West. As a loyal member of NATO, the Danish Social Democratic government supported the US in Vietnam. Yet despite Palme's harsh anti-American rhetoric, Sweden remained in a secret strategic alliance with NATO. Palme's criticism of the United States was not grounded in a historical, economic, or political analysis of the root causes of US imperialism and the Vietnam War. The war was opposed as a political stupidity that could be corrected.

Nonetheless, Palme's criticisms of the United States had consequences within the Swedish state apparatus. Elements within the SÄPO intelligence service distrusted Palme, and vice versa. Members of SÄPO suspected that Palme was a spy for the Soviet Union. The Social Democrats therefore felt compelled to create their own intelligence service, "IB" (Information Bureau). Ironically, IB primarily spied on the left, which in those years was demonstrating against US imperialism.

160. Försvarets forskningsinstitut, "Hemliga atomubåtar gav Sverige säkerhetsgaranti." Archived July 7, 2007.

161. Nils Bruzelius, "'Near friendly or neutral shores': the deployment of the fleet ballistic missile submarines and US policy towards Scandinavia, 1957–1963." Licentiate thesis, monograph. KTH, School of Architecture and the Built Environment (ABE), Architecture. 2007.

A capitalist path to socialism?

In the late 19th and early 20th century, the Swedish labor movement prioritized the struggle for the right to vote and parliamentary democracy. Once this framework was in place, they would be able to conquer government power. The next phase was social democracy: the development of the welfare state with social security and material welfare for all citizens. In the early 1980s, Sweden was in fact the country with the lowest level of income inequality in the capitalist world. The Swedish welfare state became known internationally as a middle ground between capitalism and socialism, the "Swedish model." The third phase was to be the democratization of economic power—a democratization of ownership of the means of production. This occurred during Palme's tenure as prime minister.

Economic development in Sweden in the 1950s and 1960s laid the basis for rising wages and the expansion of the welfare state. There was a widespread notion that Keynesian-inspired economic policies could regulate capitalism, avoiding future crises. At the same time, however, capital continued to be concentrated in fewer and fewer hands. To counter this tendency, the trade union movement began to foster the idea of "economic democracy" in the late 1960s. At first, there was confusion and disagreement about what exactly was meant by "economic democracy" and how it should be implemented. Was it just about having a say in important decisions in the company? Was it profit-sharing—a kind of collective capitalism which retained a market economy? Or was it something more radical—collective ownership of the means of production?

One of the reasons for this agenda was that the trade union movement had been politically radicalized as part of the '68 rebellion. Many new shop stewards were to the left of the old Social Democrats. At the 1971 congress of the Swedish Trade Union Confederation (*Lands Organization*, or LO), a majority of delegates demanded the abolition of the employer's right to direct and distribute work and the introduction of economic democracy. The Social Democratic leadership of the LO wanted to increase employees' say regarding their working conditions and company operations in general, however they were against any change in the ownership of capital itself. Nonetheless, the Metal Workers' Union managed to get majority support for a proposal that the LO should study the possibility of acquiring co-ownership of companies under the auspices of the trade union movement, through collective investment funds. This resulted in a study group being established, headed by LO economist Rudolf Meidner (1914–2005). Together with Gösta Rehn (1913–1996), Meidner had been the LO's economic strategist since the late 1940s. Meidner was convinced that economic democratization had to strike at the heart of capitalism: private ownership of the means of production.[162]

Together with Anna Hedborg (b. 1944), Meidner put together a proposal according to which every year companies with more than one hundred employees should transfer part of their profits to collective funds, in the form of new shares. These funds should belong to the trade union movement and be managed by the employees, making them active partners in the companies.[163]

Over a period of 20 to 30 years, the funds would acquire a larger and larger share of the companies, until eventually they would own a majority of all shares in major Swedish corporations. It was the first time that the Swedish labor movement had made a concrete proposal challenging private ownership of the means of production. As Meidner put it:

> We want to deprive the owners of capital of their power, which they are exercising precisely by virtue of their ownership. All experience shows that influence and

162. Henrik Berggren, *Underbara dagar framför oss - en biografi över Olof Palme* (Stockholm: Norstedts, 2010), 528.

163. Anna Hedborg and Rudolf Meidner, *Kollektiv kapitalbildning genom lontagarfonder, rapport till LO-kongressen 1976* (Lund, 1976).

control are not enough. Ownership plays a crucial role. I would like to refer to Marx and Wigforss: We cannot fundamentally change society without also changing the relations of ownership.[164]

The proposal did not suggest a traditional nationalization of capital, which would give the state ownership of the means of production, let alone a planned economy where economic priorities would be decided politically by the state. Meidner's idea was to do away with private ownership of the means of production without concentrating economic power in state institutions. It was the trade unions and their members' position that needed to be strengthened in relation to capital.[165] As such, it was not a break with the logic of capitalism. Sweden was to continue as a market economy, both domestically and internationally. Sweden would remain part of the capitalist world market, just as before. It would be a more democratic capitalism with the trade unions at the helm, a kind of "people's capitalism."

It turned out that regular trade union members supported the plan to an extent that surprised even Meidner and Hedborg; with this momentum, LO chairperson Gunnar Nilsson was convinced to support the plan. At the June 1976 LO Congress, the Meidner-Hedborg plan was approved by a large majority of delegates, who closed the debate by singing the *Internationale*.

But it soon became clear that the Social Democratic Party, which had spent the past century pursuing peaceful class cooperation, could not endorse a proposal that called into question the private ownership of the means of production. As the Social Democrats saw things, it was the role of the trade union movement to take care of the interests of the working class, while the Social Democrats, as a people's party and as

164. Rudolf Meidner, "Intervju i Fackföreningsrörelsen," *LO:s tidning*, no. 19 (1975).

165. L. Ekdahl, *Mod en tredje vej: En biografi om Rudolf Meidner. Faglig ekspert og demokratisk socialist* (Lund: Arkiv Forlag, 2005).

a government, was to manage the division of power between labor and capital.

When Olof Palme first received Meidner's proposal, he initially thought it was only a discussion paper. When he learnt it was the official policy of the national trade union, his first comment was, "They went beyond my wildest imagination." To the Social Democratic leadership, Palme made it clear that "This is a hell, but it's a hell we have to go through."[166]

Due to the longstanding close relations with the trade unions, the Social Democrats could not simply reject an important proposal passed by a large majority at the LO congress. Still, the Social Democrats avoided taking a public stand on the proposal in the 1976 parliamentary elections, in which the liberal political parties described the LO proposal as introducing "Soviet-style socialism" into Sweden.

When Olof Palme became prime minister in 1969, it seemed that economic growth and the expansion of the Swedish welfare state would continue as in previous decades. With the international oil crisis and subsequent stagflation in the early 1970s, however, it suddenly became difficult to implement new welfare reforms. Keynesian economic policies had stopped working. High-income working-class families with a house, car, lots of credit, and high consumption levels failed to support the Social Democrats. Palme lost the 1976 election and, after 44 years in power, the Social Democrats found themselves in opposition for the first time since 1931.

Palme had to find political ground between the left wing of the trade union movement and a section of the working class increasingly attracted to economic liberalism—ground from which to regain power. To achieve this, the Social Democrats and the LO leadership created a working group in 1977, tasked with drafting a bill on establishing Employee Funds.

Time was on Palme's side. The energy from the '68 rebellion was dissipating and neoliberalism was at the door. In 1978, the

---

166. Björn Elmbrant, *Palme* (Stockholm: Författarförlaget. Fischer & Rye, 1989), 211.

joint working group presented a modified compromise proposal, which limited Meidner's original plan to companies of
more than 500 employees. Furthermore, the funding should
come not just from profits but also from the wage-earners'
salaries. The question of the ownership of the means of production had disappeared completely, as the working group's
introduction made clear: "The proposal is not going to fundamentally change the economic and political environment in
which businesses operate."[167]

In the revised joint proposal, the purpose of the Employee
Funds was no longer to transform society's economic power
relations but to finance the investments needed for industrial
restructuring in the context of neoliberal globalization. In
addition, the state would pay compensation for the profits paid
into the funds, to indemnify the private shareholders from any
loss. According to Meidner, the new proposal had nothing in
common with the original except its name.[168] Despite the compromise, the Social Democratic leadership refused to support
the new joint proposal prior to the 1979 general election, so
as not to scare away voters. It made no difference: the Social
Democrats lost and the Liberals formed the new government.

In 1981, a new revised proposal was issued by the Social
Democrats and the LO, largely the work of future Social
Democratic Finance Minister Kjell-Olof Feldt and influenced
by the new neoliberal trends. The proposal got rid of any man-
datory profit-based transfer of shares to the funds. The core
mechanism for changing property relations was completely
gone. The purpose of the funds, whose capital now consisted
of joint contributions from capital and employees, was to buy
shares on the stock exchange, just like any other investor.

In the campaign leading up to the 1982 elections, the Social
Democrats tried to downplay the significance of the proposal

---

167. Niels Dalgaard, "Debatten om økonomisk demokrati i Danmark og Sverige," *Politica* 25,
no. 3 (1993): 335.

168. Ekdahl (2005).

for economic democracy. They presented it as an initiative to deal with the economic crisis in Sweden by encouraging new investments. This time the Social Democrats won the election. The new Palme government drafted a bill for Employee Funds, with five funds to be established, financed primarily by contributions from the joint capital and labor payments to future pensions. The size of the funds' total assets was limited and the funds were to own a maximum of 8 percent of each company's shares. As he presented the bill to parliament, the Finance Minister concluded:

> The Employee Funds are not an instrument intended to do away with capitalism ... . The Employee Funds are one of many corporate tools that the democratic labor movement employs to make life better for people in our country ... . The funds are a way to strengthen the common interest concerning work, production, and savings, which has existed in our country for a long time. Thus, the introduction of the Employee Funds is a reform in the traditional spirit of social democratic reform.[169]

The bill now looked like some proposal from the Liberal Party or the Employers' Association. But, despite all the compromises and changes to the LO's Meidner proposal, it seemed that the opposition could not forget the content and spirit of the original. There was still strong opposition to the Social Democrats' proposal. At the opening of parliament on October 4, 1983, approximately 75,000 people demonstrated in front of the Riksdag against the proposal. A petition against the bill received more than a half-million signatures. Opinion polls showed that 63 percent of voters were against and only 17 percent for the funds.[170] The rhetoric was over the top; the question was presented as a choice between the funds and free-

---

169. Swedish Riksdag, *Rigsdagsprotokoll*, no. 53 (1983): 49.

170. Mikael Gilljam, *Svenska folket och lontagarfonderna*, (Lund: Studentlitteratur, 1988), 155. Göran Hägg, *Välfärdsåren: svensk historia 1945–1986* (Stockholm: Wahlström & Widstrand, 2005), 192–93.

dom. Nonetheless, on December 20, 1983, the bill was passed by the Riksdag with the votes of the Social Democrats and the former Communist Party, the *Vänsterpartiet Kommunisternes*. As for the opposition, they swore to abolish the funds as soon as they were back in power. In protest, several large companies — including Ingvar Kamprad's IKEA, the Rausing family's Tetra Pak, and the Persson family's H&M—relocated their assets and headquarters out of Sweden to tax havens in Switzerland and England. There was no love lost at the time between the Swedish bourgeoisie and the Social Democrats.

In February 1986, in central Stockholm, Olof Palme was murdered, shot at close range on his way home from the cinema with his wife. As it was a spontaneous and personal outing, he did not have a bodyguard with him at the time. Despite a massive investigation, it has never been clarified whether the murder was committed by a random petty criminal or as part of a politically motivated conspiracy. The latter possibility cannot be ruled out. The Employee Funds issue had polarized the political climate in Sweden and Palme's interventionist foreign policy had earned him many enemies, both abroad and in Sweden.

The Palme government marks the high-point of the Social Democratic era in Sweden. Individuals, however, do not create the story. It was not Palme's death that changed the Swedish *folkhem*. For some time, neoliberalism had been eating away at its foundations, and it now entered the scene to restructure Swedish society.

When the Liberal Party (*Moderaterne*) formed the government in 1991 with Carl Bildt as prime minister, one of its first acts was to dismantle the Employee Funds and distribute their assets. Ten billion kroner were spent on various scientific research projects and the rest went into ordinary labor market pensions funds. As for the Social Democrats, SAP chairperson Ingvar Carlson promised that they would never again introduce wage-earner funds. (Parallel to the Swedish efforts to introduce "economic democracy," the Danish Social

Democrats had attempted something similar. Their proposal never reached parliament, however, as Social Democratic Prime Minister Anker Jørgensen threw in the towel and handed power over to a conservative government in 1982.)

The Employee Funds fiasco marks a boundary limit for the social democratic project in Sweden. In the end, the Social Democrats simply wanted to democratize capitalism, not abolish it. Imperceptibly, up through the 20th century, the Social Democrats had shifted from being a party which had some kind of socialist agenda to being a pro-capitalist party. At the beginning of the century, the Social Democrats defined socialism as their goal. It was how to reach and implement socialism that separated them from the more radical left. The Social Democratic strategy was to make a temporary compromise with capital on the path to socialism. At some point after World War II, however, socialism disappeared from the plan and the Social Democrats discovered a newfound appreciation for capitalism—maybe given what they could see of how "real existing socialism" was working or maybe out of a fascination with US consumer society and culture. For the Social Democrats, the growth of the Swedish welfare state was proof that a healthy capitalism could exist. When the health of capitalism is threatened by crises, it just needs some social democratic Keynesian medicine and care to set things right and reign in the worst excesses.

As for capital, the Employee Funds were beyond the pale, in terms of what was or was not an acceptable level of power-sharing with the Social Democrats. Although the final proposal did not challenge the private ownership of the means of production or the right of capital to direct and distribute work, the original ideas in the LO's proposal had provoked the bourgeoisie. Before parliament voted on the bill, the Employers' Association purchased full-page ads in the leading newspapers, describing the funds as the first step towards a totalitarian socialist society opposed to capitalist freedom and democracy. A slew of books were published on the relationship between capitalism and freedom. The tenor of the debate leading up to the vote had been harsh and this created cracks in the *folkhem*. Capital had drawn a line in the sand.

These conflicts in Swedish society had their origin in transformations in global capitalism in the second half of the 1970s, which made capital move from the defensive to the offensive, as we shall see.

Capitalism under pressure

By the early 1970s, a number of Swedish companies could be found among the world's 500 largest multinational corporations: Volvo, Saab Scania, LM Ericsson, Electrolux, Stora Kopparbergs Bergslags, Svenska SKF, Trelleborg Cellulosa, Nobel Industries, KF Industri, Procordia, Mo & Domsjö, Sandvik, and Esselte. The years between the Second World War and the mid-1970s had not only been the golden age of Social Democracy but also of Swedish industry—perhaps because of the partnership between the two. Even the Employee Funds, which capital had fought against tooth and nail, proved a useful tool when the economic crisis hampered growth. The funds provided venture capital for modernizing and restructuring Swedish industry to better face the challenge of increased competition as globalization evolved.

As the Social Democrats reached the peak of their power in Sweden, an opposition emerged to their left that wanted even more. There were a number of wildcat strikes at the iron mines in northern Sweden in 1969 and 1970, and Meidner's proposal to expropriate the capitalists via trade union–controlled funds was adopted by the LO. Furthermore, the spirit of '68 radicalized a section of youth, who not only wanted to abolish capitalism and imperialism but were also highly critical of the Social Democrats and the old Communist Parties— it was the emergence of a New Left. All this was not just a

Swedish phenomenon; the same trends could be found elsewhere in Europe, especially in Italy, France, and Germany. In
the US, resistance to the Vietnam War set the political agenda
in the late 1960s and early 1970s. At the same time, the Black
Liberation Movement was rapidly escalating to new levels of
struggle; this took form in a number of new organizations, the
most famous of which probably being the Black Panther Party.
Economically, these confrontations were expressed in the dollar crises of 1967–8 and 1971, which forced the US to aban-
don the gold standard. Capital was not only under pressure
in Europe and North America, however—forces in the Third
World were also demanding change.

In contrast to the relatively peaceful coexistence between
the working class and capital in the core countries after the
Second World War, strong nationalist and anti-imperialist
movements emerged in the Third World. In total, there were
about 40 revolutionary attempts to seize state power in the
Third World between 1945 and 1975.

The contradiction between neocolonialism and the Third
World also took global economic and institutional forms. In
the 1970s, a group of 77 Third World countries organized
themselves into the G77, demanding that new global institutions be established to govern the world economy, instead of
the US-dominated Bretton Woods institutions.

The raw material–producing countries in the Third World
tried to counteract the unequal terms of trade with the rich
countries by establishing oil, bauxite (aluminum), copper, and
sugar cartels. The most successful example of this strategy
was OPEC, the Organization of the Petroleum Exporting
Countries. OPEC also proved itself to be a political force. In
October 1973, during the Yom Kippur War, the Arab OPEC
countries imposed an oil embargo on the US and Western
Europe and then quadrupled the price of oil, which resulted
in the oil crisis of 1973–74. For the first time since the Second
World War, the West experienced an economic crisis with
high inflation simultaneous with stagnation in production and

consumption—stagflation.

As a result of this combined pressure, capital went on the offensive; its opportunities for expansion were far from exhausted. There were still hundreds of millions of people in the Third World and in the socialist bloc who could be incorporated as cheap labor in a globalized capitalism, if production could only be outsourced. To implement such a strategy required a showdown with the social democratic state and trade unions in Europe and North America.

From the perspective of capital, the social state had gradually changed from being part of the solution to being *the* problem. The social state's welfare programs demanded an increasing share of profits, but even worse, the social state's regulation of financial activities and trade was a hindrance to the transnational activities of capital.

If transnational capital was to be able to invest and trade globally and to outsource production to countries where wages and working conditions were optimal for accumulation, it had to break free from the grip of the social democratic state and its accomplices—the domestic trade unions. This was the rationale behind capital's counter-offensive against the social state under the banner of neoliberalism. This was a prerequisite for enrolling millions of new proletarians in the Global South into the capitalist world system. Capital had to clear away the obstacles at home before it could proceed with its global expansion.

The neoliberal breakthrough

One of the most important factors behind the neoliberal breakthrough was the development of technologies and management tools (meaning: productive forces) required for the globalization of production, to make it possible for capital to free itself from the nation-state's embrace.

Specifically, it was the development of communications and transport technology that made global neoliberalism possible. The introduction of the standard-size container for land and sea transport is one example. Instead of taking days or weeks to unload and load a ship, it now took only hours. The container reduced the costs of long-distance transport by 97 percent, to 3 percent of what they had been. Cheap container transport was a necessary precondition for the outsourcing of industrial production to the Global South, as the bulk of consumers were still in the Global North.

Another important development of the productive forces was computer technology. The computer was the prerequisite for the mobile phone and for the Internet, and thus for e-mail, all of which have revolutionized information flows globally. This was necessary for the management and control of global production and trade networks. At the same time, the new forms of transport and the development of information and communications technology laid the basis for subdividing production and coordinating it via networks and chains between factories, countries, and continents, in whatever way was most profitable for capital. The development of the productive forces made capital more independent from any one specific place, while labor was bound much more tightly to its geographical location.

Neoliberalism was not just a technical development, it was also about politics. The neoliberal breakthrough occurred when liberal think tanks and lobyists from multinational corporations connected with conservative political forces. In England, Margaret Thatcher ran against the Labour Party in the 1979 election with the slogan: "There is no alternative." She immediately set about cutting away at the services provided by the welfare state, privatizing public companies and seeking in every way to curtail the influence of the trade union movement. When Ronald Reagan won the US presidential election in 1981, it signaled the global breakthrough of neoliberalism. Neoliberalism combined a market-oriented critique of state regulation of capitalism with an emphasis on individualism rather than community. As Thatcher explained:

> There is no such thing as society. There is living tapestry of men and women and people and the beauty of that tapestry and the quality of our lives will depend upon how much each of us is prepared to take responsibility for ourselves and each of us prepared to turn round and help by our own efforts those who are unfortunate.[171]

The social democratic state was criticized for being patronizing and bureaucratic and for depriving people of responsibility and initiative. Again in the words of Margaret Thatcher:

> We should not expect the state to appear in the guise of an extravagant good fairy at every christening, a loquacious companion at every stage of life's journey, and the unknown mourner at every funeral.[172]

Thatcher wanted to replace what she called the "Nanny State" and its cradle-to-grave "coddling" with the much more bracing risks and rewards of the "competition state."

Neoliberal criticism of the social state became so pervasive that it spread to various social democratic parties. From the 1990s up to 2014, successive Danish Social Democratic governments adopted neoliberal policies, "modernizing" the workflows of the public sector according to the principles of New Public Management and Public Choice. Citizens became customers. They sold off public assets from social housing, railway and bus companies, telecommunications companies, electricity, heating—everything from the water supply to the sewers. On the international front, the main priority of the "competition state" is to secure the best possible conditions for capital, in competition with other states in the world system. From trying

---

171. Margaret Thatcher, interview for *Woman's Own*, September 23, 1987.

172. Daniel Yergin and Joseph Stanislaw, *Commanding Heights* (New York: Simon & Schuster, 1998), 107–108.

to regulate and control multinational corporations in the 1960s, the role of the state today is to serve capital as best as possible, in order to attract investments and thus jobs.

Free from the grip of the social state, from its control of the flow of capital and trade, and from the power of the trade unions, capital could initiate a new transformation of the global economy. The result was the relocation of hundreds of millions of industrial jobs from the Global North to the low-wage countries of the Global South, in search of higher profits.

To govern this new wave of globalization, neoliberalism established an informal political leadership consisting of the US, the EU, and Japan, with the United States as the "lead dog," and with biannual "G-meetings" to coordinate their policies. Europe developed from a common market towards a political union, and the former socialist bloc in Eastern Europe was absorbed by the EU. A common currency, the euro, was introduced in 1999, used by 19 countries with a population of more than 300 million. The North American Free Trade Agreement (NAFTA) was signed in 1991 and the World Trade Organization was established in 1995. These institutions and agreements, and others like them, formed the political institutional framework of the new globalized capitalism. In addition, there were a number of more informal gatherings and "clubs," such as the Davos and Bilderberg meetings between leading capitalists and politicians.

Neoliberalism in Sweden

With the neoliberal breakthrough, the contradiction between transnational monopoly capital and the social state intensified and became a driving force in the development of global capitalism. Gradually the social state aspect weakened and transnational capital became the dominant aspect. This also meant that the balance of power between labor and capital shifted in favor of the latter.

This trend spread quickly to Sweden. The Social Democrats' long-standing "monopoly" of government was broken. Parliamentary power fluctuated between the Social Democrats and Liberals, with the latter forming governments following the 1976, 1979, 1991, 2006, and 2010 elections.

Marcus Wallenberg, Sweden's top financier, switched horses in the mid-1970s, from the Stockholm School of Economics to neoliberalism. Wallenberg, whose family directly or indirectly controlled a third of the Swedish gross domestic product, was a major influence on the Swedish Employers' Association (*Svenska Arbetsgivareföreningen*, or SAF). In 1978, Wallenberg's favorite, Curt Nicolin, became head of the SAF. His aim was to tame the Swedish trade unions and force the Social Democrats to support or pursue a neoliberal economic policy. In accord with the neoliberal doctrine, Nicolin criticized the high taxes, high wages, and swollen public sector, all of which caused Sweden to lag behind in the global race to attract capital.[173]

Initially, the Social Democrats responded to this pressure with talk of the "the middle road," an adaptation of the social democratic welfare state to neoliberal criticism: there were to be no new demands for wage increases and restrictions on the movement of capital had to be relaxed, but the core—the social spending—was to be maintained.

In 1987, Britain deregulated the trade in currency, shares, and bonds. The London Stock Exchange is the center of global financial trade, so other European states quickly followed suit— Sweden in 1989. Whereas Keynesianism had been a bulwark shielding the Swedish national economy, neoliberalism now established a conveyor belt bringing global market forces into the country. Neoliberalism thus also marks a shift from the dominance of industrial capital to financial capital. In the

173 Louis Proyect, "How Swedish Social Democracy became neoliberal." Louis Proyect, The Unrepentant Marxist (blog), November 10, 2015.

article "The End of the Middle Road: What Happened to the Swedish Model?" Kenneth Hermele and David Vail describe the development of Swedish capitalism in the early 1990s:

> ... the growing profits bred speculation and inflated the prices of real estate, art, stamps, and the like. In order to find an outlet for all this speculative capital, the Social Democratic government thought it necessary to eliminate the little control over international capital flows that it had previously exerted. Within a year or two, Swedish capital had spilled over into Europe and helped push real estate prices in London and Brussels to record highs ... . The outflow of capital amounted to as much as 7 percent of Sweden's GNP, or 60 percent of its domestic investment in 1989 and 1990. Approximately 35 percent of those investments were for speculative purposes (real estate and portfolio investments) and centered on London and Brussels. Swedish capital in fact became one of the most active investors in the EC at the end of the 1980s ... . As we know now, the bubble burst sooner rather than later, and the losses turned out to be enormous. In Sweden, the banking system lost an estimated 90 billion SEK (18 billion US dollars) on the collapse of the real estate market. Here, private and public commercial banks and the normally-conservative savings and loan institutions had all participated in the scramble. Their enormous losses are now covered by the Swedish state, i.e., by the taxpayers. Thus, wage earners have paid twice for the policy of the Third Road: first, when their wages were sacrificed in favor of profits, and then again when the banks' losses are covered by the state.[174]

---

174. Kennet Hermele and David Vail, "The End of the Middle Road: What Happened to the Swedish Model?" *Monthly Review* 44, no. 10 (March 1993). Quoted from Ibid.

The deregulation of the foreign exchange market led to massive speculation on small day-to-day fluctuations between currencies. There are huge profits to be made on even small changes in exchange rates, if you trade large amounts. A political crisis in the EU in 1992 led to massive speculation against first the Italian lira, then the British pound, and then the Swedish krona. In September 1992, the Swedish National Bank had to purchase billions of Swedish kroner on the foreign exchange market to prop up the currency, before giving up in November 1992 and leaving its value be decided by the market.

The Social Democrats were forced to adapt to the neoliberal regime. As in Denmark, this meant getting rid of public monopolies, such as those on television, radio, postal services, telephone, railways, schools, and employment services. Whatever could not be sold learned to mimic the private sector. After a half a century of Social Democratic rule, the ideological and mental transformation of Swedish society was profound.

Neoliberalism changed the international division of labor, too, of course, which also had a profound impact on the Swedish labor market. Let us now return to the global perspective to review these changes.

THE GLOBAL PERSPECTIVE AND SWEDEN'S ROLE WITHIN IMPERIALISM

The new global division of labor

From the breakthrough of industrial capitalism in Northwestern Europe in the first half of the 19th century until the late 1970s, the imperialist countries mainly imported raw materials and agricultural commodities from Asia, Africa, and Latin America, and exported industrial goods. With the advent of neoliberalism, however, there was a shift. In the 1950s, industrial goods were only 15 percent of the Global South's total exports, in 2009 they accounted for roughly 70 percent.[1] The reason for this change was the outsourcing of industrial production from North to South, made possible by neoliberalism.

Between 1980 and 2011, the size of the labor force enrolled in global capitalism grew from 1.9 to 3.3 billion people, an increase of 73 percent. Three quarters of this workforce was located in the Global South. The workers in China and India alone account for 40 percent of the world's industrial workers.[2] Together with the integration of the former Soviet Union and Eastern Europe, this represented an expansion of capitalism of historic dimensions—a wave of proletarianization, the likes of which had not been seen since the dissolution of feudalism. Hundreds of millions of workers were ejected from state-owned enterprises and family-based agriculture, to be proletarians in the global capitalist low-wage sector. Not only have more than a billion new workers been incorporated within capitalism, but the division of labor between North and South itself has changed.

Figure 2 below shows the changes in the distribution of industrial workers between North and South from 1950 to 2012. In 1980, there were approximately as many industrial workers in the South as in the North. In 2010, 541 million industrial workers, corresponding to 79 percent of the global

---

1. John Smith, Figure 2.1 in *Imperialism in the twenty-first century* (New York: Monthly Review Press, 2016), 5. UNCTAD, *Handbook of Statistics, 2009* (New York & Geneva: United Nations).

2. ILO, *World of Work Report 2011* (Geneva: International Labor Organization, 2011).

industrial workforce, were in the South, while there were only 145 million industrial workers left in the North. By 2012, the share of industrial workers in the Global South had grown to 83 percent.[3] The center of gravity of the world's industrial production had moved from North to South.

It is not just industrial production: where possible, different kinds of office work and services, those that are geographically mobile, have been outsourced. Mumbai, for example, has become a global hub for cheap computer services. The cost of an Indian software engineer, programmer, or simple typist, is a fraction of the cost in North America or Europe. The Swedish company Volvo's truck division outsourced its IT department in 2016 to the Indian company HCL.[4] Call centers, bookkeeping, medical and insurance records, flight tickets, desktop publishing, proofreading, and similar jobs are being moved to low-wage countries. If China has become the world's factory, India has become the world's office.

In the 1980s, academics talked about the post-industrial society. We work more and more intangibly, with knowledge, information, communication, creativity, entertainment, and experience economics. However, if "we" is humanity, then "we" are not living in a post-industrial world. There is "somebody" who is manufacturing the monitors, computers, iPhones, and iPads which are used in the post-industrial work, and there is "someone" who is manufacturing the ever-increasing quantities of highly material goods that we consume. Globally, the number of industrial workers is growing. Industrial production is not in decline. The work has just been transferred to the South.

The industrialization of the Global South is one side of the change in the global division of labor. The other side is

---

3. Intan Suwandi and John Bellamy Foster, "Multinational Corporations and the Globalization of Monopoly Capital," *Monthly Review* 68, no. 3 (July–August 2016): 124.

4. Surabhi Agarwal, "HCL Technologies buys Volvo group's external IT business," *The Economic Times*, February 17, 2016.

FIGURE 2. THE DISTRIBUTION OF THE GLOBAL INDUSTRIAL LABOR
FORCE, 1950–2010[5]

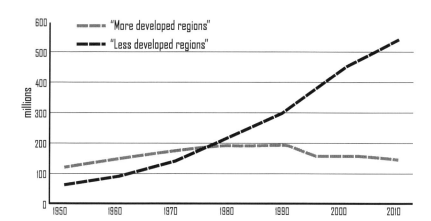

the growth of the service, administration, marketing, and
sales sectors in the North. As William Milberg has observed:
"Many [Northern] 'manufacturing' firms now do no manufacturing at all, providing only brand design, marketing, supply
chain logistics and financial management services."[6] Or, as
described in *The Economist*: "Factory floors today often seem
deserted, whereas the office blocks nearby are full of designers,
IT specialists, accountants, logistics experts, marketing staff,
customer-relations managers, cooks and cleaners."[7]

It is important to recognize that the ongoing industrialization of the South is taking place in a different context than
the industrialization of Europe and North America two hundred years ago. At that time, the industrialization process was
driven by a mutually reinforcing dynamic between growing

5. Based on a chart in John Smith, *Imperialism in the Twenty-First Century* (New York: Monthly
Review Press, 2016), 5.

6. William Milberg, "Shifting Sources and Uses of Profits: Sustaining US Financialization with
Global Value Chains," *Economy and Society* 37, no. 3 (2008): 425.

7. The Economist, "Back to Making Stuff. Special report: Manufacturing and Innovation,"
April 21, 2012. Here from Steve Knauss, *Unequal exchange in the 21th Century* (unpublished
paper), 25.

mass production and an affluent domestic market, a dynamic initiated and maintained by the additional contribution of profits from colonialism. The industrialization of the Global South is mainly based on exports to the North. Competition between suppliers in the South leaves no room for wage levels sufficient to sustain a large enough home market to balance the growth of production. The transnational "Big Brands" from the North can choose between many local manufacturers on offer. Branding has a huge impact on how value is distributed between countries and between work functions and companies. Furthermore, the South has no periphery to exploit or to which their reserve army of unemployed can emigrate, as European workers did in the 19th century. The door to the North is only open to the most attractive part of the workforce from the South.

Global production chains

The neoliberal industrialization of the South is not just a new international division of labor—the production process itself has been globalized. Capitalism is increasingly organized in global production chains—from conception, development, and design, to the manufacture of various sub-components, to the assembly of the final product, its branding and marketing, and then its final sale.[8] All these sub-processes can take place in different locations around the globe, depending on where conditions are optimal for capital accumulation. Relevant factors might include wage levels, labor and environmental laws, taxes, infrastructure, and so on. In 2017, the World Bank estimated that approximately 80 percent of world trade was

---

8. The concept of the "global commodity chain" has its origins in world-system theories and was introduced in Terence C. Hopkins and Immanuel Wallerstein, "Patterns of Development of the Modern World-System." Fernand Braudel Center. *Review* 1, no. 2: 111–45.

linked to the production chains of transnational corporations.[9]

Some transnational companies have skipped even having to have their own production facilities. Apple is an example of such a "fabless"—factory-free—enterprise. Apple develops, designs, brands, and sells products, but the actual production is completely outsourced. Apple is one of the world's most valuable companies with a stock market value of $530 billion in 2016. Its assets are not manufacturing plants, however, but patents and the brand.

The production of Apple products takes place in Asia. The subcomponents are manufactured by companies such as Toshiba and Samsung in various locations in Southeast Asia. All subcomponents are shipped to Shenzhen in China, where Foxconn, a production firm headquartered in Taiwan, has huge assembly plants.[10] In Foxconn's Longhu factory in Shenzhen, where iPhones and iPads are assembled, 400,000 workers live in barracks, working 12 hours a day, six days a week.[11] Apple management, located in California, is well aware of what is going on. They refer to Foxconn's compound in Longhu as "Mordor," a reference to hell in Tolkien's *Lord of the Rings*[12]—a number of suicides in 2010 at Foxconn's factories indicate that this is not just hyperbole.[13] In 2019, there was a broad protest movement against the so-called "996 regime" in the Chinese high-tech industry, which includes the largest

9. UNCTAD, *GVCs and Development: Investment and Value Added Trade in the Global Economy*. Summary. (Geneva: UNCTAD, 2013), iii. See also: ILO, *The Impact of Global Supply Chains on Employment and Product System*, Report no. 1, submitted to the ILO Research Department (Paris: Institut de Recherches Économiques et Sociales, 2018).

10. Foxconn is the world's largest electronics manufacturer, producing approximately 40% of the world's electronic products. In 2012, Foxconn employed 1.26 million workers in China, Taiwan, India, Malaysia, and Mexico.

11. Charles Duhigg and Keith Bradsher, "How the U.S. Lost Out on iPhone Work," *The New York Times*, January 22, 2012.

12. Nicole Aschoff, "The Smartphone Society," *Jacobin*, no. 17 (March 2015): 2.

13. Lei Guo, Shih-Hsien Hsu, Avery Holton, and Sun Ho Jeong, "A Case Study of the Foxconn Suicides," *The International Communication Gazette*, no. 74: 484–503.

companies such as Tencent, Baidu, Alibaba, Huawaei, Apple, and Byte Dance. "996" refers to working hours being 9 am to 9 pm, 6 days a week.[14]

If we dig deeper into the electronics manufacturing process, the global production chain connects to Congolese miners, some of them children, who extract the minerals contained in the electronic components produced in Southeast Asia, which are then assembled by Chinese workers into smartphones — the chain also connects to the management, designers, marketing people, and the vendors in the Apple stores. The living conditions of these various participants are very different, not because of the distances that separate them but because of the political economy of capitalism.

A characteristic feature of the transnational production chains is that although production takes place in the Global South, they are controlled by headquarters located in the Global North. It is this control that reduces the rest of the chain to being subcontractors. In addition, the companies in the North are able to claim, comfortably removed from the factory floor, that wage levels and working conditions are not their responsibility. In this way, the big brand companies in the North are able to acquire most of the value created by their subcontractors' production in the South. From 2005–2015, Foxconn's profit rate hovered around 2 or 3 percent, while Apple's was roughly 30 percent.[15]

14. Li Xiaotian, "The 996.ICU Movement in China: Changing Employment Relations and Labor Agency in the Tech Industry," *Made in China Journal* 4, no. 2 (2019).

15. Jan Drahokoupil, Rutvica Andrijasevic, and Devi Sacchetto (eds.), *Flexible Workforces and Low Profit Margins: Electronics Assembly between Europe and China* (Brussels: European Trade Union Institute, 2016), 158 and 167.

FIGURE 3. AVERAGE HOURLY COMPENSATION IN MANUFACTURING, 2007[16]

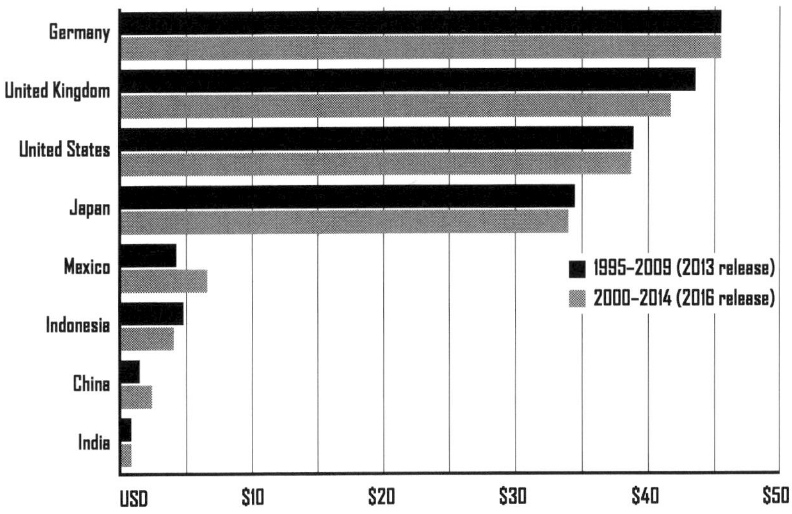

Labor arbitrage

The driving force of neoliberal globalization is the relocation of production to low-wage countries. The English political economist John Smith calls this phenomenon "labor arbitrage."[17] Arbitrage is a concept borrowed from financial transactions. Profits are made by exploiting the price differences of identical financial assets on different markets. Labor arbitrage means buying labor cheap in one market to produce goods

16. Based on the chart from Intan Suwandi, *Value Chains. The New Economic Imperialism* (New York: Monthly Review Press. 2019), 59. Data from "Socio Economic Accounts (SEA), Release 2013 and 2016," in: Marcel P. Timmer, Erik Dietzenbacher, Bart Los, Robert Stehrer, Gaaitzen J. de Vries, "An Illustrated User Guide to the World Input–Output Database: The Case of Global Automotive Production," *Review of International Economics* 23, no. 3 (August 2015): 575–605. On exchange rates, see: Robert C. Feenstra, Robert Inklaar, Marcel P. Timmer, "The Next Generation of the Penn World Table," *American Economic Review* 105, no. 10 (October 2015). On USD Conversion Factors, see: Robert Sahr, "Individual Year Conversion Factor Tables," Oregon State University, 2019.

17. John Smith, "Imperialism & the Globalization of Production." Ph.D. dissertation. Department of Politics, University of Sheffield, 17.

and then selling the goods on another market where wages are higher. The more separate the markets are, the greater the price difference can be for the same product, and the greater the profit that can be obtained. There is hardly a market more segregated and thus "imperfect" (in the liberal sense) than the global labor market.

Labor arbitrage can exist in two forms: relocating production to low-wage countries or importing immigrant workers from low-wage countries. The former is by far the most important form, because labor mobility is limited by the rules and regulations of the nation-state. The latter is used in branches that are difficult or impossible to relocate to countries with cheap labor, e.g. local transport and construction and various service industries, such as cleaning and catering. These migrant workers in the North still earn significantly more than their colleagues in the South, though. According to the World Bank, in 2013, each of the 210,000 Bangladeshi immigrants living in England sent an average of $4,058 back to family and friends in Bangladesh. By way of comparison, a worker in the textile industry in Bangladesh earned an average of $1,380 that year. Thus, on average, the immigrant could save three times as much money by working and living in England as he or she could earn by working in the textile industry in Bangladesh.[18]

As the table on the preceding page shows, the relocation of millions of industrial jobs to the Global South, coupled with ever-stronger immigration barriers to North America, Europe, Japan, and Australia, is based on large global wage differences.

According to the World Bank, the price difference of the commodity labor is greater than any other price difference created by borders.[19] In order to maintain this divided labor

18. John Smith, "Marx's Capital and the Global Crisis" (Paper presented at the conference, Imperialism: Old and New, New Delhi, 2015), 6.

19. Michael Clemens, Claudio Montenegro and Lant Pritchett, *The Place Premium: Wage Differences for Identical Workers Across the US Border*. Background Paper to the 2009 World Development Report (Policy Research Working Paper 4671). (New York: World Bank, 2009), 1, 56.

market, physical structures, military, and police are necessary at the borders between Europe, the United States, Australia, and the Global South. An important function for the nation-state is to maintain border controls—not for goods and capital but for labor.

The happy and sad smiley curves

As part of the neoliberal offensive, the establishment of trans-national production chains was tantamount to an integration of imperialism into a globalized capitalism. Simultaneously, it represented the heightened exploitation of the proletariat in the South. The outsourcing of industrial production created new forms of "unequal exchange," more extensive than the exchange of raw materials and agricultural commodities from the periphery for industrial products from the core that had characterized imperialism prior to the 1970s. This new source of superprofits saved capitalism from its crisis in the mid-70s and granted the system forty golden years.

Through transnational production chains, a huge amount of value created in the Global South is transferred to the Global North in the form of profits and cheap goods. In official statistics and in the companies' accounting ledgers, however, this value appears as created in the North. The reason for this "disagreement" on where value is created is due to the fact that the value transfer is disguised by the market price of the goods in question.

The formation of the market price—for example, the retail price of a computer—can be described as a process whereby each part of the production process contributes a part of the final price. Such a production chain typically starts in the North with design, after which the production of subcomponents and the assembly take place in the South, from where the goods are exported and sold to consumers in the North.

FIGURE 4. THE SMILEY CURVE[20]

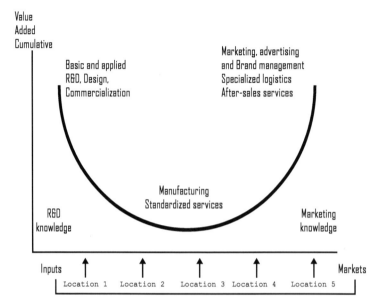

FIGURE 5. HOW WAGE LEVELS INFLUENCE VALUE AND PRICE FORMATION IN THE GLOBAL ECONOMY

20. Based on a chart in R. Mudambi, "Location, Control and Innovation in Knowledge-Intensive Industries," *Journal of Economic Geography* 8, no. 5 (2008): 707.

A graph showing "value added" (sic) in such a global production chain will be described as a "smiley curve" by mainstream economics.[21]

"Value added" is high in the first part of the chain: highly
paid development and design tasks, financial and general management, which are located in the North. By contrast, "value
added" is low in the middle of the chain: poorly paid labor
physically producing the product, located in the South. "Value
added" rises again in the latter part of the chain, when the
product returns to the North, where branding, marketing, and
sales take place.

According to the smiley curve of neoclassical economics,
most of the product's "value" is created in the North, while
the labor force in the South only contributes a small part. The
wage levels in the various parts of the production chain are
what determine the shape of the curve.

According to Marxist economics, the curve of value added
in such a production chain looks exactly the opposite. This
does not mean that the happy smiley curve is "wrong." It simply
illustrates the process by which the market price is established,
while the sad-face smiley illustrates the labor value contribution to the different steps in the production chain. The Marxist
conception of value added is defined by the contribution of a
certain amount of socially necessary labor, not by the size of
the wage paid for this labor.

What the capitalist buys with the wage is the labor-power
of the worker: the skills, the energy, the knowledge, the commitment of a specific quantity of time. Blood, sweat, and tears.
What interests capital is the capacity of labor to produce an
amount of commodities that can be sold at a higher price than
the wage and other expenses that it takes to produce them. The
higher the productivity of the work, the longer the extension

21. Jason Dedrick, Kenneth L. Kraemer, and Tony Tsai, *ACER: An IT Company Learning to Use Information Technology to Compete.* Center for Research on Information Technology and Organization (California: University of California, 1999), 156.

of the working day, the lower the wage—the higher the profits.

While the working class in the Global North has managed to reduce the amount of weekly working hours to around 40, between 50 and 60 hours is normal in the Global South, and the intensity is certainly not lower. The productivity of Southern labor is as least as high as in the North, as the neoliberal industrialization of the Global South has involved the most advanced production technologies.

This global contrast between the more or less equal value of labor and the huge difference in the price (wage) of labor-power is the crucial factor in the international value transfer—this is imperialism. The price of labor—the wage—is determined by historical developments as well as the current level of class struggle, this is what Marx referred to as the "historical and moral element." When Marx formulated this concept, capitalism consisted of distinct national economies. In today's neoliberal capitalism, on the other hand, there is a global market for capital and commodities with globalized production-chains linking labor-power in the North and South together. Furthermore, with the industrialization of the Global South over the last decades, the level of technology and management regimes are also becoming increasingly similar on a global level. The value of a commodity is no longer based on varied and isolated national conditions. The value is based on global conditions, and as such, labor-power has a globalized *value*.[22] As Samir Amin explained:

> My major contribution concerns the passage from the law of value to the law of globalized value, based on the

---

22. I am aware that elements of the cost of reproducing labor power are cheaper in the Global South than in the North—for instance, food and certain services. Others are more expensive, such as education and healthcare. Some elements are difficult to compare, such as housing. A simple flat in a slum is cheaper that an apartment in a European city. However, a flat that is up to European standards, with hot water, heating, or air conditioning, is often more expensive in the Global South than in the North. Yet concerning most consumer products, there is a tendency towards the formation of one global market price.

hierarchical structuring—itself globalized—of the price of labor-power around its value … this globalized value constitutes the basis for imperialist rent.[23]

The seaport worker who loads containers in Shanghai creates as much *value* as the port worker in Rotterdam who unloads them, assuming that the work is of the same intensity and uses the same technology. The *price* of labor-power—the wage—varies due to the different histories, social relations, and political conditions, and the limited mobility of labor, as Samir Amin noted:

> Capitalism is not the United States and Germany, with India and Ethiopia "only halfway" capitalist. Capitalism is the United States and India, Germany and Ethiopia, taken together. This means that labor-power has but a single value, that which is associated with the level of development of the productive forces taken globally. In answer to the polemical argument that had been put against him—how can one compare the value of an hour of work in the Congo to that of a labor-hour in the United States?—Arghiri Emmanuel wrote: just as one compares the value of an hour's work by a New York hairdresser to that of an hour's labor by a worker in Detroit. You have to be consistent. You cannot invoke "inescapable" globalization when it suits you and refuse to consider it when you find it troublesome!

> However, though there exists but one sole value of labor-power on the scale of globalized capitalism, that labor-power is nonetheless recompensed at very different rates.[24]

---

23. Samir Amin, *The Law of Worldwide Value* (New York: Monthly Review, 2010), 11.

24. Ibid., 84.

The combination of globalized value and low wages in the South is the basis for the extraction of *super-surplus-value*, which generates super-profits for capital and relatively low commodity prices relative to Northern wage levels. The difference between the value of labor and its price therefore corresponds to a transfer of value from the South to both capital and labor in the North.

The global distribution of value[25]

So what is the global value of labor-power? Roughly speaking, it is the average wage calculated according to the number of workers receiving different wage levels in different parts of the world. Where an average wage level lies in comparison to the global value of labor-power indicates whether you are in the core or the periphery of the world system. The difference in wages between the USA and China is roughly 10:1, between Sweden and Bangladesh 50:1.

This definition of the global value of labor-power also allows us to quantify the size of transnational value transfer and allows us to measure whether a given wage level generates or consumes value in the global context.

I specified the method for calculating the average wage factor between the Global South and North in the book, *Unequal Exchange and the Prospects for Socialism in a Divided World*, published in 1986.[26] There I measured the extent of unequal exchange at $353 billion (USD) in 1977. Zak Cope, in his book *Divided World Divided Class: Global Political Economy and the*

25. See also: Torkil Lauesen, "Marxism, Value Theory, and Imperialism." In Immanuel Ness and Zak Cope (eds.), *Palgrave Encyclopedia of Imperialism*, 2nd Edition (New York: Palgrave Macmillan, 2019).

26. Manifest-Communist Working Group, *Unequal Exchange and the Prospects for Socialism in a Divided World* (Denmark: Publishing House Manifest, 1986), 110–13 and 131–40.

Stratification of Labour under Capitalism, made the same calcula-
tion using figures from 2008.[27] He reached a wage ratio of 11
to 1 between OECD workers and non-OECD workers, which
gives an average global wage factor of 6.5 if you take the number of workers in the different parts of the world into account.
If we apply the wage factor to the figures of trade running
from South to North, it comes up to a transfer of $4.9 trillion
in 2008. To this must be added corporate profits on capital
invested in the Global South, estimated at $2.6 trillion.[28]

The value transfer from the Global South to North in the
form of profit is commonly accepted in Marxist theories of
imperialism, yet value transfer in the form of commodities produced by low-wage labor being consumed by high-wage workers is controversial, as it calls into question the idea of global
working-class unity and solidarity against global capitalism.

When viewed in a global context, however, the fact that
you are a wage earner does not necessarily mean that you are
exploited in the Marxist sense of the term. Some wage workers consume more value that they create. In concrete terms:
the hidden value (in the relatively cheap price) of the smartphones, iPads, sneakers, t-shirts, IKEA furniture, chocolate
bars, bananas, coffee, etc. produced in the Global South and
consumed by workers in the Global North, may be greater
than the value the wage earners in the North create.

The level of exploitation through the consumption of goods
produced by low-wage labor depends on the concrete relationship between the national price of labor-power (wage) and the
global value of labor-power (the global average wage).

Already in 1857, Marx discussed the possibility of workers drawing advantages from the labor of other workers. This
happens when the goods some workers produce are sold for
less than their value and consumed by other workers who can

27. Zak Cope, *Divided World Divided Class. Global Political Economy and the Stratification of Labour under Capitalism* (Montreal: Kersplebedeb, 2015), 254–56.

28. Ibid., 262.

afford them because of the higher wages they are paid. As he wrote in the *Grundrisse*:

> As regards the other workers, the case is entirely the same; they gain from the depreciated commodity only in relation (1) as they consume it; (2) relative to the size of their wage, which is determined by necessary labour.[29]

Therefore, it is possible for a wage earner to consume more value than she or he produces. This is not a matter of morals but of mathematics. I have made a rough estimate of the threshold above which workers receiving that income cease to be exploited in the global context. I base this rough estimate on the wage ratio between OECD countries and non-OEDC countries, which is 1 to11, combined with OECD figures on average wages.[30] The average annual wage in the OECD in 2019 was $48,587; a wage ratio of 11:1 between OECD and non-OECD countries gives a non-OECD annual wage of $4,417.[31] The average wage factor is calculated to be 6.5, which gives us $28,710 as the average global wage. There are many uncertainties and sources of error in information on wages and the number of wage-workers in different countries, and the OECD average wage covers all wages, high and low. Even with these caveats, it is interesting to estimate the approximate range of the global value of labor in cash terms.

Let us now look at how Sweden fits into this global framework of imperialism.

---

29. Karl Marx, "Notebook IV—The Chapter on Capital, The general rate of profit. The section: The general rate of profit.—If the capitalist merely sells at his own cost of production, then it is a transfer to another capitalist. Worker gains almost nothing thereby." In *Grundrisse: Foundations of the Critique of Political Economy (Rough Draft)* (Baltimore: Penguin, 1973; in association with New Left Review).

30. Manifest-Communist Working Group (1986), 131–40. Cope (2015), 254–56.

31. OECD, "Average wages."

Sweden's position in globalized capitalism

In 1776, Adam Smith explained how the international division of labor was the source of the wealth of nations. If we all just do what we are best at and what nature gives us the best prerequisites to do then, according to Smith, the "invisible hand" of economics will make sure that we all become rich. In reality, however, it was not just the "invisible hand" of economic transactions that established the global division of labor and apportioned the wealth of nations—the very "visible hand" of brute force also played a part. All through the history of capitalism, violence has played a significant role in the creation and distribution of wealth. To take one contemporary example: at every step, from the extraction of minerals and metals for its electronic components to the final assembly of a smartphone, elements of oppression and exploitation are present, from the miners in the Congo guarded by militias to Foxconn's factories in China, where workers are subjected to an inhumane work regime.

Swedish capitalism is not an innocent bystander standing outside of globalized capitalism—it is an active participant. Swedish investments abroad are larger than foreign investments in Sweden. Huge parts of Swedish industrial production have been outsourced in search of higher profits. The Swedish company Electrolux, which is one of the world's leading producers of household appliances and tools, had by 2010 outsourced roughly 70 percent of its production to low-wage countries. The car industry is another example—it is difficult to produce cars at Swedish wage levels and make a profit. In 1999, Ford Motor Company purchased Volvo's passenger car division; Ford then sold Volvo in 2010 to the Chinese car company Geely, which today produces Volvo's passenger cars. In 2018, Geely also purchased shares worth $3 billion in Volvo's truck and bus division. Volvo trucks and busses are still produced in Gothenburg in Sweden—but also in India, France, and the USA.[32] Failing to outsource, after years of economic difficulties, Saab Automobile went bankrupt in 2011.

In 2018, the 3,103 Swedish transnational companies employed 2.16 million people, 1.5 million abroad and the other 660,000 at home in Sweden. Swedish transnational capital is highly concentrated. The 30 largest companies had 1,053,381 employees in 2018, 773,611 abroad and 279,770 in Sweden. These companies had a turnover of 3,713 billion SEK ($445.56B USD) abroad compared to 2,263 billion SEK ($271.56B USD) in Sweden.

Outside of Sweden, most employees of these Swedish companies were located in the USA (235,899), Germany (103,820), and China (102,748). There are differences in the types of jobs carried out in the Global North and South. In the North most jobs were in management, branding, sales, and services, while in the South most were in production.

Approximately half of investments are inter-imperialist— Swedish investments in North America and the EU, and vice versa—this is an expression of the level of integration of global capital. Swedish Electrolux products are sold in the EU and the USA, and German Siemens and US Apple products are sold in Sweden; what is important is that Electrolux, Siemens, and Apple products are all physically produced in low-wage countries. It is the investments in low-wage countries that are key from the perspective of imperialism.[33]

Sweden is integrated into the imperialist labor arbitrage regime. According to Statistics Sweden, approximately 576,000 people living in countries with low wage levels worked for Swedish companies through subsidiaries in 2018. Of these, 252,000 were living in Asia, with 103,000 in China and 46,000 in India. South and Central America had 125,000 such

32. Pamela Ambler, "Volvo & Geely: The Unlikely Marriage Of Swedish Tech And Chinese Manufacturing Might That Earned Record Profits," *Forbes*, January 23, 2018.

33. Statistiska Centralbyrån, *Svenska koncerner med dotterbolag i utlandet 2018* (Östersund: Tillvaxtanalys, 2020),, 10.

workers, with 27,000 in Brazil and 33,000 in Mexico. Africa had 25,000, with 12,000 in South Africa. Eastern Europe had 144,000, with 64,000 in Poland.[34] These Swedish subsidiaries in low-wage countries had a turnover of 93 billion SEK ($11.16 billion USD) in 2018 alone.[35]

Parallel with outsourcing, the number of industrial workers in Sweden decreased from roughly 370,000 in 1996 to 161,367 in 2018. During the same period, the number of employees in the service sector increased from roughly 275,000 in 1996 to 408,437 in 2018.[36]

The private service sector employs the largest share of the workforce, with more than 30 percent of employed persons. Manufacturing employs 11 percent of the workforce and agriculture accounts for 2 percent. The rest are public employees.[37]

As a result of outsourcing, in China and India *alone*, the number of workers directly employed by Swedish transnational companies is the same as the number of industrial workers employed by these companies in Sweden.

To the number of workers in low-wage countries working for Swedish transnational companies must be added the number of workers in independent local companies in the South to which Swedish companies have outsourced their production. For example, textile companies like Hennes and Mauritz, MQ and Dressman, which have thousands of textile workers around the world who manufacture their clothes. The same goes for the furniture company IKEA. Hundreds of thousands of workers labor for these "fabless" companies. Let's take a look at some specific examples of this kind of Swedish company.

---

34. Ibid., 19–20.

35. Ibid., 32.

36. Ibid., 11.

37. Ekonomi Fakta, "Strukturförändringar i sysselsättningen," *Ekonomi Fakta*, Dec. 19, 2019.

FIGURE 6. EMPLOYEES OF TRANSNATIONAL SWEDISH COMPANIES, 1990–2018[38]

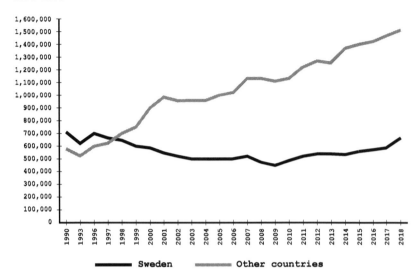

FIGURE 7. EMPLOYEES IN SWEDISH COMPANIES IN SWEDEN 1996–2018, BROKEN DOWN BY MANUFACTURING, SERVICE SECTOR, AND OTHER[39]

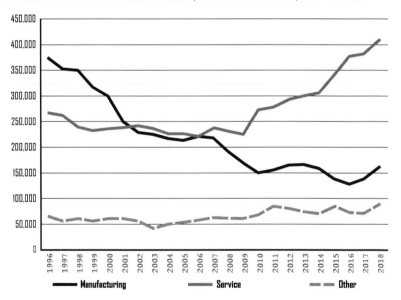

38. Based on a chart in Ibid. 8.

39. Based on a chart in Ibid., 11.

H&M

H&M opened its first clothing store in the small town of Västerås in Sweden in 1947. As of 2016, it had 3,900 outlets with 87,000 employees in 61 countries, mainly in Europe, North America, and Japan. H&M has no production of its own. All production is outsourced to 900 suppliers at 1,900 factories with 116,000 workers—80 percent of H&M's production takes place in Asia.[40]

H&M's outsourcing is at "arm's length" and "consumer driven." Employees of H&M's suppliers are on short-term, flexible contracts; they can be hired and fired at short notice and working hours can vary from week to week. H&M denies any responsibility for how production is managed and it is the workers in the factories who directly bear the brunt of fluctuations in consumer demand.

In 2016, the UN's International Labour Organization published a report on work conditions at textile factories in Cambodia, India, and Bangladesh that are suppliers to H&M.[41] In Cambodia, approximately 700,000 people work in the apparel industry, 90–95 percent of whom are women between the ages of 18 and 35. The monthly wages at the Cambodian factories supplying H&M average $187 USD. At the factories in India, the monthly wages were $114, while the monthly salary in Bangladesh was approximately $87. According to the ILO report, these wage levels are enough to pay for approximately half of the basic necessities of life and a simple dwelling.[42]

---

40. T. Donaldson, "H&M to source more garments from Bangladesh," *Sourcing Journal*, March 14, 2016.

41. Shikha Silliman Bhattacharjee, *Precarious Work in the H&M Global Value Chain.* A Report to the ILO (2016). Empirical findings on working conditions in H&M factories are based upon data collection and analysis of working conditions in 17 H&M supplier factories, including 12 supplier factories in Phnom Penh, Cambodia, and 5 supplier factories in the Delhi-NCR, India. The report is based on interviews, collected between August and October 2015, with 251 workers in Cambodia and India engaged in H&M supply chains.

42. Ibid.

The textile industry in Bangladesh, which has the lowest labor costs in the region, employs roughly 3 million workers, 90 percent of whom are women. Almost all of its output is geared to exports.

A 2010 German investigation published in the newspaper *Die Zeit* described conditions in a factory where workers produced 125,000 shirts a day, half of which were sold to H&M, the rest to other western retailers.[43] Workers at the factory earned 1.36 euros *a day*, for 10–12 hours work. The journalists described the price formation of a t-shirt manufactured in Bangladesh and sold by H&M in Germany. The price of the t-shirt was 4.95 euros in the store in Berlin. This is what this sale price represents:

> 0.40 euros: the cost of 400g of raw material (cotton) bought by the factory in Bangladesh
>
> 1.35 euros: the price H&M paid per t-shirt to the Bangladeshi company
>
> 1.41 euros: after adding 0.06 euros per shirt for shipping costs from Bangladesh to Hamburg in Germany
>
> 3.40 euros: after adding 1.99 euros for transport within Germany, storefront rent, wages to sales employees, and marketing and administrative expenses within Germany
>
> 4.16 euros: after adding 0.76 euros net profit for H&M
>
> 4.95 euros: after adding 19 percent VAT, paid to the German state

This breakdown of price formation reveals that H&M paid the manufacturer in Bangladesh €1.35 for each t-shirt, corresponding to 28 percent of its sales price. From that share

---

43. Wolfgang Uchatius, "Das Welthemd." *Die Zeit*, December 17, 2010. Here from: Tony Norfield, "The China Price," Economics of Imperialism (blog), June 4, 2011.

one must deduct €0.40, the cost of cotton fabric for each t-shirt. That leaves €0.95 of the sales price to be split between capital and the workers in Bangladesh. That covers salaries, power, materials needed other than cotton, depreciation of the machinery, buildings, and other assets, plus the local manufacturer's profit. A reasonable estimate would be that the average labor cost to produce one t-shirt is roughly €0.10–0.15.

That leaves €3.55, corresponding to 72 percent of the sales price, to be distributed in Germany. This includes €2.05 for transport, sales, and marketing expenses. H&M's profit is €0.76 per t-shirt, which is four to six times what is paid to the workers in Bangladesh who actually make the t-shirts. The German state receives 19 percent of the sales price, equivalent to €0.79, in VAT.

So a t-shirt produced in Bangladesh is a cheap commodity for consumers, one which generates profits for H&M and tax revenue for the German state. The sales tax alone is significantly higher than the wages workers receive to produce the clothes. Among other things, this tax is used to pay for welfare benefits, such as financial support in case of unemployment, illness, etc. In Denmark, a "cash beneficiary recipient" gets the equivalent of between $1,500 and $2,300 per month. The level of social benefits is similar in Sweden. In 2018, the textile worker in Bangladesh received a salary of roughly $87 per month.[44]

In February 2018, Swedish state television reported that factory workers at H&M's Hawassa supplier in Ethiopia earned only 300 SEK a month ($36 USD). Meanwhile, H&M is participating in a new major development aid project: the Swedish state development aid organization Swedfund has granted favorable loans of 125 million SEK to a Bangladeshi company, DBL, which is building a new textile factory that will provide 4,000 jobs in Ethiopia. H&M will act to

44. Danish Ministry of Employment, "Satser for 2021." Bizvibe, "Minimum Wages in Asia's Textile and Apparel Industry."

guarantee sustainable conditions, committing to be a long-term buyer from the factory. In the interview with Swedish television, Swedfund's CEO did not want to say whether he thinks that 2 SEK an hour—300 SEK a month—is a decent wage in Ethiopia. Swedfund intends to try and arrange for higher wages in the country, they say, but even though the joint project was started in 2014, there are still no requirements as to what wages will be at the factory. This is not covered by the agreements, according to Swedfund.[45]

IKEA

The IKEA furniture company is another example of a company that has outsourced its entire production. As previously mentioned, Ingvar Kamprad founded IKEA in 1943. Like H&M, IKEA moved their financial activities out of Sweden in 1983 in protest against the wage earners' capital funds. Today, IKEA's management and financial headquarters is located in Delft in the Netherlands, though the design department is still headquartered in Sweden. In 2013, IKEA had 349 "mega stores" in 43 countries with 139,000 employees.

IKEA began to outsource to low-wage countries as early as the 1960s. Kamprad was in constant disputes with Swedish suppliers about prices—at one point the Swedish Federation of Wood and Furniture Industry simply boycotted all deliveries to IKEA. As a result, IKEA outsourced its production to Poland, Czechoslovakia, Romania, and Hungary, achieving a 50 percent reduction in production costs.

Time and time again, in interviews Ingvar Kamprad has repeated how significant the conflict with the Swedish furniture manufacturers was for IKEA's decision to become a

---

45. STV Nyheter, "H&M satsar i Etiopien—med svenska biståndspengar," STV Nyheter, February 18, 2018.

"pioneer" in terms of outsourcing, and as a consequence to its becoming a global company. In the 1990s, IKEA transferred much of its production to China, India, Pakistan, Bangladesh, Vietnam, Malaysia, Thailand, and Indonesia, all of which have lower wage levels than Eastern Europe.[46]

The wealth and power of IKEA is based on control of "brand" design, patents on fittings, and production rights. They can transfer the production of popular designs—like the "Billy" shelf unit, "Pax" cabinets, "Lack" tables, and "Sultan" beds—to locations where conditions are optimal. In recent years, IKEA has centralized its production to 43 companies in 12 countries, in order to streamline production and reduce transport costs. The low price of IKEA products has even made them available to middle-class consumers in the Global South. In 1978, Ingvar Kamprad established the Ikano Group financial company, which is primarily engaged in banking and real estate speculation.

Lundin Petroleum

There are also Swedish examples of a more "classic" kind of imperialism. In the Middle East, as well as geopolitical concerns, imperialism's aim has been to secure access to oil. The US-led attacks on Iraq and Libya are examples of this.

In the Second Sudanese Civil War (1983–2005), the oil wells were of interest. French, Austrian, Italian, German, and Swedish oil companies were involved in the conflict; they contributed to the displacement of farmers and were complicit with the military regime carrying out war crimes. The Swedish participant was Lundin Petroleum; as journalist Kerstin Lundell

46. Jens Hultman, Susanne Hertz, Rhona Johnsen, and Thomas Johnsen, *Global Sourcing Development at IKEA—A Case Study*. Paper prepared for the 25th IMP conference (Jönköping International Business School, 2009), 9–11.

states in their book *Affärer i blod och olja: Lundin Petroleum i Afrika* (Business in Blood and Oil: Lundin Petroleum in Africa), the company was complicit in several crimes against humanity between 1997 and 2003, including the murder of local farmers and the burning of villages.[47]

Adolf H. Lundin was a pioneer in the Swedish oil and mining industry, and the Lundin family still owns his company today. Lundin Energy's main area of operations is offshore production in Norway. In 2002, Lundin acquired the Coparex oil company, which came with exploration and production assets in France, the Netherlands, Tunisia, Sudan, Venezuela, Indonesia, and Albania. Since its very first days in Sudan in the 1990s, Lundin had the backing of powerful institutional investors, including major Swedish banks and state pension funds, and its board has included the likes of former Prime Minister Carl Bildt. Many of these actors continued to invest in the company even after connections between Lundin and war crimes were made public.[48]

In June 2010, the European Coalition on Oil in Sudan published a report, *Unpaid Debt*, which called upon the government of Sweden to investigate allegations that Lundin had been complicit in war crimes and crimes against humanity whilst operating in South Sudan (then Sudan), specifically during the 1997–2003 period.[49] The crimes in question include the indiscriminate and intentional targeting of civilians, burning of dwellings, pillage, destruction of objects necessary for survival, unlawful killing of civilians, rape of women, abduction of children, torture, and forced displacement. Approximately 12,000 people died and 160,000 were violently displaced from

47. Kerstin Lundell, *Affärer i blod och olja: Lundin Petroleum i Afrika* (Stockholm: Ordfront, 2010).

48. Olof Björnsson, *Fuel for Conflict, Investors and the Case of Lundin Petroleum in Sudan.* Swedwatch Report 85 (2017).

49. European Coalition on Oil in Sudan, *Unpaid Debt: The Legacy of Lundin, Petronas, and OMV in Block 5A, Sudan, 1997–2003*, European Coalition on Oil in Sudan, 2010.

their land and homes, many unable to ever return. Satellite images taken between 1994 and 2003 show that the activities of the oil company in Sudan coincided with a spectacular drop in agricultural land use in their area of operation.

In June 2010, the Swedish public prosecutor for international crimes opened a criminal investigation into connections between Lundin Petroleum and these crimes. On 1 November 2018, the Swedish Prosecution Authority notified Lundin Petroleum AB that the company may be liable for a corporate fine of 3,285 SEK million (almost $400 million USD) for involvement in war crimes and crimes against humanity. On 15 November 2018, the suspects at Lundin Petroleum were informed that they might be indicted for aiding and abetting international crimes and could face life imprisonment if found guilty. The Swedish Prosecution Authority announced on 10 June 2020 that the Lundin investigation was complete. "We believe we have sufficient grounds to prosecute," Chief Prosecutor Henrik Attorps told the leading Swedish daily newspaper *Dagens Nyheter*, expressing his firm intention to take the case to court.[50] Since then, Lundin's lawyers have tried to postpone the court hearings as much as possible; proceedings may nonetheless start as soon as summer 2021 and could take up to two years.

This is the first time since the Nuremberg Trials that a multibillion-dollar company has been charged with international crimes.[51] On 13 February 2019, the Swedish Prosecution Authority in Gothenburg announced that a second criminal investigation had been opened into threats and acts of violence against witnesses in the investigation, who have allegedly been

50. Dagens Nyheter, "Lundinutredningen klar—åklagaren: 'Tillräckliga skäl för åtal'," October 1, 2020.

51. Isabel Schoultz and Janne Flyghed, "Denials and confessions. An analysis of the temporalization of neutralizations of corporate crime," *International Journal of Law, Crime and Justice* 62 (September 2020). Once court hearings commence the Swedish NGO Global Idé will provide daily English language coverage of proceedings, expert analysis and commentary at: www.unpaiddebt.org.

pressured not to testify in court.[52] Several witnesses have been granted asylum in safe countries through UNHCR-supported emergency protection procedures. *Dagens Nyheter* has also reported that there are ongoing parallel investigations into Ian Lundin and Alex Schneiter, for harassment and witness tampering. According to Thomas Alstrand, Deputy Chief Prosecutor in Gothenburg, who is leading the investigation, the Covid-19 pandemic has also prevented him from interviewing witnesses.

Swedish Imperialism in the Baltic

The economic and political pressures of neoliberalism, combined with the need to compete with the US in the arms race, contributed to the internal collapse of "real existing socialism." The fall of the Berlin Wall in 1989 was followed by the dissolution of the Soviet Union in 1991. The EU quickly swallowed Eastern Europe and the Baltic parts of the Soviet economic sphere. While Germany grabbed the biggest piece of the cake in Eastern Europe, it provided Sweden with the opportunity to resume its historic imperialist role in the Baltic countries of Estonia, Latvia, and Lithuania.

Sweden is the largest foreign investor in Estonia, accounting for 27 percent of all foreign investments in the country in 2016.[53] The largest Swedish companies in Estonia are Swedbank and the Wallenberg-owned SEB Bank, which together make up 63 percent of the banking sector in Estonia. Luminor, a Finnish-owned bank, controls 14 percent of the sector and Danske Bank controls 6 percent. Scandinavian banks therefore controlled a total of 83 percent of the Estonian

52. Dagens Nyheter, "Lundintoppar misstänks för anstiftan till övergrepp i rättssak," February 13, 2019.

53. Sveriges Kommunistiska Parti / Uppsala (2016), *De svenska monopolkapitalisterna i Baltikum.*

banking sector in 2019.[54] The Danske Bank in Estonia is at the moment the object of a criminal investigation; from 2007 to 2015, DKK 1,500 billion ($236B USD) flowed through the bank's foreign clients' branch in Estonia. These billions are believed to come from criminal and secret arms deals. Danske Bank's Estonian branch has been an important node in a large Russian money-laundering network that includes one of the world's biggest money launderers, Altaf Khanani, and the infamous arms smuggler Iurii Lunov.

The largest Swedish manufacturing company in Estonia is LM Ericsson, which produces communication equipment. With a turnover of more than one billion euros in 2013, Ericsson was the largest company in Estonia, its production representing 11 percent of Estonia's total exports.[55] There are also the Wallenberg companies Stora Enso (timber industry) and ABB (solar energy), as well as the Lundberg family's ICA/Rimi supermarkets, which control approximately 17 percent of the retail market in the country.[56] One reason for these investments is the low wage level in Estonia. The minimum wage in 2015 was 500 euros a month and the average industrial wage is approximately 1,100 euros a month, less than a third of the Swedish wage level.[57]

In Latvia, direct Swedish investments amounted to approximately 19 percent of total foreign investment in 2015.[58] Swedish banks have a market share of 53 percent, local Latvian banks only around 15 percent.[59] Two Swedish companies, Telia Sonera and the Stenbeck family's Tele2, control approximately 60 percent of the Latvian telecommunications market.[60] The

54. China-cee Institute, "Estonia economy briefing: A story of a Danish bank in Estonia: the bowing out part. To be continued?"

55. Crunchbase, "Estonia Companies."

56. Sveriges Kommunistiska Parti / Uppsala (2016).

57. Ibid.

58. Investment and Development Agency of Latvia, "FDI in Latvia," April 7, 2020.

59. OECD, *Latvia: Review of the Financial System* (April 2016).

60. Sveriges Kommunistiska Parti / Uppsala (2016).

Swedish ICA/Rimi supermarkets account for approximately 30 percent of the retail market in Latvia.[61]

In Lithuania, Swedish investments also represent approximately 19 percent of total foreign investments, though with greater concentration in manufacturing than in financial services, unlike Estonia and Latvia.[62] This is due to Lithuania's Klaipeda and Kaunas Free Economic Zones, where Tele2, Telia Sonera, ABB, and IKEA have investments. Lithuania is the fourth largest manufacturer of IKEA products, while Tele2 and Telia Sonera together control about 70 percent of the Lithuanian telecommunications market, and the two Swedish banks SEB and Swedbank control 59.7 percent of the banking sector.[63] To sum up: Swedish capital dominates banking, telecommunications, and the supermarket retail market in the Baltic States.

The Swedish arms industry

Not all forms of industrial production are outsourced to low-wage countries. For strategic reasons, the arms industry and the related aircraft and missile industries are retained in the Global North. The United States has by far the world's largest military budget: $649 billion in 2018. That is more than the next nine countries combined: China, Saudi Arabia, Russia, India, France, England, Japan, Germany, and South Korea. The United States is also the world's largest arms manufacturer and exporter. In addition to supplying its own domestic market, the US military-industrial complex accounts for 36 percent of global arms exports, focusing on high-end products

61. ICA, "Market development in Baltic."

62. Sveriges Kommunistiska Parti / Uppsala (2016).

63. The Baltic Course, "SEB ranks 1st among Lithuanian banks by assets, loans, Swedbank leads in deposits."

like fighter aircraft and missiles. The ten largest arms manufacturers and their annual revenues, as of 2019, were:

Lockheed Martin ($44.9 billion, USA)

Boeing ($26.9 billion, USA)

Raytheon ($23.9 billion, USA)

BAE Systems ($22.9 billion, UK)

Northrop Grumman ($22.4 billion, USA)

General Dynamics ($19.5 billion, USA)

Airbus Group ($11.3 billion, Europe)

Thales ($9 billion, France)

Leonardo ($8.9 billion, Italy)

Almaz-Antey ($8.6 billion, Russia)[64]

Sweden's longstanding military neutrality has provided the basis and need for the development of a substantial national arms industry, not only for the Swedish military but also for export to countries that would like to be independent of the United States (and, for much of the twentieth century, the Soviet Union) concerning arms purchases. The most important Swedish arms manufacturers are Bofors—which it partly state-owned—and Saab, which no longer produces cars but concentrates on advanced fighter aircraft and missiles. Bofors manufactures missiles, anti-tank weapons, anti-aircraft and artillery cannons, tanks and armored vehicles, naval vessels, torpedoes, sea mines, explosives, and small arms and related ammunition.

In the year 2000, Bofors's activities were split between Saab Bofors Dynamics AB (missiles and anti-tank weapons)

---

64. SIPRI, "Global Arms Trade: USA Increases Dominance; Arms Flows to the Middle East Surge," March 11, 2019.

and BAE Systems Bofors AB (artillery systems and medium-caliber/heavy ammunition), which is a subsidiary of the UK company BAE Systems Ltd. In this way, the Swedish arms industry is connected to the NATO alliance, despite the country's formal neutrality.

The arms trade is a special form of commerce, where what counts is not just price and quality but also politics. Who does the government want the industry to deliver arms to and who does the customer want to buy weapons from? Because the market is not open but is dependent on political factors, the arms trade enjoys extraordinary profits. At the same time, the trade is often associated with corruption. According to Transparency International, one CIA report concluded that "arms trafficking accounted for 40–45 percent of the corruption in world trade."[65]

Besides corruption, the trade is full of secret agreements. Bofors has been involved in several arms deals that under Swedish law were illegal. In May 1984, Bofors was reported to the police for smuggling 300 Robot 70 anti-aircraft missiles via Singapore to Dubai and Bahrain in 1979 and 1980. After a long trial, in 1989 Bofors finally received a fine from the Stockholm District Court for illegal arms exports.

In the early 1980s, India wanted to equip its army with new heavy artillery from Bofors. Olof Palme had personally negotiated a deal with Prime Minister Indira Gandhi, whereby Sweden offered credit for the purchase and promised delivery even if India should be in armed conflict. In 1983 and 1985, however, the Indian government complained that Bofors used intermediaries who made the deal much more expensive. In 1985, Bofors announced that it had liquidated all its intermediary agents in India, and in 1986 India finally placed an order for 410 Haubits FH77 howitzers, at a cost of approximately

---

65. Andrew Feinstein, "Corruption and the Arms Trade," *War Resisters' International* (2015). See also: Joe Roeber, *Parallel Markets: Corruption in the International Arms Trade* (London: Campaign Against Arms Trade, 2005).

$1.4 billion. In 1987, however, Sweden's national radio revealed that Bofors had bribed key decision-makers in India to get the order. Bofors denied the charges, but the Swedish Ministry of Foreign Affairs asked the Auditor General to investigate the transaction.

The report from the Office of the Auditor General showed that Bofors had paid at least 260 million SEK to a company in Switzerland owned by W. N. Chadha, who had been a Bofors agent in India for many years. While no charges were laid in Sweden, in India a corruption case was filed. Bofors director Martin Ardbo refused to answer his subpoena, however, and it came to nothing.

Sweden remains an important arms exporter. In the fall of 2018, Sweden hosted peace talks between the warring parties in Yemen's civil war. Yet since 1998 Sweden had been selling arms to Saudi Arabia, a key player in the conflict and one which has carried out frequent airstrikes.[66] As recently as 2017, Saab opened an office in Abu Dhabi, United Arab Emirates to promote arms sales in the region. In August 2019, media reported that Saab's Erieye radar and combat management system, as well as Swede Ship's patrol vessels, were being used by Saudi Arabia in the war in Yemen.[67] The Danish arms company Terma is also under investigation, facing similar charges. Terma has sold equipment and provided maintenance for the Archangel fighter aircraft, which have been used by the United Arab Emirates in attacks on Yemen.

Following this survey of the position of Swedish capital within global capitalism, let us now turn to the position of the Swedish working class.

66. Louise Gårdemyr, "Kan Sveriges samtaler bane vejen for fred i Yemen?" *Om Världen*, November 21, 2018.

67. Svenska Freds, "Nya avslojanden om svenska vapen i kriget i Jemen," *Svenska Freds*, August 14, 2019.

More than their chains to lose

In 1848, in *The Communist Manifesto*, Marx and Engels called on the proletariat to abolish capitalism, declaring that "The proletarians have nothing to lose but their chains." At the time, wages in Europe were around subsistence level, covering only what was needed in terms of food and shelter for workers to recover and return to work. Nineteen years later, however, in 1867, Marx noted in *Capital*, in a discussion about the level of the subsistence wage, that the question of "necessary wants" was not straightforward:

> On the other hand, the number and extent of his so-called necessary wants, as also the modes of satisfying them, are themselves the product of historical development, and depend therefore to a great extent on the degree of civilisation of a country, more particularly on the conditions under which, and consequently on the habits and degree of comfort in which, the class of free labourers has been formed. In contradistinction therefore to the case of other commodities, there enters into the determination of the value of labour-power a historical and moral element.[68]

This qualification was derived from the fact that wage levels during this period had begun to rise and detach themselves from the physical subsistence level. It was precisely in the second half of the 19th century that significant wage differences began to develop between the imperialist countries and the colonies. This wage gap continued to grow throughout the 20th century.

When labor is paid significantly more than the physical subsistence level, so that it becomes possible to transform a part of the wage into means of production or financial capital, the dividing line between the proletariat and capitalists becomes blurred. Whether the worker uses the share of the wage that

---

68. Marx [1867], *Capital*, vol. 1 (Moscow: Progress Publishers, 1962), 121.

exceeds subsistence needs as capital or uses it for consumption is a personal choice. This non-subsistence part can be used to go on vacation, buy consumer goods, private property, or shares, or else the worker can become an entrepreneur and start up their own business.

One's status of being a wage earner is therefore not sufficient to determine one's class position; furthermore, it would be logical to assume that wage levels have an influence on political consciousness and action. The global wage gap, which developed as a result of colonialism and imperialism, presents an obstacle to working-class unity. This is a historical fact. The working class in the North and South do not have the same interests in confronting the capitalist system. The classic Marxist understanding of the working class being one big family across nations cracks into pieces.

The socialist movement underestimated the forces of nationalism, as reformism turned the "dangerous classes" into citizens. Nationalism created a sense of loyalty between citizen and state, which was more important than international class solidarity. Nationalism in Europe developed into national chauvinism; as a consequence of which, feelings of superiority, distrust, and sometimes hatred towards foreigners took root. When nationalism was linked to colonialism, it developed into racism towards the people of Asia, Africa, and Latin America.

A crude and simple division between capitalists and the working class masks the global differences in the living conditions of the working class, and thus in their interest in radical systemic change. The low wage levels in countries like China or Bangladesh benefit not only capital—in countries like Sweden, they also benefit consumers. Products like smartphones and other electronic devices, cars, refrigerators and washing machines, shoes, clothes, furniture, toys, bananas, coffee, tea, spices, and chocolate are produced by workers with monthly wages between $100 and $1,000, and are consumed by workers in Sweden earning monthly wages between $3,000 and $5,000.

As a result of the history of colonialism and the structures of imperialist exploitation, an "imperial mode of living" developed in the parasite states. As Ulrich Brand and Markus Wissen have explained, people in the Global North are born and socialized into this way of life.[69] Their actions and choices are not just made under conditions of their own choosing but also under conditions inherited from the past. The imperial mode of living is normalized in daily acts of production and consumption, so that its violent character and consequences are kept at a distance from those who benefit from it. It is not only the consumption of cheap consumer goods and food; the infrastructure underlying everyday life, in areas such as transport, electricity, heating, and telecommunications, relies heavily on material flows from abroad. People in the Global North draw on these flows, not just because they consider them to be essential to a good life, but because they are dependent on them.[70]

It is not just an individual choice that makes us purchase cheap goods without caring about how they are produced, or drive cars or heat and light our homes with power that is generated by burning fossil fuels without regard for the consequences to the climate. Rather, we do so in order to live our lives in comfort, to get to work, or because the government where we live does not offer renewable alternatives. We choose the imperial norms of consumption because they are convenient and attractive. The imperial mode of living in the Global North creates economic and social problems in the Global South and global ecological and climate catastrophes. For generations it has also allowed the economic crises and social conflicts of the Global North to be externalized.

---

69. Ulrich Brand and Markus Wissen, *The Limits to Capitalist Nature. Theorizing and Overcoming the Imperial Mode of Living* (London: Rowman & Littlefield, 2018).

70. Ulrich Brand and Markus Wissen, *The Imperial Mode of Living and the Political Ecology of Labour*. Paper presented at the Conference on International Solidarity and Relational Inequality Amsterdam, September 13, 2020, 4–5.

Furthermore, as neoliberalism privatized and individualized our patterns of consumption and finance capital penetrated the lifestyles of the middle class and large sections of the working class, it became common for Global North citizens to invest a large part of their income in real estate. Former tenants became owners. In the US, roughly 64 percent own their home. In Western Europe, it ranges between 50 and 85 percent. In Sweden it is roughly 64 percent.[71] It is not the ownership of a home itself that is the problem. To own your home as "use value"—a roof over your head, so to speak—is widespread all over the world, even amongst poor people. The problem arises when ownership turns into an investment and speculation and becomes an important source of income. Since the 1970s, there has been a huge increase in the price of real estate, especially in major cities. A *yearly* increase in prices of 10–15 percent is not unusual. There was a slump during the financial crisis of 2007–8, but prices have been rising steadily since. Regular wage earners developed an interest in the real estate market and property tax rates. Today, there is a real estate agent on every corner of the city. Political parties are very hesitant to tax gains on real estate because they know they will lose votes if they do. If they make the right decisions selling and buying houses or flats, ordinary workers can make more money on the real estate market than they can on the job, using their increased equity to fix up the bathroom or kitchen or for consumption. Just as one can have a career on the labor market, many have a career on the real estate market, increasing their square footage and seeking better neighborhoods. Sections of the working class become property speculators as financial neoliberalism makes its way into our everyday life.

---

71. Trading Economics, "Sweden Home Ownership Rate."

Pensions

Another link chaining the working class in the Global North to capitalism is the growth of the pension system. The Swedish trade union movement did not succeed in establishing collective capital funds to promote "economic democracy." Like a consolation prize, however, they did win pension capital funds, through the introduction of a statutory occupational retirement provision, to supplement the state-financed age-based public pension. Historically, only state employees from whom special loyalty was required—such as police, military officers, railroad and postal employees—received occupational pensions. But today, occupational pensions are an essential part of collective bargaining, in both public and private labor markets in the Global North.

An occupational pension is generated by payments of a certain percentage of the wage by the employer into an individual account for each employee, in a pension fund. The percentage varies from country to country and according to the labor agreement, but it is typically between 10 and 20 percent. The pension fund invests this as ordinary capital in shares, equities, bonds, or real estate investments, with the aim of getting the highest profit for the individual wage earner's account. Occupational pension funds are thus part of the accumulation process, just like all other capital. Pension funds generate profits for capital and interest for the wage earner and thus social security in old age—provided capitalism is doing well.

To give a personal example: I retired in 2017. I only managed to have steady work with a pension plan from 1999–2017. During this period, 17–18 percent of my wage was deposited into an account in a pension fund. In this way, it has generated a sum of approximately $150,000, which gives me approximately $1,000 a month, after taxes, for the rest of my life, in addition to the state-financed old-age pension of approximately $1,000 after taxes, which are approximately 36 percent in my case.

In Sweden and Denmark, over 90 percent of wage earners

have an occupational pension. The breakdown between public old-age and occupational pensions is different in the two countries: the Swedish public pension is higher, while the employers' payments to the Danish occupational pensions are higher. The total size of Danish occupational pensions is growing so quickly that by 2030 they will exceed the value of the public old-age pension. Already today, the assets of the pension funds amount to $600 billion, 1.5 times Denmark's gross domestic product.[72] The assets of the Swedish pension funds are worth the same amount, $600 billion.[73]

Employers, employees, and representatives of the state usually manage the pension funds jointly. They manage huge sums of money. In North America, approximately 30 percent of financial capital comes from pension funds. In Western Europe, it is approximately 40 percent.[74]

If we look at pensions in a global perspective, it is not surprising to see that there is considerable variation in pension coverage and size. Total private pension assets in the 36 OECD countries amounted to $42.5 trillion at the end of 2018. By contrast, 52 non-OECD countries, where more than two thirds of the global population lives, held approximately $1.9 trillion in pension fund assets.[75] In other words, roughly 75 times more wealth per capita is invested in pension funds in OECD countries than in the rest of the world. OECD countries have the highest pension coverage in the world—in most cases, it is estimated to be more than 90 percent of wage earners. South Asia and sub-Saharan Africa have the lowest coverage, less than 10 percent of working-age people.[76]

72. Forsikring & Pension, "Pensionsformuer."

73. F. Norrestad, "Financial Assets of Pension Funds in Sweden in 2019, by Asset Type," *Statista*, November 20, 2020.

74. Allianz, *Allianz Wealth Report*. Nationale Zentralbanken und Statistikämter (2014).

75. OECD, "Pension Markets In Focus 2019, Table A B.2" (2019).

76. Carolina Romero-Robayo, Robert Palacios, Montserrat Pallares-Miralles, and Edward Whitehouse, *World Bank Pension Indicators and Database. Social Protection and Labor*. (Washington, DC: World Bank, 2012), 81.

A nation of rentiers

With the neoliberal breakthrough in the 1980s, trade in equities, bonds, and currencies was liberalized and speculation increased dramatically. Capital that could not be invested profitably enough in commodity production flowed into the financial sector to turn a quick profit. Financial capital moved globally, around the clock, from stock exchange to stock exchange, in what came to be known as casino capitalism. Between 1980 and 1986, the turnover at the Stockholm Stock Exchange increased from 7 billion to 140 billion SEK. At the turn of the millennium, as much was being traded every day as had been traded every year in the early 1980s. The new shareholders are not just a few yuppie capitalists. Membership in the Swedish Shareholders Association grew from 1,780 in 1969 to 142,000 in 2000. The Association has 122 local branches in Sweden where shareholders meet to share experiences and sharpen their investment skills, as the association writes on its website:

> In 2014/2015, the association developed a new four-part training model called "Millionaire as a pensioner". The education plan covers examples of how the pension fortune can be managed, how the pension system works, what the traditional "pension pyramid" looks like, and what an optimized "pension pyramid" should look like. The training is free if you are (or become) a member of Swedish Shareholders' Association.[77]

One reason why Sweden is the country that has the highest percentage of shareholders is that many companies offer their employees opportunities to buy shares on favorable terms. As early as 1988, more than 200,000 employees in 200 companies had acquired assets worth 13 billion SEK.[78]

---

77. Aktiespararna, "Kort om Aktiespararnas historia" (2019).

78. Mats Lindqvist, *Is I magen. Om ekonomins kolonisering av vardagen* (Stockholm: Natur och Kultur, 2001), 42.

In 1993, the Social Democrats and the Moderates (the liberal party) implemented a labor market pension reform. Both employees and employers deposit contributions into pension funds, investing them in shares and bonds at market rates.

In addition, many employees invest in private pension funds to supplement the public old-age and occupational pensions. Out of a population of 10 million, today approximately 1.3 million Swedes own shares directly purchased on the stock market. 5.5 million own shares via private pension funds and 7.5 million own shares via their occupational pension savings.[79] I am well aware that capital is still very unequally distributed in Sweden and that most are small shareholders; nevertheless, they are literally invested in capitalism.

The fact that large parts of the working class have invested in real estate and shares is not a step on the road to socialism, neither as a mode of production nor in terms of consciousness. On the contrary, it binds the working class to a desire for the comforts of capitalism.

The hourglass society

Not everyone is included in this "bourgeoisification" of the working class. While in its glory days Swedish social democracy managed to attain the highest level of equality in the capitalist world, neoliberalism generated greater inequality. An "hourglass-shaped" distribution of income developed, not only between the bourgeoisie and the working class but also within the working class itself. There has been an increase in the number of people living on social benefits and workers with insecure jobs and relatively low pay, the so-called precariat. At the same time, there has been an increase in the number of people employed at the high end of the global production

79. Aktiespararna (2019).

chains, in finance, research and development, branding, and so on—and these people earn more and more. The middle group of skilled and unskilled industrial workers is shrinking in size. These income disparities are amplified by the fact that the upper middle class is able to to invest more in real estate and finance and thus obtain additional benefits and tax deductions.

We have seen the labor market increasingly polarized between those parts of the workforce that can find attractive positions in the global division of labor and that part of the traditional Swedish working class that has been incapable of doing so. These workers, who must now compete with the proletariat in the Global South and with immigrant workers in the Global North, have not accepted this development passively.

THE GLOBAL PERSPECTIVE: GEOPOLITICAL DEVELOPMENTS AND THE CRISIS OF NEOLIBERALISM

The political crisis of neoliberalism in the Global North

Neoliberalism gave capitalism thirty golden years; however, beneath the surface of "the end of history" and the final victory of liberal capitalism, resistance was growing. Outsourcing of industrial production to the Global South made goods cheaper but also led to job losses and pressure on wages in the Global North. Neoliberal reforms and privatizations eroded the capitalist welfare state. Imperialist wars in the Middle East and the huge global inequalities created flows of refugees and immigrants and, as a result, pressure on the borders of the Global North. Immigrants and refugees were perceived as competitors for wages and welfare, not least by the sectors of the working class most affected by the erosion of the welfare state.

As a response to the consequences of neoliberal globalization and its institutions, there has been a steady increase in nationalism. This made its popular breakthrough in the wake of the 2007–8 financial crisis. Greedy financiers and banks constituted the straw that broke the camel's back.

Although trade unions and the labor movement in general had been weakened by decades of neoliberalism, and the state's ability to act as a mediator between capital and the working class was compromised, the Global North working class was not powerless. It had a weapon left: parliamentary democracy. While investments, production, and markets had been globalized, and a host of supranational institutions had been created, the parliaments of the nation-state remained the basic political entity and framework for political decision-making. Nation-states were still the building blocks of the transnational institutions. Governments were still an essential instrument of power and governments were won by elections.

The pressure on wage levels, the erosion of the welfare state in the North, immigration and "integration problems" created a desire for a return to the strong nation-state and its borders, as a bulwark against the consequences of neoliberal globalization. The financial crisis and the scandals surrounding banking and financial capital led to demands for regulation and control of capital as well as a more equitable distribution of wealth— things that require a stronger state. In most European countries, however, the demand for more state involvement changed character, ceasing to be the purview of social democracy and being increasingly linked to forms of right-wing populist nationalism. A political line the Social Democrats later sought to emulate, to win back the electorate they had lost thanks to their having taken up neoliberal positions during the previous decades.

Thirty years of neoliberalism also changed the balance of power within the world system of states. US hegemony, which was initially reinforced by the collapse of the Soviet Union, suddenly found itself challenged. The industrialization of the Global South, primarily China, shifted the center of gravity of industrial production from the North. China was no longer at the periphery of global capitalism but had become its center. The US had expected to maintain its political hegemony despite outsourcing, but China was able to maintain its national economic and political project in spite of its opening up to the capitalist world market. The US had hoped that global neoliberalism would have the same effect on China as on the former Soviet Union—however, the effect was very different. While neoliberal shock therapy devastated the economy of the former Soviet Union, leading to a huge decline in production, the Chinese government used the wave of neoliberal globalization to develop its productive forces and maintain a high growth rate. Within a few years, China surpassed the US as the largest economy in the world. Today, China is a leading force in telecommunications, robotics, artificial intelligence, and sustainable technology. Twenty years ago, the US could easily compete with China on the global market, because the products from US companies were better. Today, the US has to employ all kinds of political maneuvers and dirty tricks to fight against Chinese Huawei and the Chinese G5 telecommunications network, because Chinese products are better and cheaper. As American hegemony has weakened, the economic and political trend towards globalization has been replaced by growing national rivalry in a more multipolar world order.

We are thus in a period of growing tensions and change in the contradiction between neoliberal globalization and the nation-state. The political crisis of neoliberalism has divided both the working class and capital, between those who want to return to a more nation-based capitalism and those who wish to continue with neoliberal globalization. Some of the world's largest companies—such as Apple, Google, Amazon, Microsoft, and the electronics industry—want neoliberal globalization to continue. This is also what the companies that form the backbone of the Swedish economy want. They have established transnational production chains, logistics networks, and international organizations, which cannot be easily rolled back. Nationalist forces, on the other hand, want a stronger state, as a bulwark against the consequences of global neoliberalism. This aspect of the contradiction has become increasingly important in the North through parliamentary struggle. Nationalists have won government power, often in alliance with national-conservative sections of capital. In power, they seek to break down the supranational institutions built up in the heyday of neoliberalism. We thus have a situation where large parts of the production apparatus—and, as a consequence, economic power—lie within transnational companies, while political power is increasingly reinforcing a more nation-based capitalism.

The contradiction between neoliberalism and different forms of nationalism has been the principal contradiction since the financial crisis of 2007–8. This was expressed politically in the United States by the election of Donald Trump, in the EU by Boris Johnson and Brexit, in France by political forces represented by Marine Le Pen, in Italy by Matteo Salvini, in Hungary by Viktor Orbán, and in Australia by Scott Morrison. In Sweden this trend is represented by the Swedish Democrats, a nationalist anti-immigration party with direct roots in Sweden's historical facist movement.

The class base for a more nationalist capitalism is found in the "old" industrial working and lower middle class, people whose jobs have been outsourced and whose welfare benefits are at risk. These groups feel let down by the social democratic parties' concessions to neoliberalism and are attracted to nationalist populist parties.

In smaller European countries such as Sweden, the old political parties are desperately trying to overcome the split between neoliberal capital's demands for continued globalization and the demand of a large part of the electorate for a stronger nation-state—a very difficult task. Alongside right-wing populism, left-wing populist parties in Europe have had some success by taking up old social democratic positions. However, it is just as difficult for them as it was for the social democrats to implement a Keynesian control of the national economy, in a world where decades of neoliberalism have blunted the traditional economic tools of the nation-state.

The right-wing nationalist currents seek to write a new social contract between workers and capital. Unlike the compromise between social democrats and capital, however, this new compromise is based on an alliance between national-conservative sections of capital and right-wing populism, and thus on a more authoritarian state. This authoritarian state is also legitimized by the increasing military rivalry in the world system. As a spillover from this new nationalist constellation, direct territorial control and political force are taking on a renewed importance within imperialism, as compared to market forces, which were the main instrument used to achieve economic dominance under neoliberalism.

The crisis of neoliberalism and the rise of China

The contradiction between neoliberalism and resurgent nationalism is not limited to the Global North. Right-wing nationalism also has its representatives in the Global South: Narendra Modi in India, Jair Bolsonaro in Brazil, Rodrigo Duterte in the Philippines, Erdogan in Turkey, amongst others. Increased national consciousness in the Global South is also expressed in new international institutions opposed to US-dominated neoliberalism. Brazil, Russia, India, China, and South Africa have formed the economic-political association called BRICS. It is a very diverse group of countries that share a common ambition to achieve independence from the old neoliberal Triad, the US, the EU, and Japan—i.e., who hope to bring about a more multipolar world.

How the contradiction between neoliberalism and nationalism unfolds in China is of no less importance. China's opening to the world market in the 1990s created a class of capitalists linked to neoliberalism. The outsourcing of industry from the Global North created an enormous private sector in which migrant workers from rural areas are brutally exploited by transnational companies and their Chinese partners. All this has been endorsed by the Communist Party and the state-controlled trade unions as a way to use neoliberal globalization to develop the Chinese economy and acquire new technology. The result has been an economic leap forward with a growth rate of between 6 and 10 percent annually, compared to 1 to 4 percent in the Global North.

China's opening to the capitalist world system has been implemented under tight political control and is integrated within the framework of a national development strategy.[1] What gets exported has changed gradually to the point that,

---

1. Rémy Herrera and Zhiming Long, "The Enigma of China's Growth," *Monthly Review* 70, no. 7 (December 2018): 52–62. See also: Rémy Herrera, Zhiming Long, and Tony Andréani, "On the Nature of the Chinese Economic System," *Monthly Review* 70, no. 5 (October 2018), 32–43.

today, high-tech goods and services represent more than half of the total value of merchandise exported by China. Technological innovations in all areas—including robotics, nuclear power, and the space program—increasingly dominate independent Chinese production; the country's productive structures have managed to evolve from being made *in* China to being made *by* China.[2]

Contrary to the fate of the Soviet Communist Party, the Chinese Communist Party managed to stay in power throughout the neoliberal offensive. In no small part because, unlike the Soviet party, the CCP retained the support of most of the population.[3] The CCP has a dense network of cells through which the party can communicate its policy and get feedback. The recent Chinese measures against Covid-19, employing popular self-organization on the ground, have been a success, pointing to the internal "solidity of the polity."[4] Moreover, China still has a significant state-owned industrial sector and public service, state control of finance and currency through state-owned banks, and the continuing absence of the private ownership of land. State ownership of basic industry, infrastructure, and finance has allowed for the continuation of economic planning concerning the location and nature of foreign investments. State ownership of banking has made it possible for China to control its own currency and defend itself against the financial hegemony of the dollar.[5] Through state ownership and household responsibility for cultivating farmland, China produces food for 22 percent of the world's population on 6

---

2. Zhiming Long, Zhixuan Feng, Bangxi Li, and Rémy Herrera, "U.S.-China Trade War, Has the Real 'Thief' Finally Been Unmasked?" *Monthly Review* 72, no. 5 (October 2020): 11.

3. Dan Harsha, "Taking China's pulse," *Harvard Gazette*, July 9, 2020.

4. Wang Hui, "Revolutionary Personality and the Philosophy of Victory: Commemorating Lenin's 150th Birthday," Reading the China Dream (blog), April 21, 2020. Here from John Bellamy Foster, "China 2020: An Introduction," *Monthly Review* 72, no. 5 (October 2020): "There is no doubt, as Wang Hui indicates, that local officials in Wuhan initially tried to suppress the first signs of the SARS-CoV-2 epidemic, but the response of the CCP nationally was rapid and the unleashing of a bottom-up peoples' war strategy was enormously effective."

5. Samir Amin, "China 2013," *Monthly Review* 64, no. 10 (March 2013): 14–33.

percent of the world's arable land.

In recent years, both collective land ownership and state ownership of the means of production and banks have come under attack from a section of the state administration and from Chinese capitalists. Nonetheless, they have been defended by the majority line in the Communist Party. If neoliberal globalization had bounced back after the 2007 financial crisis, the Chinese bourgeoisie, and thus China itself, might have become fully integrated within global capitalism. The political crisis of neoliberalism allowed China to avoid such a development, however.

It would seem that Xi Jinping and the Communist Party have come to the conclusion that neoliberalism has lost its vitality and is no longer capable of developing the productive forces in China. The engagement with neoliberal globalization is also a threat to social peace and a burden for the environment. In August 2020, Xi Jinping emphasized the importance of Marxist political economy and criticized neoliberal economics in conjunction with a reassertion of the importance of state ownership and rural revitalization:

> Nowadays, there are various kinds of economic theories, but the foundation of [China's] political economy can only be Marxist political economy, not other economic theories ... . Some people believe that Marxist political economy and "Das Kapital" are both outdated. This conclusion is arbitrary, and indeed, wrong. Putting aside the long term, just from the international financial crisis, many capitalist countries have continued to suffer economic downturns, serious unemployment problems, increased inequalities, and deepening social conflicts. The facts show that the inherent contradiction between the socialisation of production and the private possession of the means of production still exists in capitalism.[6]

---

6. In August 2020, the CCP journal *Qiushi* published an article by Xi on political economy, quoted here from Yun Jiang and Adam Ni, "Neican: 23 August 2020," The China Story *(*blog) August 23, 2020.

It seems that the Chinese Communist Party is now sliding to the left, partly because of the crises of neoliberalism, partly as a response to the growing hostility of the US, and partly because of internal class struggle and growing environmental problems.

The industrialization of China in the context of neoliberal globalization was based on exporting to the Global North—an international division of labor that generated unequal exchange to the benefit of the latter. A group of Chinese and French economists has measured the unequal trade:

> The results we obtained for the last four decades (from 1978 to 2018) highlight the existence of an unequal exchange between the United States and China ... . We then find that between 1978 and 2018, on average, one hour of work in the United States was exchanged for almost forty hours of Chinese work. However, from the middle of the 1990s—a period of deep reforms in China, especially in fiscal and budgetary matters—we observed a very marked decrease in unequal exchange, without it completely disappearing. In 2018, 6.4 hours of Chinese labor were still exchanged for 1 hour of US labor.[7]

In the last decade, there has been a significant rise in industrial wages in China, reducing the extent of unequal exchange. China has managed to reduce the level of imperial rent that the US, the EU, and Japan have exacted from Chinese workers as the price for economic growth while simultaneously breaking the technological monopoly of the transnational corporations. China's economic development has reached a point where it is challenging US hegemony.

So far as the US was concerned, everything was fine so long as China exported cheap toys, household appliances, shoes, and textiles and provided low-wage labor to US computer and cell phone companies. Things started to become problematic once China began to compete in sectors such as railway equipment,

---

7. Long, et al. (2020), 8.

construction machinery, and cars. Today there is a serious problem, now that independent Chinese products are gaining a share of the market in electronic devices, biotechnology, 5G networks, robotics, aircraft engineering, and online shopping. At the same time, China is setting up infrastructure projects in Asia, Africa, and even Latin America—America's backyard. What's more, China is challenging the US dollar as "world currency" and is pursuing an independent fiscal policy. Losing these markets and benefits is unacceptable to the United States, especially in the face of a looming economic crisis.

As to China, it too has its own problems on the home front. Neoliberal globalization has lost its momentum and the negative externalities accumulated over three decades are making themselves felt in Chinese society, in the economy, and environmentally. Access to cheap labor from rural areas is running dry and this has led to demands for wage increases. This intensifies the class struggle between the neoliberal bourgeoisie and the proletariat, which wants a greater share of the value that has been flowing to the US and the EU. Moreover, people are increasingly dissatisfied with the holes in the Maoist social safety net—"the iron bowl"—and skyrocketing housing prices. Industrial air pollution has become a nuisance in the big cities and water shortages are causing discontent in the countryside. The US trade war with China has aggravated these problems. Neither Xi nor Biden can back down, and political conflicts and military tensions between China and the United States are increasing.

The situation has led China to seek development within its own borders and, thereby, a degree of *delinking*, as Samir Amin called it.[8] Delinking is defined as reducing participation in the world market with its logic of profit and instead prioritizing a people's development agenda. China was in a similar situation in 1949, but today it has a completely different level of productive forces with which to meet the needs of the people.

---

8. Samir Amin, *Delinking: Towards a Polycentric World* (London: Zed Books, 1990), 62.

In July 2020, the CCP proposed a new economic strategy centered on expanding "internal circulation," backed by an increase in the domestic effective demand. This enlarged internal circulation will generate a "dual circulation" growth model, in which "internal circulation" and "international circulation" will promote one another.[9] This focus on internal development has been coming for some time. From 2014 to 2018, $586 billion USD has been invested in the construction of social housing and major infrastructure, such as high-speed railways, highways, and airports. China has also invested in so-called "new smart infrastructure," i.e., information-based infrastructure such as 5G, the Internet, cloud computing, data centers, artificial intelligence, and smart transportation. These are infrastructures that support scientific research and technological development.[10] Concerning 5G technology, China possesses twelve times more 5G base stations than the US.[11]

For decades, Chinese rural society has served as the buffer absorbing negative externalities generated by the urban economy, in terms of draining value and labor and in terms of pollution.[12] In 2017, the Chinese government put forth its Rural Revitalization strategy, with the intention to move away from accelerating urbanization and towards beginning to prioritize agriculture and the countryside. The strategy also involves a turn toward eco-friendly growth and development. At the same time, the "new infrastructure" projects aim to bridge the gap between China's urban and rural areas. For example, fast-growing rural e-commerce to help farmers sell products via

9. China Daily, "China to Form New Development Pattern Centered on 'Internal Circulation'," August 7, 2020.

10. CGTN, "Getting to Know China's New Infrastructure Projects," May 6, 2020.

11. Dan Littmann, "5G: The chance to lead for a decade." Deloitte Consulting (2018).

12. Wen Tiejun, *Ten Crises: The Political Economy of China's Development*. See also his lecture series, *Ten Cyclical Economic Crises in China (1949–2016)*, Global University for Sustainability Book Series, (London: Palgrave Macmillan, 2021). Here from: Sit Tsui, Erebus Wong, Lau Kin Chi, and Wen Tiejun, "Toward Delinking: An Alternative Chinese Path Amid the New Cold War," *Monthly Review* 72, no. 5 (October 2020): 15–31.

livestreams on the Internet.[13] Rural revitalization is to be an important factor supporting internal circulation.

Rural families have seen their incomes rise in recent years. The income gap between urban and rural is continuing to narrow. The growth rate of rural residents' per capita disposable income surpassed urban residents' by 2.2 percentage points in the first half of 2020.[14]

The crisis of neoliberalism and the conflict with the US have forced the CCP to reconsider China's dependence on an economy oriented towards exporting to the imperialist countries and to instead pursue a strategy of delinking. To be effective, however, the CCP leadership's current articulations of internal circulation, rural revitalization, and prioritizing the environment and the climate will have to be integrated with bottom-up popular participation. The peasantry and the working class have to be re-politicized. Without a strong popular mobilization, participation in, and support for the delinking strategy, it will not be able to prevail over its internal and external adversaries.

The Covid-19 pandemic provided an opportunity for the popular forces in China to organize and mobilize to recover their rights to public health care. The residents' committees and the rural village committees have played an important role during the pandemic, stepping in where broader state capacity was lacking. These committees constitute the lowest level of state administration, each overseeing four to five thousand people. They were given the primary responsibility for managing the pandemic on the local level—as the Chuang blog explained: "They were the ones you reported to if you arrived in the area, they oversaw your quarantine, you provided your health data to them, and they also had the final

13. CGTN, "Getting to Know China's New Infrastructure Projects."

14. CGTN, "Rural China Sees Robust Income and Consumption Growth," September 30, 2020.

say as to whether you could return to your home or not."[15] In addition to these residents' committees, there was plenty of other grassroots mutual aid activity taking place to provide healthcare workers with personal protection equipment or to establish local quarantine checkpoints.

As people undergo this experience of self-organization, they tend to become more involved in political debates and mobilize for social change. The possibility of renewed radical, egalitarian change in China depends on the ongoing class struggle between the neoliberal capitalists and the workers' and peasants' demands for an economy oriented towards popular needs.[16] This struggle will either take place within or against the Communist Party, depending on what policies the CCP adopts.

Spontaneous rebellion

Economically and politically, the Chinese experience of neoliberal globalization has been very different from that of the rest of the Global South. In parts of the Global South, the crisis of neoliberalism resulted in spontaneous rebellions against deteriorating living conditions, high fuel prices, unemployment, corruption, and a lack of democracy. The rebellions spread around the world: Thailand, Indonesia, Egypt, South Africa, Iraq, Lebanon, Iran, Argentina, Chile, and the list goes on. These uprisings differed in many ways as to their specific context and immediate demands; what they all had in common, however, was that they had no clear vision of an alternative or a strategy to reach it. They lacked any organization capable of moving from demonstrations in the streets and squares to the

---

15. Chuang, "Covid, Capitalism, Strikes & Solidarity: An Interview with Asia Art Tours," November 20, 2020.

16. Tsui, et al. (2020), 1515.

kind of struggles and alliances that can lead to radical social change.

Such protest movements, despite the radical forms they take, often operate with a short-term perspective and are reformist. They demand work, cheaper gasoline, a new government, another president, and liberal political reforms. They represent the economic and political crisis of neoliberalism and the desperation of the people. It is not without danger that people participate in these revolts. They disrupt society and are uncomfortable for the system; yet, without a clear anticapitalist strategy, developed organization, and a diversity of forms of struggle, the powers that be can just wait for people to get tired or else can introduce some reforms and then continue to rule. These are the lessons of the Arab Spring.

Rivalry

The transition from neoliberal globalization under US hegemony towards a world of growing nationalism is reflected in increased rivalry between states, primarily between the United States, China, and Russia. Rivals do not necessarily accept competition on market terms but may use more substantive means to promote their interests.

The United States is ramping up a hybrid war strategy of political, ideological, technological, and financial interventions, combined with military pressure, designed to halt China's advance and retain hegemonic power.[17]

There has been a significant arms build-up over the last decade. US military spending is greater than the seven runner-up states combined, despite Russia and China rearming. In December 2019, Trump declared that military control of space

---

17. Michael R. Pompeo, "Communist China and the Free World's Future," July 23, 2020, Richard Nixon Presidential Library, Yorba Linda, CA.

is essential for the United States. The Trump administration requested a $705 billion military budget for the 2021 fiscal year, directed explicitly against China and Russia.[18] The Biden administration is continuing this policy of military build up.

The United States is trying to obstruct China's presence around the world. In South America, the US has developed a program called Growth in the Americas (or América Crece), the purpose of which is to encourage US private sector funding, in order to squeeze out Chinese public investments.[19] In Africa and Asia, the US has developed the Millennium Challenge Corporation to provide funds to counter China's Belt and Road Initiative. Apart from these financial initiatives, the United States has established a military alliance with Australia, India, and Japan, known as the Quadrilateral Security Dialogue ("the Quad"), which is intended to encircle China.[20] India and the United States signed a Basic Exchange and Cooperation Agreement (BECA) when US Secretary of State Mike Pompeo and Defense chief Mark Esper visited the country in October 2020, with the purpose of cementing a close alliance against China.

China has not been marginalized by the US diplomatic offensive, however. In November 2020, 15 countries centered around the Association of Southeast Asian Nations, plus China, Japan, and South Korea, signed the Regional Comprehensive Economic Partnership (RCEP) trade agreement. The 15 RCEP participant countries account for nearly a third of the world's population and approximately thirty percent of the global gross domestic product.[21]

---

18. Darius Shahtahmasebi, "2021 Pentagon Budget Request Hints at Russia and China as New Focus of US Empire," *Mint Press*, February 24, 2020.

19. US Department of State, *Growth in the Americas* (2020).

20. US Department of State, *United States, Australia, India, and Japan Consultations (QUAD)* (2020).

21. M. K. Bhadrakumar, "India's Farewell to ASEAN as it Boards RCEP Train," *Indian Punchline*, November 14, 2020.

Over the past two decades, China has become one of the most important trading partners for Latin American countries. China has indicated that it will do what it can to provide a shield to prevent regime change operations against Cuba and Venezuela. China has openly criticized the US sanctions against Venezuela, and the Chinese government is currently holding talks with Venezuela about a new oil-for-loans deal.[22]

A Cold War–style "containment" of China is no longer possible, as Chinese production is vital and integral to the entire global economy. It is not easy for US transnational companies to leave China, which has become the workshop of the world. Half of the world's electronics manufacturing capacity is located in China, and the country benefits from infrastructure and labor skills that are not easily matched. Former US Secretary of State Pompeo was well aware that "China is already within our borders," in the sense of the US consuming huge amounts of goods produced in China. The US strategy is therefore to break the hold of the CCP over China, to replace it with a liberal pro-US regime. The aim is to damage the CCP's credibility, exploiting its external and internal contradictions—and in so doing, to weaken the Chinese state. US support for the Hong Kong rebellion is one example of this, hoping that the demand for liberal democracy will spread to the rest of China. This would allow the United States and global monopoly-finance capital to move in to support its internal Chinese allies and to restructure China's state and economy in such a way as to ensure ongoing US dominance and the interests of transnational capital.[23]

This imperial strategy will not be as easy as dismantling the Soviet Union was, however. Unlike the Soviet Union in the 1980s, China has a strong and technologically developed economy. Beijing's Belt and Road Initiative is expanding China's

22. Vijay Prashad and John Ross, "China is working to expand its ties to Latin America," *Peoples Dispatch*, November 10, 2020.

23. Pompeo (2020).

global role. If China is able to develop equal relations with the countries of the Global South, as opposed to the hierarchical-imperialist mode of relations, China will gain allies and its economic model will be a source of inspiration.

The position of Scandinavia in a multipolar world system

One consequence of a more nationalist form of capitalism is the resurgence of imperialist rivalry based on territorial domination. This is the context in which Scandinavia must navigate, both politically and economically. Sweden is located on the Baltic, an important seaway for Russia; with the Faroe Islands and Greenland, Denmark holds strategic territories in the Atlantic Ocean. The Scandinavian countries are drawn into the conflict between the US and China and Russia.

It is in this perspective that we should view Trump's interest in buying Greenland from Denmark in 2019. Climate change means that shipping routes south and north of Greenland will become strategically important, and the territory would be perfect for launching and detecting intercontinental missiles. While the offer to buy Greenland was declined, the US is taking steps to strengthen ties there as part of an attempt to exert more influence in the Arctic region.

China was on the agenda in October 2020 meetings between the US, the Greenland Government (Home Rule), and Denmark, which concluded in an agreement on issues ranging from new military initiatives to trade and investment programs in Greenland, including new airports.[24] In the future, American warships will be able to use ports in Greenland and the Faroe Islands for repairs, refueling, replacement of

---

24. Wall Street Journal, "U.S. Holds Talks Over Economic, Security Arrangements with Greenland," *Wall Street Journal,* October 28, 2020.

crewmembers, and other service and maintenance tasks.[25] Other measures by the US are designed to blunt Chinese investments by "assisting Greenland politicians to assess foreign investments." "We cautioned them about how the [People's Republic of China] is trying to gain a foothold in the Arctic," one US official said. "We pointed out that China is not an Arctic country and they should be aware of that."[26]

In February 2021, Denmark decided to spend $250 million (not including related operating expenses) to install new military surveillance equipment in the Arctic, consisting of air warning radars, satellite monitoring systems, and surveillance with long-range drones, stationed in Greenland and on the Faroe Islands.[27]

In another effort to weaken the Chinese economy, the US has targeted the Huawei telecom company, China's largest private capitalist corporation. Huawei is considered to have the best and cheapest 5G technology; Nokia (Finland) and Ericsson (Sweden) are the only European suppliers of similar 5G infrastructure, and experts say they cannot provide 5G kits as quickly or inexpensively as Huawei.[28]

It is difficult for the US to compete in terms of quality and price, so the government resorts to political pressure. In December 2018, Canada arrested Meng Wanzhou, the chief financial officer of Huawei, on an extradition request from the United States. Meng is currently under house arrest in Vancouver. Her extradition hearings are currently scheduled to wrap up in August 2021, although the potential for appeals means the case could drag on for years. European governments have been tightening controls on Chinese companies building 5G networks following diplomatic pressure from Washington,

25. Politiken, "USA forhandler om aftale for krigsskibe i Nordatlanten," October 28, 2020.

26. Wall Street Journal (2020).

27. Oliver Batchelor, "Forsvaret i Arktis får halvanden milliarder kroner til droner, satellitudstyr og uddannelse," Denmark Radio, February 11, 2021.

28. Lucy Fisher, "Downing Street Plans New 5G Club of Democracies," *Times*, May 29, 2020.

which alleges Huawei equipment could be used by Beijing for spying. No evidence has been presented to sustain these allegations. The US wants a monopoly on such activity, as the whistleblower Edward Snowden has documented.[29]

A similar Danish whistleblower reported in August 2020 that the Danish Defense Intelligence Agency (FET) had entered into a secret agreement with the US National Security Agency (NSA), by means of which the FET granted the NSA access to large amounts of raw data from electronic cables used for all forms of digital communication, including phone calls, the Internet, and text messaging. The claims were confirmed by a government agency commissioned to supervise the activity of the Danish Intelligence Service.[30] The various targets of this espionage included the Danish Ministry of Foreign Affairs and the Ministry of Finance, the manufacturers of the Eurofighter fighter jet, and the Swedish arms company Saab, which produces the Gripen fighter jet, as well as the Danish arms company Terma, which supplies parts for the American fighter Joint Strike Fighter (F-35).

The Americans would do anything to get a five billion dollar contract for fighter jets from the Danish Air Force—which they did.

The Danish Intelligence Service, whose mission should be to protect Denmark against such espionage, apparently gave the NSA a free pass to spy on Danish ministers and companies. The affair caused a scandal, of course. The chief and other high-ranking officers in the service were "sent home," and the former head of the service, who had become director of the Ministry of Defense, was relieved of his duties while

29. James Ball and Dominic Rushe, "NSA Prism Program Taps in to User Sata of Apple, Google and Others," *The Guardian*, June 6, 2013. Glenn Edward Greenwald, *No Place to Hide: Edward Snowden, the NSA, and the U.S. Surveillance State* (New York: Metropolitan Books, 2014).

30. Forsvarets Efterretnings Tjeneste, "Tilsynet med Efterretningstjenesterne afslutter særlig undersøgelse af Forsvarets Efterretningstjeneste (FE) på baggrund af materiale indleveret af én eller flere whistleblowere." Press release. (2020).

the Danish government set about preparing an investigation into the affair. What makes the case even more embarrassing is that the Danish intelligence service also granted the NSA access to data from Norway, Sweden, Germany, and France—to the consternation of the neighboring Scandinavian countries. High-ranking politicians' and ministers' communications were tapped.

The United Kingdom, Canada, Australia, New Zealand, and France have de facto bans on Huawei. Germany is reducing its purchases from Huawei but has not yet banned them. Bulgaria, Northern Macedonia, and Kosovo are also amongst the countries that have signed a "Clean Network" agreement with the United States on the security of high-speed wireless 5G networks. The deal was part of the Trump administration's plan to exclude Huawei and other Chinese companies from 5G networks. US government officials campaigned across Europe, as well as in other regions, agitating against the use of Huawei's equipment.[31]

In October 2020, Sweden joined other European nations in passing a ban on telecommunications equipment from Huawei. The decision came following recommendations from the country's armed forces and security service, which described China as "one of the biggest threats against Sweden."[32] However, another explanation has been suggested by *The Economist*:

the Huawei fallout could lead to the bifurcation of global markets into two incompatible 5G camps. ... In this scenario, Sweden's Ericsson, Finland's Nokia and South Korea's Samsung would supply a pricier network comprised of kit made outside of China.[33]

31. Nicolas Fredriksen, "5G: Bulgarien og Sverige ekskluderer kinesiske selskaber," 5G-Netværk.dk (website), October 26, 2020.

32. Supantha Mukherjee and Helena Soderpalm, "Sweden Bans Huawei, ZTE from Upcoming 5G Networks," *Reuters*, October 20, 2020.

33. The Economist, "Companies Must Get Ready for a Riskier World," July 13, 2019.

Following political pressure, Danish telecommunications companies decided to drop Huawai and buy Ericsson.[34] Swedish companies depend on open access to the global market and are traditionally in favor of free trade, but a politically motivated ban on Huawai would be a windfall.

Denmark and Sweden are being dragged into the US-China conflict on the side of the declining US Empire, with all the military and economic risks this implies. Scandinavia may be on the losing side—the IMF's latest global projections indicate that in 2020–21, China will account for the absolute majority, 51 percent, of world growth, and the US only 3 percent.[35]

Besides the rivalry between the US and China, there are numerous regional conflicts. Parts of the Arab world have been plagued by wars for the past half century. Entire nations lie in ruins. Denmark participated as a loyal partner on the US side in Libya, Iraq, Afghanistan, and Syria. New wars loom on the horizon. In the conflict between Iran and the United States/Saudi Arabia, Denmark deployed a frigate to the Strait of Hormuz and from January 2021 will take command of the European-led maritime surveillance mission in the area.

The climate crisis

Besides the evolving economic and political crises—and threatening the basis for all human development—there are the growing environmental and climate problems. The predatory exploitation of raw materials, the depletion of the land, and the burning of fossil fuels to meet the demands of capital's ever-expanding accumulation and growing individual consumption have gradually sharpened the contradiction up through the

34. E. H. Mortensen and Marcel Mirzaei-Fard, "Sidste danske teleselskab dropper 5G fra Huawei: Nu går kineserne efter 6G," Danish Radio and Television, November 19, 2020.
35. IMF, "World Economic Outlook Update," June 2020.

20th century. In the 1950s, the contradiction assumed a qualitative new dimension—the so-called Anthropocene, defined as "the period of Earth's history during which humans have a decisive influence on the state, dynamics, and future of the Earth System."[36]

This coincided with the breakthrough of consumer society in countries like Sweden, with a substantial increase in the consumption of oil and other raw materials, and consequently of carbon emissions and the pollution of land, air, and water. What Brand and Wissen call "the Imperial mode of living." This way of life is reaching its limits, however:

> [T]he Imperial mode is in the process of succeeding even at the cost of self-destruction. By its nature it implies disproportionate access to natural and human resources on a global scale—in other words: an "elsewhere."[37]

The current ecological, economic, and political crises of neoliberalism are reflected in the contradiction of the imperial mode of living, which presupposes a periphery to exploit, a periphery which must therefore abstain from enjoying the fruits of their own labor and natural resources. As Arghiri Emmanuel wrote 45 years ago, at the dawn of neoliberalism:

> 6% of the world's population already consumes over 40% of the world's raw materials. Present world production in physical terms could only feed, clothe, house, etc., about 600 million people on the American level … . Just as their inhabitants can still travel by air and fly the world's skies only because the rest of the world does not have the means to fly and leaves the world's air routes to them alone. And so on … [38]

---

36. Anthropocene Working Group, "Results of Binding Vote by AWG," *Subcommission on Quaternary Stratigraphy*, May 21, 2019.

37. Brand and Wissen (2021).

38. Arghiri Emmanuel, "Unequal Exchange Revisited," *IDS Discussion Paper* no. 77 (August 1975).

This inequality is also reflected in carbon emissions. In the history of capitalism, the United States, Canada, Europe, Japan, and Australia have contributed 61 percent, China and India 13 percent, Russia 7 percent, the rest of the world 15 percent, with international shipping and air transport accounting for the remaining 4 percent. This inequality is further amplified if we calculate emissions based on where consumption takes place, rather than where production is located.[39] This applies, for example, to China, which is a major consumer of energy and raw materials. However, as China is the world's largest exporter of manufactured products—primarily to the United States, Western Europe, and Japan—it is the consumers in this part of the world who bear the responsibility for a large part of China's carbon emissions.

There is therefore a connection between the ecological and climate problems and imperialism. The global production chains do more than just bring profits to capital and cheap smartphones, t-shirts, and sneakers to consumers—intrinsically, these goods are a transfer of energy and raw materials. There is not only economic unequal exchange but also ecological unequal exchange. Pollution and climate change interact with imperialism and its division of the world into producer economies in the South and consumer economies in the North.

Air, water, and soil pollution have moved to the Global South along with the relocated industries. Likewise, the consequences of climate change, in the form of hurricanes, droughts, and floods, are also greater in the poorer part of the world than in the rich countries. The ecological and climate problems cannot be solved independently of the problem of imperialism.

The development of imperialism is in the process of undermining the very existence of the imperial mode of living. In China, India, and Brazil the upper class and an expanding middle class have adopted the imperial mode of living as their

39. Glenn P. Peters, "From Production-Based to Consumption-Based National Emission Inventories," *Ecological Economics* 65, no. 1 (2008): 13–23.

own. More importantly, however, in recent years, the working class in China, consisting of hundreds of millions of people, has experienced rising wages. From being a periphery, which contributed to the imperial mode of living in the North, China has become a competitor in economic and ecological terms. This is what is behind the hybrid war between the US and China.

Fewer and fewer people in the South are prepared to suffer for the sake of the imperial mode of living of others. If they cannot improve their living conditions at home because of ruthless exploitation or imperial wars, many become migrants or refugees. They risk their lives to reach North America or the European Union in the hope of been integrated into the imperial mode of living. They seek the security and the welfare goods that the imperial mode of living in the core has to offer. However, this push from the South brings out the repressive and violent aspects of the capitalist welfare state. The imperial mode of living is not meant for everyone, it is exclusive. In fear of "diluting" the welfare state, the majority of the population in the Global North refuses to share its benefits.

An isolated national defense of the capitalist welfare state is a defense of a privileged position within global capitalism and thus translates into support for imperialism. To defend the imperial mode of living, refugees and migrants are met with hostile national chauvinism and racism. The fact that more and more people are trying to achieve the imperial mode of living and at the same time others find themselves unable to benefit from it in the way they used to, can be seen as the cause underlying the rise in social and political protest from both left- and right-wing populism. However, it is a losing game. The imperial mode of living cannot be preserved nor can it be universalized, as there is no exploitable periphery to Mother Earth. As Brand and Wissen state:

> We are aware of the hegemonic character of the impe-
> rial mode of living—that is, the breadth and depth of its

acceptance in society. In that mode, the global North is attempting to maintain something that cannot be maintained, and something that cannot exist on a universal basis is expanded and universalized in many countries of the global South. Therefore, in the face of growing upheaval and increasingly brutal externalizations, we recognize—politically and analytically—the urgent need for genuine alternatives that lead to a solidary mode of living, justice (both social and ecological), peace and democracy.[40]

In the near future, the contradiction between capitalism and the earth's ecosystem will make another bid for being the principal contradiction, in the form of conflicts around access to energy and raw materials, amplified by natural disasters and related flows of climate refugees, all because of centuries of misuse of nature.

In recent years, public demands for greater efforts to combat climate change have grown around the world. However, even the most radical parts of the movement still formulate their demands toward the existing political apparatus, in the belief that it can and will change capitalism in a green direction. The Swedish activist Greta Thunberg is invited to Davos to lecture the elite, and they are inspired—green capitalism might even provide answers to the current economic problems. Just as the social state saved capitalism from its inherent contradictions in the 1930s, a green state might save the capitalist system from its contradictions. "Green transition" has been a buzzword in business circles in recent years. Such an escape route is in fact a blind alley, however.

The climate and ecological problems are by their nature global. They affect all humans and other living species. The solutions have to be made collectively and on a global basis. Due to the imperialist nature of capitalism, however, the

---

40. Brand and Wissen (2021).

political world system is increasingly torn apart by national rivalries. The rival national interests constitute an obstacle to the necessary compromises. The green state would have to contend with both populist nationalism as well as the interests of neoliberal globalized capitalism.

A crucial turning point for the climate movement will be the recognition that these problems cannot be solved within the framework of capitalism, leading to a political turn against the system.

The multiple crises of capitalism

The economic contradictions of global capitalism, the political contradiction between neoliberals and nationalists, and the growing contradiction between the capitalist mode of production and nature, are all interacting with one another with increasing intensity.

A major economic crisis has been underway for some time. Large quantities of "liquid capital" cannot find profitable investment opportunities in production. This surplus of liquid capital is expressed in low or even negative interest rates. Instead of productive investments, to secure its value this surplus capital is drawn towards financial assets, real estate, gold, diamonds, art, and other objects of speculation. This creates bubbles, which can burst into crises.

The principal contradiction between neoliberal globalization and different kinds of nationalism spills over into interstate rivalry, such as the US-China trade war and political confrontations. The combination of economic crises and growing nationalism could trigger wars.

In the past, imperialist wars have led to revolutionary upheavals. World War I opened the window of opportunity for the Russian Revolution. World War II and Japan's defeat contributed to the success of Chinese Revolution. Inter-imperialist rivalry opened the window for decolonization and national liberation struggles in the 1960s and 70s. The proliferation of nuclear weapons, however, could make 21st-century wars fatal for humanity. Consequently, the struggle against war, when the ruling class calls for war, has a revolutionary perspective.

The growing ecological and climate problems, as well as the scramble for the earth's natural resources, may also trigger revolutionary situations, in the context of sudden changes in living conditions, natural disasters, and refugee flows. A "lifeboat socialism" may well be the only model able to solve the climate crisis, once the idea of green capitalism is deflated by reality. A global planned emergency action plan, whereby a socialist state organizes and carries out the necessary steps to ensure human survival in a severely damaged planetary biosphere.

All this has been temporarily pushed aside by the Covid-19 pandemic. Covid-19 will pass, but what about the next pandemic? There is a connection between the emergence of pandemics and the way capitalism relates to nature. A concrete example: Denmark breeds mink for fur; 16 million mink live in small metal cages in big farms. Some of these were infected with Covid-19, and when the infections went back from mink to humans it mutated into a new variant, which antibodies generated by the original Covid-19 do not respond to. As a result, in November 2020, Denmark killed all 16 million mink, closed all mink farms, and locked down the part of the country where they were located, in an effort to avoid a second global pandemic.

For years, scientists have warned about the threat of what they call "zoonotic spillover"—the process by which a virus can leap to humans from another species. Outbreaks of infectious diseases caused by zoonotic spillover have been on the rise since the 1980s. Besides Covid-19, which originated with bats, other diseases such as HIV/AIDS, Ebola, SARS, MERS, and Zika all originated in animals. The risk of spillover is heightened due to deforestation and urbanization, which bring wild animals into closer contact with human populations. Modern livestock industries, which cram thousands of animals into confined spaces, are perfect breeding grounds for pathogens that can jump to humans.

These various contradictions will have a critical impact on Sweden. The current pandemic will most likely slide into a world economic crisis. In an article in the *Financial Times*, Jacob Wallenberg, of Sweden's leading financial dynasty, cautioned governments against weighing the risk of economic depression and social unrest as less than the health threat represented by the coronavirus. If the crisis goes on for too long, unemployment could hit 20–30 percent while economies could contract by 20–30 percent, he warned:

> There will be no recovery. There will be social unrest. There will be violence. There will be socio-economic consequences: dramatic unemployment. Citizens will suffer dramatically: some will die, others will feel awful. … Right now, we're just going on one path … We have to weigh the risks of the medicine affecting the patient drastically … How does tomorrow look like? One of these days there is a tomorrow. We have to prepare ourselves as well.[41]

Wallenberg added that concern about what would happen after "the acute phase of the crisis" was shared by the European Round Table for Industry, a body which consists of 50 leading industrialists, representing companies with revenues of €2tn.

During the Covid-19 pandemic Sweden had fewer restrictions than most European countries—keeping the economy running, but with a higher death rate. Sweden's Social Democrats sought a balance between the social aspect—the *folkhem*—and the needs of capital. The government's enormous relief packages and budgetary measures reflected Wallenberg's concerns, aiming to preempt economic breakdown and social

41. Financial Times, "Coronavirus 'Medicine' Could Trigger Social Breakdown," March 26, 2020.

upheaval. Indeed, throughout the Global North, govenrments have pumped out dollars in historically unprecedented quantities to ease the economic effects of the pandemic. Money they were unwilling to invest in projects to solve the climate or social problems.

While a solution to climate problems would challenge the very existence of capitalism, a solution to the Covid-19 pandemic is intended to save the system. The government's measures to stop the spead of Covid-19 represent a serious disruption to capital accumulation, but they are just temporary measures. By contrast, action to address climate problems must be permanent. A radical response to climate change is a challenge to private property, the commodification of nature, and the capitalist mode of production itself.[42]

Despite its former neoliberal criticisms of state intervention, capital is happy to receive massive support from state funds via Corona-Keynesianism, in an effort to rescue capitalism. Such policies might give social democracy another chance in Scandinavia, but we will not see a return to the old *folkhem*. The world economy has changed a lot since the 1960s and 70s, when social democrats were at the height of their power. Neoliberal globalization cannot just be rolled back: industry has been outsourced and production chains established, and the nationalist response to neoliberalism has damaged the political governance framework, which is meant to manage the global economy. The current crises reveal capitalism's lack of global leadership. Trump was a catastrophe and Joe Biden is an uninspiring figure with nothing new to offer in terms of how to revive neoliberalism. Nor is Europe capable of responding adequately to the crisis, thanks to the rising nationalist EU-skepticism.

It seems the ruling classes have not yet grasped the extent of the recession that awaits us. The economy will not get back to

---

42. Andreas Malm, *Corona, Climate, Chronic Emergency: War Communism in the Twenty-First Century* (London: Verso, 2020).

normal in 2021 or 2022. Many will lose their jobs, while those who keep them will struggle to find customers and clients. Meanwhile, someone will have to pay the astronomical bill for massive state spending to support capitalism. Governments around the world are currently pumping thousands of billions of dollars into the economy to keep demand up and thereby keep accumulation going. The cash flow is sustained by printing banknotes and issuing government bonds. But can and will the financial markets absorb a debt bubble of hitherto unseen dimensions? There is reason to be concerned about the health of the financial markets, which are more and more "disengaged" from the real economy—the production of goods and services.

The Covid-19 virus did not cause these economic problems; it just aggravated them in a system that was already unhealthy. The "medicine" that governments and their central banks used to treat the 2008 financial crisis was not curative but was merely a life-extending and pain-relieving drug. This treatment resulted in low interest rates on "available capital." Falling interest rates indicate that there is too much capital and too few possibilities of finding profitable opportunities for the exploitation of people and nature.

The declining profit rate results in investments being shifted from production to speculation in (among other things) financial securities, including government bonds, which are being issued en masse at the moment. A government bond is an IOU in which the government commits to repay a loan with interest after a certain number of years. For the moment, these government bonds are an attractive investment for "available" capital, as investors do not generally expect governments to go bankrupt. US government bonds are considered a valuable "safe haven" for disposable capital, with the consequence that the United States has been able to increase its public debt to astronomical heights. The surplus of capital in general has allowed states to issue bonds with very low interest rates and still find buyers for them. This has created a "mountain" of government debt, on the one hand, and giant bubbles of financial capital, on the other.

Global production has stagnated since the financial crisis. With the exception of China, the GNP growth rate worldwide has been lower than in any decade since World War II. One consequence has been that total debt worldwide doubled between 2008 and 2018. The Covid-19 pandemic occurred at the worst possible moment: the growth rate in the Euro area had already shrunk to zero and the neoliberal economic world order was already in trouble due to the US-China trade war.

Companies in the production sector need capital to carry on, but they find it difficult to borrow, despite the banks being flooded with money, because the banks don't think the businesses will survive. Whole nations like Italy are heading towards bankruptcy. No one wants to buy Italian government bonds if the EU will not guarantee them. An Italian state bankruptcy will be another nail in the EU coffin.

A debt bubble without historical precedent is at risk of bursting in a devastating blast. In the end, dollar bills, like bonds, are just pieces of paper. As trillions in banknotes flow into the market without any parallel production of goods backing them, the day is approaching when investors will lose confidence that their dollars or euros can buy goods. Money does not grow on trees. Capitalism cannot escape the crisis, no matter how many trillions of dollars governments borrow or central banks print. Capitalism is entering a dramatic era. How are the political forces in Sweden prepared to meet this challenge?

CURRENT SITUATION
AND PROSPECTS

The current political landscape in Sweden

Large sections of the Swedish population consider neoliberalism to be a threat to the welfare state. This has led to changes in the political landscape in Sweden in the last decade. The working class is pursuing three different strategies to regain their foothold, backing the neoliberal Social Democrats, the right-wing populist Swedish Democrats, and the Left Party.

The political crisis of neoliberalism was reflected in the difficult 131 days of negotiations that followed the November 2018 election; with 28.5 percent of the vote, the Social Democrats finally managed to form a government. Prime Minister Stefan Löfven had to bridge the gap between neoliberal business interests and the working-class demand for more welfare, under external pressure from the growing right-wing nationalism represented by the Swedish Democrats, who received 17.5 percent of the vote.

Social Democratic policy has changed a lot since the 1960s, when the trade union movement was on the offensive. Already in 2005, the Employers' Association published a report entitled "The Swedish model has capsized," in which they singled out the excessive power of the Swedish trade unions for criticism.[1] In 2010, the Employers' Association launched a counter-strategy called "Advantage Sweden," calling for a commitment to ensuring peace and order on the Swedish labor market, and thus to ensure the competitiveness of Swedish business.[2] The Social Democratic government immediately agreed.

The Swedish Employers' Association, the large trade unions, and Minister of Labor Ylva Johansson drew up a proposal for extended peace obligations. This made strikes, blockades, and other actions illegal, in cases where an agreement existed between a trade union and the employer. Only in cases where there was no collective agreement at a workplace were actions

1. Svenskt Näringsliv, "Den svenska modellen har kantrat" (April 2005).
2. Svenskt Näringsliv "Advantage Sweden" (2010).

lawful, and even then, only after prior negotiations. According to the proposal, employers do not have to enter into an agreement with the trade union that organizes a majority of workers. Employers can decide for themselves which trade union they want to sign an agreement with—including company unions—and this agreement is then binding on everyone else.[3] Furthermore, Swedish labor law interprets the concept of "actions" broadly. In some cases, handing out flyers and writing opinion pieces in the press have been classified as actions directed against an employer and are thus potentially illegal. The proposal for extended peace obligations was adopted by parliament on June 18, 2019.

Right-wing populism

A significant section of the working class is leaving the Social Democrats. The best-paid workers are moving toward the Liberal Party. Their relatively high salaries allow them to acquire real estate, private retirement savings, etc. This part of the working class is attracted to the Liberal Party's attempt to reduce property and progressive income taxes. The lower strata of the working class are attracted to the right-wing populists or to the left. An opinion poll from November 2020 gave the Swedish Democrats 20 percent and the Social Democrats 24 percent of the vote.[4]

The class basis for right-wing populism is found partly among sections of the old low-skilled industrial working class, those whose jobs have been outsourced to the Global South; partly among artisans, construction workers, truck drivers, and other groups who are feeling the competition from immigrants and low-paid workers from the EU's eastern edges; and

---

3. Gabriel Kuhn and Micke Nordin, "Class War in Sweden." CounterPunch (website), Jan. 4, 2019.

4. Dick Erixon, "Op til oppositionen I demoskop," *Samtiden,* November 7, 2020.

finally, partly among sections that depend on social welfare benefits, such as cash benefits, elder care, etc., who see immigrants and refugees as competitors in relation to social welfare goods. In addition to the economic aspects, right-wing populism sees migration and cultural pluralism, especially Islam, as introducing a foreign element that threatens Swedish national culture, and sees immigrant youth as the "new dangerous class," a threat to law and order.

The national-conservative Swedish Democrats are demanding a total end to immigration from "non-Western countries" and greater national control of the economy and borders, in order to re-establish the old homogenous Sweden. But the Swedish *folkhem* was not established within a closed national economy. Although it was based politically on a national compromise between capital and the working class, the creation of the *folkhem* was only possible thanks to Sweden's position in the global capitalist system.

Like the Social Democrats, the Swedish Democrats fail to recognize the historical, economic, and political basis for Sweden's privileged position in the international division of labor. On the national level, class consciousness has been replaced by the consciousness of being a citizen of a "European civilization," with all the benefits that entails. National citizenship has become more important than class solidarity.

In some European countries, such as Denmark and Austria, Social Democrats are cooperating with right-wing populist parties in parliament. The populist right wing has moved closer to the Social Democrats on welfare issues, while the Social Democrats have aped right-wing positions towards immigrants and integration. In Sweden, things are not yet so far gone. Neither the Social Democrats nor the Liberals want to cooperate with the Swedish Democrats, perhaps because of that party's historical links to fascism.

The situation was more or less the same in Denmark ten years ago. The Danish People's Party was not considered "socially acceptable," and the Social Democratic prime minister declared that they would never cooperate with them. That would soon change, however: as Social Democratic voters switched to the Danish People's Party, the Social Democrats changed their attitude towards immigrants, refugees, and integration. Today, the Danish People's Party is viewed as an acceptable and attractive partner by both the Social Democrats and the Liberals. The Danish People's Party is no less dangerous than the Swedish Democrats, despite the latter's ideological roots in fascism—on the contrary. The Danish People's Party has become mainstream in Denmark, both in the parliamentary system and in the media—the populist right wing is now considered respectable in Denmark.

The left

The former Swedish Communist Party—now called the Left Party (*Vänstrepartiet*)—has also benefited from the Social Democrats' decline, receiving 7.9 percent of votes cast in the November 2018 election. In a November 2020 opinion poll they received 9.6 percent support. The main strategy of the Left Party is to take up old social democratic positions, which means saying goodbye to any previous radicalism that might scare voters away. In the 1970s, Communists in parliament often used their position as a platform for extra-parliamentary work; today, extra-parliamentary actions are considered an uncomfortable embarrassment that might cost votes. Any form of "old-fashioned revolutionary romanticism" is to be abandoned. The focus is on parliamentary politics—to attract as many voters as possible. The main strategy is to compete with the right-wing populists, using a defense of the welfare state to try to pick up voters who are dissatisfied with the Social Democrats' neoliberal policies. A more radical confrontation with capitalism is put off to the distant future. The task at hand in the current crisis is to save the system rather than to use the crisis as an opportunity to demand radical change. The extensive financial support to capital during the pandemic has been adopted unanimously in parliament.

On November 1, 2020, Nooshi Dadgostars, the newly elected chairperson of the Left Party, said in her first speech to the party:

> Just a few generations ago, people in Sweden were only small peasants and farmworkers, and poverty was such that over a million people had to flee to America. Our small country in Northern Europe—how is it that we have become one of the most successful nations in the world? Those who established the trade unions in this country had no legal protections. On the contrary, they were ruthlessly persecuted. Employers enjoyed support from the police and the military to prevent people from organizing in trade unions. We continued anyway. And succeeded, step by step, in building a more equal society. Universal suffrage, the 8-hour working day, general pensions, and the Employment Protection Act. Sweden has a long tradition of prominent industries. In places like Sandviken, Degerfors, and Grums, the foundation was laid for modern Sweden. Everything that creates our future continues to be made in our industrial areas. And development is moving forward. In the basic industries, exports range from pulp and ore to more advanced paper products and special steels. High-tech industries producing machinery have grown in importance. With the right efforts, Swedish products can compete with virtually any country. We have perhaps the world's best industrial workers.[5]

The reformist agenda is limited to redistributing the "cake" between capital and labor. In a purely national perspective this might be seen as a step in the right direction. In globalized cap-

5. Nooshi Dadgostars, Speech at the 43rd Vänsterpartiets Congress, November 1, 2020.

italism, however, much of the cake being sliced up in Sweden has been baked in the Global South and Eastern Europe. This has been left out of the equation by the Left Party.

When discussing anti-imperialist strategy in the Global North, I have often encountered the argument that the best way to fight imperialism is to fight the capitalist class in your own country. When you weaken capital at home, you contribute to the global anti-imperialist struggle. An argument that is sometimes even echoed by movements in the Global South. But this is not how things work in an imperialist world of globalized capitalism. A purely national struggle in the Global North, for a bigger share of profits in the form of higher wages and more welfare, simply amounts to dividing up the loot.

It seems to be taboo and controversial to mention the fact that the vast majority of people living in Scandinavia benefit from how global capitalism works and that our imperial mode of living is reflected in our political choices. The American dream and the idea that "every man is the master of his own destiny" dominate the collective consciousness, making us believe that the citizens of the Swedish welfare state owe their privileges to their hard work. In reality, however, privilege is generally inherited, whether directly within a family or structurally within a nation thanks to the history of colonialism and the current imperialist system.

The imperial mode of living has political implications. Sweden is a parliamentary democracy. The electorate has interests and the political parties take care of those interests. Voters are not "innocent sheep" who have been deceived and manipulated into "false consciousness." While manipulation certainly occurs, to explain Swedish working-class support for reformism—and worse—for decades, if not a century, as a manifestation of "false consciousness," amounts to calling historical materialism into question. They have been defending their interests, like all classes do.

The reason why I insist on breaking this taboo is the need to face reality, if we are to develop a realistic and effective strategy. Marx and Engels did not pull any punches in their description of the connection between colonialism and national chauvinism, racism, and reformism in the English working class.[6] Lenin was quite blunt in his description of the connection between imperialism and opportunism in the European working class in the years leading up to World War I.[7] He did so because an assessment of class interests was crucial in order to be able to choose the right partners in the struggle for socialism.

There is nothing wrong with welfare in and of itself. The current *capitalist welfare state*, however, is reserved for a limited number of people at the expense of others. In addition, our imperial mode of living is certainly not sustainable on a global scale. We can only consume energy and raw materials and fly in the skies the way we do because others do not. It is not wrong to defend the principle of public and free healthcare, education, unemployment support, etc.—but the struggle has to be fought in a global context. An isolated national defense of the capitalist welfare state is a defense of a privileged position within global capitalism, and thus amounts to support for imperialism.

In the US context: capital may accept certain healthcare and educational reforms, even if this cuts into their profits. They will embrace Corona-Keynesianism and perhaps even the "New Green Deal," and this may fuel accumulation just as the social New Deal did in the 1930s. Dismantling US imperialism, however, will remain unacceptable. The economic exploitation and related political and military domination of the Global South is necessary for the system to survive. Capital will fight any step in the direction of anti-imperialism, by all means necessary.

---

6. Torkil Lauesen and Zak Cope, Preface to *Marx & Engels on Colonies, Industrial Monopoly & the Working Class Movement* (Montreal: Kersplebedeb, 2016).

7. Torkil Lauesen, Preface to *V.I. Lenin on Imperialism and Opportunism* (Montreal: Kersplebedeb, 2019).

Toward a transnational anti-systemic movement

To combat globalized capitalism we need a strategy that corresponds to the existing conditions. In *The Communist Manifesto*, Marx and Engels urged: "Proletarians of all countries, unite!" However, the experience of the three Internationals and the ongoing struggle against colonialism and imperialism shows that it has been difficult to unite the different national struggles into a common world revolutionary process. Nationalism has been a Trojan horse that has divided the global proletariat. The very fact that the Third International was created because the Social Democratic parties of the Second International each supported their own national bourgeoisie in the imperialist war to divide up the world illustrates the scale of the problem.

Working-class parties in Europe and North America have prioritized the national class struggle and this has obstructed the struggle for global socialism. During the Third International, which supported decolonization, the Communist Parties of England and France did not oppose the colonialism of their own countries nor did they support national liberation movements, out of fear of alienating the workers in their own countries. The world revolution was of secondary importance in relation to the national political struggle.[8] Another example is the American AFL-CIO trade union, which has always supported US imperialism.[9]

The struggle for socialism has unfolded within the nation-state because the nation-state is the primary political unit in the world system. The strategy of national struggles must be based on the global perspective, however, because capitalism is a global system. Even if some kind of "socialist transition" were to occur in a country within a capitalist world system, it would still be part of the global division of labor, it would

---

8. Lauesen (2018), 114–30.

9. Ibid., 153–54.

still be part of the transnational production chains, it would have to compete in the global market, which means implementing all the exploitative and discriminatory practices that ensue from the capitalist world economy. Production is organized in transnational productions chains. Goods are traded on a highly integrated world market. Global capitalism has an inherently imperialist character, which has divided the world system into a core and a periphery. As a consequence, the contradictions of globalized capitalism largely determine the outcome of national and local struggles, and national struggles can contribute to moving the world system's principal contradiction in the correct direction. National struggles must have a clear global perspective.

To escape the problem of narrow nationalism in the struggle for socialism we need to move from internationalism towards transnational struggle. Whereas the concept of internationalism refers to the priority of the national class struggle which will then somehow be united in an international struggle, the concept of transnationalism has the global perspective as its foundation and priority. According to the global perspective, the principal contradiction in the world system determines the strategy of national struggles. In a world in which the economy and politics are interconnected and integrated, "internationalism" based on prioritizing national struggles is a dead end, whereas "transnationalism" maintains the original spirit of *The Communist Manifesto*: a proletariat with no "fatherland" but united as a global class.

The specific forms of transnational struggle can be multiple: transnational trade union struggles (across global commodity chains); transnational climate and ecological struggles; movements against imperialist wars, transnational anti-racist, anti-fascist, anti-colonial struggles; global movements for basic living conditions, etc.

Besides transnationalism, the struggle has to have a radical anti-capitalist perspective. There is no social democratic road leading to socialism, nor can we join with the social democrats for the first part of the transformation. It has to be a radical break with the system, because it has to break with the imperialist character of the system. If healthcare, social welfare, or educational reforms are not accompanied by dismantling imperialism—economically, politically, and militarily—then they are not a step towards a more equal and democratic world. National moves towards "socialism" which co-exist with a defense of capital's global interests are not progressive in any sense. Furthermore, time is running out for reforms. The capitalist mode of production threatens the balance of the global ecosystem and, as such, the entire human species. We do not have all the time in the world. We therefore need a *transnational anti-systemic movement.*[10]

How do we organize such a movement? To begin with, in a network through which participants would share experiences and information; coordinate protests, strikes, and demonstrations; mobilize solidarity and support; in short, organizationally erase the boundaries between isolated struggles and connect them into one common struggle.

In our daily political work, we often feel that what we are doing is too little—unimportant in terms of changing the world. But it is important to keep in mind that there are no "small" struggles, no "small" resistances. There are separate sets of actions and interventions that sometimes converge to force "big" changes. Now is not the time for compromise. In this chaotic world of declining US hegemony, every action affects the outcome. Collective and continuous action is the decisive element for building a better world.

Solidarity is rooted in a common struggle against capitalism. The majority in the Global North has a material interest in maintaining the capitalist system in the short and middle term. The left in our part of the world will not be the driving force in the transition toward global socialism. The struggle in "the

10. Samir Amin, "It is Imperative to Reconstruct the International of Workers and Peoples," *Ideas*, July 3, 2018.

belly of the beast" can play an important role, however, as we saw during the resistance against the Vietnam War. There is and has always been a counter-stream of anti-imperialism, even in the Global North—resistance against imperialist wars, support for liberation movements. Solidarity is more than a word: solidarity is something material you can hold in your hand. Solidarity is practical help in common struggle. Solidarity is also changing our way of life, so we do not participate in the exploitation of others or damage our shared environment.

Bibliography

Åbom, Eva Ersson. "Ett folkhem i Liberia." *Företagshistoria*, no. 4 (2013). bizstories.se/foretagen/ett-folkhem-i-liberia

Agarwal, Surabhi. "HCL Technologies buys Volvo group's external IT business." *The Economic Times*, February 17, 2016. https://economictimes.indiatimes.com/tech/ites/hcl-technologies-buys-volvo-groups-external-it-business/articleshow/51009129.cms

Aktiespararna. "Kort om Aktiespararnas historia," *Aktiespararna*, 2019. aktiespararna.se/om-aktiespararna/var-organisation/historia

Algott, Stig. *Stockholms fondbörs 100 år*. Stockholm: Nordiska bokhandeln, 1963.

Allianz. *Allianz Wealth Report*. Nationale Zentralbanken und Statistikämter, Allianz SE, 2014. allianz.com

Ambler, Pamela. "Volvo & Geely: The Unlikely Marriage of Swedish Tech and Chinese Manufacturing Might That Earned Record Profits." *Forbes*, January 23, 2018.

Amin, Samir. "China 2013." *Monthly Review* 64, no. 10 (March 2013): 14–33.

——— "It is Imperative to Reconstruct the International of Workers and Peoples." *Ideas* July 3, 2018. http://www.networkideas.org/featured-articles/2018/07/it-is-imperative-to-reconstruct-the-internationale-of-workers-and-peoples

——— *Delinking: Towards a Polycentric World*. London: Zed Books, 1990.

——— *The Law of Worldwide Value*. New York: Monthly Review, 2010.

Anderson, Karen and Steven Snow. "Forestalling the Business Veto: Investment Confidence and the Rise of Swedish Social Democracy." *Social Science Quarterly* 84, no. 1 (March 2003).

Andersson, Rainer. *Vad gjorde du i Finland, far? Svenska frivilliga i finska inbördeskriget 1918.* (Stockholm: Sahlgrens förlag, 1999).

Anthropocene Working Group. "Results of Binding Vote by AWG." *Subcommission on Quaternary Stratigraphy,* May 21, 2019.

Arnstad, Henrik. *Skyld.* Oslo: Forlaget Spartacus, 2010.

Aschoff, Nicole. "The Smartphone Society." *Jacobin,* no. 17 (March 2015).

Bäckström, Knut. *Götrek och Manifestet.* Stockholm: Gidlund, 1972.

Ball, James and Dominic Rushe. "NSA Prism Program Taps in to User Data of Apple, Google and Others." *The Guardian,* June 6, 2013. https://www.theguardian.com/world/2013/jun/06/us-tech-giants-nsa-data

Batchelor, Oliver. "Forsvaret i Arktis får halvanden milliarder kroner til droner, satellitudstyr og uddannelse." Denmark Radio, February 11, 2021. https://www.dr.dk/nyheder/politik/forsvaret-i-arktis-faar-halvanden-milliarder-kroner-til-droner-satellitudstyr-og

Bauer, Otto, "Proletarische Wanderungen." *Die neue Zeit: Wochenschrift der deutschen Sozialdemokratie* 1907, no. 41 (1907): 476–494.

BBC. "Ex-Congo PM Declared dead." *BBC,* February 13, 1961.

Beckerts, Sven. *Empire of Cotton: A New History of Global Capitalism.* New York: Vintage, 2015.

Bengtsson, Erik. *Värdens Jämligste land?* Stockholm: Arkiv, 2020.

Berg, Magnus. *Förlåta men inte glömma. Röster om rasism, nationalism och det mångkulturella samhället i Namibia och i Sverige.* Stockholm: Carlsson, 2004.

Berggren, Henrik. *Underbara dagar framför oss - en biografi över Olof Palme.* Stockholm: Norstedts, 2010.

Berman, Sheri. *The Primacy of Politics: Social Democracy and the Making of Europe's Twentieth Century.* Cambridge: Cambridge University Press, 2006.

Bernstein, Eduard (1889). *Die Voraussetzungen des Sozialismus and die Aufgaben der Sozialdemokratie.* Hamburg: Rowoht, 1969.

Bhadrakumar, M. K. "India's Farewell to ASEAN as it Boards RCEP Train," *Indian Punchline* November 14, 2020. https://indianpunchline.com/indias-farewell-to-asean-as-it-boards-rcep-train

Bhattacharjee, Shikha Silliman. *Precarious Work in the H&M Global Value Chain.* A Report to the ILO (2016).

Bizvibe. "Minimum Wages in Asia's Textile and Apparel Industry." https://www.bizvibe.com/blog/minimum-wages-asias-textile-apparel-industry

Björnsson, Olof. *Fuel for Conflict, Investors and the Case of Lundin Petroleum in Sudan.* Swedwatch Report 85 (2017). https://swedwatch.org/wp-content/uploads/2021/01/fuel-for-conflictfull-report.pdf

Boëthius, B. "Swedish Iron and Steel 1600–1955." *Scandinavian Economic History Review* 6, no. 2 (1958): 144–175.

Brand, Ulrich and Markus Wissen. *The Imperial Mode of Living and the Political Ecology of Labour.* Paper presented at the Conference on International Solidarity and Relational Inequality. Amsterdam, September 13, 2020.

—— *The Limits to Capitalist Nature. Theorizing and Overcoming the Imperial Mode of Living.* London: Rowman & Littlefield, 2018.

—— *The Imperial Mode of Living: Everyday Life and the Ecological Crises of Capitalism.* Verso: London, 2021.

Bromé, Janrik. *Nasafjäll, ett norrländskt silververks historia,* Stockholm: A-B Nordiska Bokhandeln, 1923.

Brum, Mauricio. "How Belgium cut off hands and arms, and killed over 15 million in Africa." *Gazeta do Povo,* February 12, 2019. https://www.gazetadopovo.com.br/wiseup-news/how-belgium-cut-off-hands-and-arms-and-killed-over-15-million-in-africa

Bruzelius, Nils. "'Near friendly or neutral shores': the deployment of the fleet ballistic missile submarines and US policy towards Scandinavia, 1957–1963." Licentiate thesis, monograph. KTH, School of Architecture and the Built Environment (ABE), Architecture. 2007.

Byttner, Karl-Johan. "Världens rikaste svensk fyller 90— Ingvar Kamprads karriär kantas av mysterier," *Veckans affärer,* March 24, 2016.

Carlson, Benny and Lars Jonung. "Knut Wicksell, Gustav Cassel, Eli Heckscher, Bertil Ohlin and Gunnar Myrdal on the Role of the Economist in Public Debate." *Econ Journal Watch* 3, no. 3, September 2006.

Carlsson, Sten and Jerker Rosén (eds.). *Den svenska historien, band 13: Emigrationen och det industriella genombrottet.* Stockholm: Bonniers, 1992.

Césaire, Aimé. *Discourse on Colonialism*. New York: Monthly Review Press, 2000.

CGTN, "Getting to Know China's New Infrastructure Projects." CGTN, May 6, 2020. https://news.cgtn. com/news/2020-05-06/Getting-to-know-China-s-new-infrastructure-projects-QfIOLy9khq/index.html

—— "Rural China Sees Robust Income and Consumption Growth." CGTN, September 30, 2020. https://news. cgtn.com/news/2020-09-30/Rural-China-sees-robust-income-and-consumption-growth-UcOtY6qh2M/index. html

Che Guevara. "December 11, 1964, 19th General Assembly of the United Nations in New York." In Che Guevara, *Che Reader*. New York: Ocean Press, 2005. marxists.org/ archive/guevara/1964/12/11.htm

China-cee Institute, "Estonia economy briefing: A story of a Danish bank in Estonia: the bowing out part. To be continued?" China-cee Institute, March 6, 2019. https:// china-cee.eu/2019/03/06/estonia-economy-briefing-a-story-of-a-danish-bank-in-estonia-the-bowing-out-part-to-be-continued

China Daily. "China to Form New Development Pattern Centered on 'Internal Circulation'." *China Daily*, August 7, 2020. http://en.people.cn/n3/2020/0807/ c90000-9719373.html

Chuang. "Covid, Capitalism, Strikes & Solidarity: An Interview with Asia Art Tours." *Chuang* (blog), November 20, 2020. https://chuangcn.org/2020/11/ interview-with-asia-art-tours

Clemens, Michael, Claudio Montenegro and Lant Pritchett. *The Place Premium: Wage Differences for Identical Workers Across the US Border.* Background Paper to the 2009 World Development Report (Policy Research Working Paper 4671). New York: World Bank, 2009.

Cope, Zak. "German Imperialism and Social Imperialism 1871–1933." In *The Palgrave Encyclopedia of Imperialism and Anti-imperialism,* vol. 1. Edited by Immanuel Ness and Zak Cope. New York: Palgrave Macmillan, 2017.

—— *Divided World Divided Class. Global Political Economy and the Stratification of Labour under Capitalism.* Montreal: Kersplebedeb, 2015.

Crunchbase. "Estonia Companies." https://www.crunchbase. com/hub/estonia-companies

Dadgostars, Nooshi. Speech at the 43rd Vänsterpartiets Congress, November 1, 2020. https://www. vansterpartiet.se/app/uploads/2020/11/Nooshi-Dadgostars-kongresstal.pdf

Dahlqvist, Hans. "Folkhemsbegreppet: Rudolf Kjellén vs Per Albin Hansson," *Historisk Tidsskrift* 122, no. 3 (2002): 452.

Dalgaard, Niels. "Debatten om økonomisk demokrati i Danmark og Sverige." *Politica* 25, no. 3 (1993). tidsskrift.dk/politica/article/view/67736/97980

Danish Ministry of Employment. "Satser for 2021." https:// bm.dk/satser/satser-for-2021

Davis, Mike. "The Origin of the Third World." *Antipode* 32, no. 1 (2000).

—— *Late Victorian Holocausts: El Nino Famines and the Making of the Third World.* London: Verso, 2002.

De Witte, Ludo. *The Assassination of Lumumba*. London: Verso, 2001.

Dedrick, Jason, Kenneth L. Kraemer, and Tony Tsai. *ACER: An IT Company Learning to Use Information Technology to Compete.* Center for Research on Information Technology and Organization. California: University of California, 1999.

Donaldson, T. "H&M to source more garments from Bangladesh." *Sourcing Journal*, March 14, 2016.

Drahokoupil, Jan, Rutvica Andrijasevic, and Devi Sacchetto (eds.). *Flexible Workforces and Low Profit Margins: Electronics Assembly between Europe and China*. Brussels: European Trade Union Institute, 2016.

Duhigg, Charles and Keith Bradsher. "How the U.S. Lost Out on iPhone Work." *The New York Times*, January 22, 2012.

Dagens Nyheter. "Lundintoppar misstänks för anstiftan till övergrepp i rättssak." *Dagens Nyheter*, February 13, 2019. dn.se/ekonomi/lundintoppar-misstanks-for-anstiftan-till-overgrepp-i-rattssak

———— "Lundinutredningen klar—åklagaren: 'Tillräckliga skäl för åtal'." *Dagens Nyheter*, October 1, 2020. https://www.dn.se/ekonomi/lundinutredningen-klar-aklagaren-tillrackliga-skal-for-atal

Edvinsson, Rodney, Tor Jacobson, and Daniel Waldenström (eds.). *Exchange Rates, Prices, and Wages, 1277–2008*. Stockholm: Ekerlids Förlag, 2010.

Ekdahl, L. *Mod en tredje vej: En biografi om Rudolf Meidner. Faglig ekspert og demokratisk socialist*. Lund: Arkiv Forlag, 2005.

Ekonomi Fakta. "Strukturförändringar i sysselsättningen."
Ekonomi Fakta, December 19, 2019. https://www.
ekonomifakta.se/fakta/arbetsmarknad/sysselsattning/
strukturforandringar-i-sysselsattningen

Elmbrant, Björn. *Palme*. Stockholm: Författarförlaget. Fischer
& Rye, 1989.

Emanuelsson, Kjell. *Den svensk-norska utrikesförvaltningen
1870–1905. Dess organisations-och verksamhetsförändring.*
Lund: CWK Gleerup, 1980.

Emmanuel, Arghiri. "Unequal Exchange Revisited." *IDS
Discussion Paper*, no. 77 (August 1975). anti-imperialist.
net/2019/05/31/arghiri-emmanuel-unequal-exchange-
revisited

Engdahl, Per Hans. "Majestät Konungen och pressen."
Arbetartidningen, October 20, 1949. https://tidningar.
kb.se/2698156/1949-10-20/edition/149508/part/1/page/2

Engdahl, Per. *Fribytare i folkhemmet*. Stockholm: Cavenfors,
1979.

Engels, Frederick. "Letter to Schmidt, C. London,
October 27, 1890." In *Marx and Engels Correspondence*.
Moscow: International Publishers, 1968. marxists.org

Erixon, Dick. "Op til oppositionen I demoskop." *Samtiden*,
November 7, 2020. https://samtiden.nu/2020/11/
uppat-for-oppositionen-i-demoskop/

European Coalition on Oil in Sudan. *Unpaid Debt: The Legacy
of Lundin, Petronas, and OMV in Block 5A, Sudan, 1997–
2003*. European Coalition on Oil in Sudan, 2010.

Feenstra, Robert C., Robert Inklaar, Marcel P. Timmer. "The
Next Generation of the Penn World Table." *American
Economic Review* 105, no. 10 (October 2015).

Feinstein, Andrew. "Corruption and the Arms Trade." *War Resisters' International* (2015). https://wri-irg.org/en/story/2015/corruption-and-arms-trade

Financial Times. "Coronavirus 'Medicine' Could Trigger Social Breakdown." *Financial Times*, March 26, 2020. ft.com/content/3b8ec9fe-6eb8-11ea-89df-41bea055720b

Fisher, Lucy. "Downing Street Plans New 5G Club of Democracies." *Times*, May 29, 2020.

Fleetwood, Gwendolyn and Wilhelm Odelberg (eds.). *Carl Georgsson Fleetwood: Från studieår och diplomattjänst. Dagböcker, brev och skrifter 1879–1892*, vol. 1, 1879–1887. Stockholm: P. A. Norstedt & söner, 1968.

Forsikring & Pension. "Pensionsformuer." https://www.forsikringogpension.dk/statistik/pensionsformuer

Forsvarets Efterretnings Tjeneste. "Tilsynet med Efterretningstjenesterne afslutter særlig undersøgelse af Forsvarets Efterretningstjeneste (FE) på baggrund af materiale indleveret af én eller flere whistleblowere." Press release. (2020). https://www.tet.dk/wp-content/uploads/2020/08/PRESSEMEDDELELSE.pdf

Försvarets forskningsinstitut. "Hemliga atomubåtar gav Sverige säkerhetsgaranti." Archived July 7, 2007. Retrieved from the Wayback Machine.

Foster, John Bellamy. "China 2020: An Introduction." *Monthly Review* 72, no. 5 (October 2020). https://monthlyreview.org/2020/10/01/china-2020-an-introduction

Foucault, Michel. *Security, Territory, Population*. London: Palgrave Macmillan, 2008.

Fredriksen, Nicolas. "5G: Bulgarien og Sverige ekskluderer kinesiske selskaber," 5G-Netværk.dk (website), October 26, 2020. https://xn--5g-netvrk-m3a. dk/2020/10/26/5g-bulgarien-og-sverige-ekskluderer-kinesiske-selskaber

Gamby, Erik. *Per Götrek och 1800-talets svenska arbetarrörelse.* Stockholm: Tiden, 1978.

Gårdemyr, Louise. "Kan Sveriges samtaler bane vejen for fred i Yemen?" *Om Världen,* November 21, 2018. https://www.omvarlden.se/Branschnytt/nyheter-2018/kan-sverige-samtalen-bana-vag-for-fred-i-jemen

Gibbs, David N. "Dag Hammarskjold, the United Nations, and the Congo Crisis of 1960–1: A Reinterpretation." *The Journal of Modern African Studies* 31, no. 1 (March 1993): 165.

Gillis Bildts, "Letter from Bildt to Oscar December 17, 1884." *RA: Gillis Bildts arkiv,* Vol. 1.

Gilljam, Mikael. *Svenska folket och lontagarfonderna.* Lund: Studentlitteratur, 1988.

Gondola, Didier. *The History of Congo.* Westport: Greenwood Publishing Group, 2002.

Götrek, Per. *Om proletariatet och dess befrielse genom den sanna kommunismen: Jämte bihang: Om kommunisternas beslutade stora emigration till Icarien.* Reprinted in: *Frilansens urkundsamling* 5 (1944).

Gramsci, Antonio [1929–35]. *Prison Notebooks,* vol. 2, Notebook 4. New York: Columbia University Press, 1996.

Greenwald, Glenn Edward. *No Place to Hide: Edward Snowden, the NSA, and the U.S. Surveillance State.* New York: Metropolitan Books, 2014.

Guo, Lei, Shih-Hsien Hsu, Avery Holton, and Sun Ho Jeong. "A Case Study of the Foxconn Suicides." *The International Communication Gazette*, no. 74: 484–503.

Hägg, Göran. *Välfärdsåren: svensk historia 1945–1986*. Stockholm: Wahlström & Widstrand, 2005.

Hämäläinen, Pekka. "Revolution, Civil War, and Ethnic Relations: The Case of Finland." *Journal of Baltic Studies* 5, no. 2 (1974): 117–25.

Hanson, Sven Ove. "Från Engdahl till Åkesson." *Tiden Magasin*, February 6, 2013.

Hansson, Per Albin. "Klasskampsbegreppet." *i Från Fram till folkhemmet* (1929).

Harsha, Dan. "Taking China's pulse." *Havard Gazette*, July 9, 2020. https://news.harvard.edu/gazette/story/2020/07/long-term-survey-reveals-chinese-government-satisfaction/

Hermele, Kennet and David Vail. "The End of the Middle Road: What Happened to the Swedish Model?" *Monthly Review* 44, no. 10 (March 1993).

Herrera, Rémy and Zhiming Long. "The Enigma of China's Growth." *Monthly Review* 70, no. 7 (December 2018): 52–62.

Herrera, Rémy, Zhiming Long, and Tony Andréani. "On the Nature of the Chinese Economic System." *Monthly Review* 70, no. 5 (October 2018), 32–43.

Hintjens, Helen M. and Serena Cruz. "Continuities of
    Violence in the Congo: the Legacies of Hammarskjöld
    and Lumumba." In *Peace Diplomacy, Global Justice and
    International Agency: Rethinking Human Security and Ethics
    in the Spirit of Dag Hammarskjöld*, edited by Carsten
    Stahn and Henning Melber. Cambridge: Cambridge
    University Press, 2014.

Hjelte, Roland, Ingrid Dahlberg, and Lars Hjelm. *Svart vecka i
    Nimba : Kring en svensk industri i ett u-land, Lamco i Liberia.*
    Dokumnetarfilm. STV (1966).

Hobsbawm, Eric J. *Industry and Empire.* New York: Penguin
    Books, 1968.

Hochschild, Adam. *King Leopold's Ghost: A Story of Greed, Terror,
    and Heroism in Colonial Africa.* Boston: Houghton Mifflin
    Company, 1998.

Holtet, Christian. *Dobbeltmordet i Køge bugt.* København:
    Forlaget Solidaritet, 2014.

Hopkins, Terence C. and Wallerstein, Immanuel. "Patterns of
    Development of the Modern World-System." Fernand
    Braudel Center. *Review* 1, no. 2: 111–45.

Horne, Gerald. *The Apocalypse of Settler Colonialism: The Roots
    of Slavery, White Supremacy, and Capitalism in Seventeenth-
    Century North America and the Caribbean.* New York:
    Monthly Review Press, 2018.

Hui, Wang. "Revolutionary Personality and the Philosophy
    of Victory: Commemorating Lenin's 150th
    Birthday." Reading the China Dream (blog), April 21,
    2020. https://www.readingthechinadream.com/wang-
    hui-revolutionary-personality.html

Hultman, Jens, Susanne Hertz, Rhona Johnsen, and Thomas Johnsen. *Global Sourcing Development at IKEA—A Case Study*. Paper prepared for the 25th IMP conference. Jönköping International Business School, 2009.

ICA. "Market development in Baltic." 2021. https://www.icagruppen.se/en/investors/#!/growth-factors/lb//investerare/tillvaxtfaktorer/marknadsutveckling-i-baltikum

ILO. *The Impact of Global Supply Chains on Employment and Product System*. Report no. 1, submitted to the ILO Research Department. Paris: Institut de Recherches Économiques et Sociales, 2018.

—— *World of Work Report 2011*. Geneva: International Labor Organization, 2011.

IMF. "World Economic Outlook Update." June 2020. https://www.imf.org/en/Publications/WEO/Issues/2020/06/24/WEOUpdateJune2020

Investment and Development Agency of Latvia. "FDI in Latvia." April 7, 2020. liaa.gov.lv/en/invest-latvia/investor-business-guide/foreign-direct-investment

Jiang, Yun and Adam Ni. "Neican: 23 August 2020." The China Story (blog) August 23, 2020. https://www.thechinastory.org/neican-23-august-2020

Jonung, Lars. "Knut Wicksell's Norm of Price Stabilization and Swedish Monetary Policy in the 1930s." *Journal of Monetary Economics* 5 (1979): 459–96.

Kalb, Madeleine G. "The CIA and Lumumba." *The New York Times*, August 2, 1981. https://www.nytimes.com/1981/08/02/magazine/the-cia-and-lumumba.html

Kelly, Mark G. E. *Biopolitical Imperialism*. Winchester: Zero Books, 2015.

Kettle, Martin. "President 'Ordered Murder' of Congo Leader." *The Guardian*, August 10, 2000. https://www. theguardian.com/world/2000/aug/10/martinkettle

Kjellén, Rudolf. "Nationalism och socialism." *Nationell samling* (1915): 42–57. Here from Dahlqvist (2002).

——— "Fredens fariséer" (1910). Here from Dahlqvist (2002).

Kjerland, Kirsten Alsaker and Bjørn Enge Bertelsen, *Navigating Colonial Orders, Norwegian Entrepreneurship in Africa and Oceania*. New York: Berghahn Books, 2014.

Knauss, Steve. *Unequal exchange in the 21th Century* (unpublished paper).

Koninckx, Christian. *The First and Second Charters of the Swedish East India Company (1731-1766): A contribution to the Maritime, Economic and Social History of North-Western Europe in its Relationship with the Far East*. Kortrijk, Belgium: Van Ghemmert Publishing Company, 1980.

Krooth, Richard. *Arms and Empire: Imperial Patterns before World War II*. California: Santa Barbara Harvest Press, 1980.

Kuhn, Gabriel and Micke Nordin. "Class War in Sweden." CounterPunch (website), January 4, 2019.

Kumar, Arun. "A Scandinavian 'Nabob' of the British Empire: The Discovery of a New Colonial Archive." *The Wire*, January 2, 2021. https://thewire.in/history/ sweden-british-empire-joseph-stephens

Lauesen, Torkil and Zak Cope. Preface to *Marx & Engels on Colonies, Industrial Monopoly & the Working Class Movement*. Montreal: Kersplebedeb, 2016.

Lauesen, Torkil. "Marxism, Value Theory, and Imperialism." In *The Palgrave Encyclopedia of Imperialism and Anti-imperialism*, vol. 1. Edited by Immanuel Ness and Zak Cope. New York: Palgrave Macmillan, 2017.

———— Preface to *V.I. Lenin on Imperialism and Opportunism.* Montreal: Kersplebedeb, 2019.

———— *The Global Perspective: Reflections on Imperialism and Resistance.* Montreal: Kersplebedeb, 2018.

Leitz, Christian. *Sympathy for the Devil: Neutral Europe and Nazi Germany in World War II.* Manchester: Manchester University Press, 2000.

Lenin, V. I. [1917]. *Imperialism, the Highest Stage of Capitalism.* In *Lenin Collected Works*, vol. 22. Moscow: Progress Publishers, 1972. marxists.org

———— [1916]. "Imperialism and the Split in Socialism." In V. I. Lenin, *Collected Works*, vol. 23, 105–120. Moscow: Progress Publishers, 1964. marxists.org

———— [1917]. "Imperialism, the Highest Stage of Capitalism." In *Lenin Collected Works*, Volume 22. Moscow: Progress Publishers, 1972. marxists.org

———— [1916]. "Ten 'Socialist' Ministers!" In *Lenin Collected Works*, vol. 23. Moscow: Progress Publishers, 1964. marxists.org

Lindorm, Erik. *Ny svensk historia, Gustaf V och hans tid 1938–1947.* Side 355. Stockholm: Wahlström & Widstrand, 1979.

Lindqvist, Herman. "Kungens order: Skjut på demonstranterna," *Aftonbladet* October 4, 2008.

Lindqvist, Mats. *Is I magen. Om ekonomins kolonisering av vardagen.* Stockholm: Natur och Kultur, 2001.

Littmann, Dan. "5G: The chance to lead for a decade." Deloitte Consulting (2018). us-tmt-5g-deployment-imperative.pdf

Ljungberg, Jonas. "The Impact of the Great Emigration on the Swedish Economy." *Scandinavian Economic History Review* 45, no. 2 (1997): 159–89.

Long, Zhiming, Zhixuan Feng, Bangxi Li, and Rémy Herrera, "U.S.-China Trade War, Has the Real 'Thief' Finally Been Unmasked?" *Monthly Review* 72, no. 5 (October 2020).

Lööw, Heléne. *Nazismen i Sverige 1924–1979: pionjärerna, partierna, propagandan*. Stockholm: Ordfront Förlag, 2004.

Lumumba, Patrice [1960]. "Speech at the ceremony of the proclamation of Congo's independence, June 30 1960." In *The Truth about a Monstrous Crime of the Colonialists*, 44–47. Moscow: Foreign Languages Publishing House, 1961.

Lundahl, Mats. *Knut Wicksell on Poverty: No Place is Too Exalted for the Preaching of these Doctrines*. London: Routledge, 2005.

Lundahl, Mikkelä. "Symboliserar Göteborg verkligen det vi vill?" In *I skuggan av samtiden: En vänbok till Sven-Eric Liedman och Amanda Peralta*, edited by Kärnfelt Johan. Göteborg: Forlaget Arachne, 2006.

Lundell, Kerstin. *Affärer i blod och olja: Lundin Petroleum i Afrika*. Stockholm: Ordfront, 2010.

Lundgren, Rasmus. "100 000 svenskar i Chicago," i *Säkthistoria*, no. 8 (2018).

Lundsjo, Olle. *Fattigdomen på den svenska landsbygden under 1800-talet*. Stockholm: Stockholm Universitet, Ekonomisk-historiska institutet, 1975.

Makko, Aryo. "I imperialismens kölvatten? Ett maritimt perspektiv på stormaktsspel, kolonialism utan kolonier och den svensk-norska konsulsstaten, 1875–1905." *Historisk Tidsskrift* 134, no. 3 (2014).

Malm, Andreas. *Corona, Climate, Chronic Emergency: War Communism in the Twenty-First Century.* London: Verso, 2020.

Manifest-Communist Working Group. *Unequal Exchange and the Prospects for Socialism in a Divided World.* Denmark: Publishing House Manifest, 1986. snylterstaten.dk

Mannerheim, Ylva and Johan Mannerheim. *Lamco:s Liberia.* Stockholm: Unga filosofer, 1968.

Martínez-Alier, Juan (ed.). *Ecological Economics: Energy, Environment and Society.* Oxford: Basil Blackwell, 1987.

Marx, Karl [1850]. "The Class Struggles in France, 1848 to 1850, Part II. From June 1848 to June 13, 1849." In *Marx and Engels Selected Works*, vol. 1. Moscow: Progress Publishers, 1969. marxists.org

—— [1867]. *Capital*, vol. 1. Moscow: Progress Publishers, 1962. marxists.org

—— [1857–61}. *Grundrisse: Foundations of the Critique of Political Economy (Rough Draft).* Baltimore: Penguin, 1973; in association with New Left Review. marxists.org

Marx, Karl and Frederick Engels [1848], "The Communist Manifesto." In *Marx and Engels Selected Works*, vol. 1, 98–137. Moscow: Progress Publishers, 1969. https://www.marxists.org

—— [1875]. "Critique of the Gotha Programme." In *Marx and Engels Selected Works*, vol. 3, 13–30. Moscow: Progress Publishers, 1970. marxists.org

———— [1847]. *Kommunismens röst: förklaring af det kommunistiska partiet.* Translated by Götrek Per (1848). Solna: Pogo Press, 1976.

Meidner, Rudolf. "Intervju i Fackföreningsrörelsen." *LO:s tidning*, no. 19 (1975).

Mies, Maria. *Patriarchy and Accumulation on a World Scale: Women in the International Division of Labour.* London: Zed Books, 1986.

Milberg, William. "Shifting Sources and Uses of Profits: Sustaining US Financialization with Global Value Chains." *Economy and Society* 37, no. 3 (2008): 420–451.

Mitchell, B. R. (ed.). *European Historical Statistics: Europe, 1750-1970.* London: Macmillan, 1975.

Mortensen, E. H. and Marcel Mirzaei-Fard. "Sidste danske teleselskab dropper 5G fra Huawei: Nu går kineserne efter 6G." Danish Radio and Television, November 19, 2020. https://www.dr.dk/nyheder/viden/teknologi/sidste-danske-teleselskab-dropper-5g-fra-huawei-nu-gaar-kineserne-efter-6g

Mounir, Karadja and Erik Prawitz. "Emigrationen till Amerika och den svenska arbetarrörelsen." *Ekonomisk Debatt* 46, no. 8 (2018): 19–29.

Mount Vernon. "Ten Fact about Washington & Slavery." mountvernon.org/george-washington/slavery/ten-facts-about-washington-slavery

Mudambi, R. "Location, Control and Innovation in Knowledge-Intensive Industries." *Journal of Economic Geography* 8, no. 5 (2008): 699–725.

Mukherjee, Supantha and Helena Soderpalm, "Sweden Bans Huawei, ZTE from Upcoming 5G Networks," *Reuters*, October 20, 2020. https://www.reuters.com/article/sweden-huawei-int-idUSKBN2750WA

Müller, Leos. "Svenska ostindiska kompaniet och den europeiska marknaden för te." In Bertil S. Olsson and Karl-Magnus Johansson, eds., *Sverige och svenskarna i den ostindiska handeln 2: Strategier, sammanhang och situationer*, 237–61. Göteborg: Riksarkivet, 2019.

Müller, Leos and Göran Rydén, "Nationell, transnationell eller global historia." *Historisk Tidsskrift* 129, no. 4 (2009): 559–667.

Ness, Immanuel and Zak Cope (eds.). *Palgrave Encyclopedia of Imperialism*. 2nd Edition. New York: Palgrave Macmillan, 2019.

Nilsson, David. *Sweden-Norway at the Berlin Conference 1884–85: History, National Identity-Making and Sweden's Relations with Africa*. Current African Issues 53. Uppsala: Nordiska Afrikainstitutet, 2013.

Norfield, Tony. "The China Price." Economics of Imperialism (blog), June 4, 2011. economicsofimperialism.blogspot.com

Norrestad, F. "Financial Assets of Pension Funds in Sweden in 2019, by Asset Type." *Statista*, November 20, 2020.

Nyanseor, Siahyonkron. "My LAMCO-Buchanan Experience." 2015. http://theliberiandialogue.org/2015/09/25/my-lamco-buchanan-experience

Nzongola-Ntalaja, Georges. *The Congo: From Leopold to Kabila: A People's History*. London: Zed Books, 2002.

OECD. "Average wages." https://data.oecd.org/earnwage/average-wages.htm

——— "Pension Markets In Focus 2019, Table A B.2."
2019. http://www.oecd.org/daf/fin/private-pensions/
PensionMarkets-in-Focus-2019.pdf

——— "Latvia: Review of the Financial System." April 2016.
http://oecd.org/finance/Latvia-financial-markets-2016.
pdf

Office of the Historian. *Foreign Relations of the United States,*
1964–1968, vol. 23, *Congo, 1960–1968.* history.state.gov

Olsen, Erling. *Danmarks økonomiske historie siden 1750.*
København: Gads forlag, 1962.

Olsson, Bertil S. and Karl-Magnus Johansson, eds., *Sverige*
och svenskarna i den ostindiska handeln 2: Strategier,
sammanhang och situationer. Göteborg: Riksarkivet, 2019.

Oscar II, "King Oscar II letter to Gillis Bildt." *I Gillis Bildts*
arkiv, vol. 1: *Brevväxling kungliga personer.* Avskrift
av brev—utdrag. Från Oscar II till Gillis Bildt.
Stockholm, December 7, 1884.

Palme, Olof. "En borgerlig regering—ett steg tillbaka,"
i Fackföreningsrörelsen, no. 17/18 (1968). Here from
Andersson, Stellan. "Biografiska notiser 1948." http://
www.olofpalme.org/personen/biografiska-notiser/1948

Palmstierna, Erik. *Orostid: politiska dagboksanteckningar,* vol. 2.
Stockholm: Tidens förlag, 1952.

Parner, Mats. *Tusentals stenkast från Storkyrkobrinken.*
lindelof.nu

Peters, Glenn P. "From Production-Based to Consumption-
Based National Emission Inventories." *Ecological*
Economics 65, no. 1 (2008): 13–23.

Pettersson, Thomas and Ewa Stenberg. "CIA villa värve den
unge Olof Palme." *Dagens Nyheter,* January 12, 2008.

Politiken. "USA forhandler om aftale for krigsskibe i
    Nordatlanten." *Politiken*, October 28, 2020. https://
    politiken.dk/udland/art7976578/USA-forhandler-om-
    aftale-for-krigsskibe-i-Nordatlanten

Pompeo, Michael R. "Communist China and the Free World's
    Future." July 23, 2020. Richard Nixon Presidential
    Library, Yorba Linda, CA. https://www.state.gov/
    communist-china-and-the-free-worlds-future

Prados, John. *Safe for Democracy: The Secret Wars of the CIA.*
    Chicago: Rowman & Littlefield, 2006.

Prandy, K., A. Stewart, and R. M. Blackburn. *White Collar
    Unionism.* London: Macmillan, 1983.

Prashad, Vijay and John Ross. "China is working to
    expand its ties to Latin America." *Peoples Dispatch*
    (website), November 10, 2020. https://peoplesdispatch.
    org/2020/11/10/china-is-working-to-expand-its-ties-to-
    latin-america

Proyect, Louis. "21st Century Socialism." CounterPunch
    (website), January 31, 2020. counterpunch.
    org/2020/01/31/21st-century-socialism

——— "Adalen 31." Louis Proyect, The Unrepentant
    Marxist (blog), April 15, 2015. https://louisproyect.
    org/2015/04/15/adalen-31

——— "Getting to the bottom of Swedish social democracy."
    Louis Proyect, The Unrepentant Marxist (blog),
    August 27, 2015. https://louisproyect.org/2015/08/27/
    getting-to-the-bottom-of-swedish-social-democracy

——— "How Swedish Social Democracy became neoliberal."
    Louis Proyect, The Unrepentant Marxist (blog),
    November 10, 2015. https://louisproyect.org/2015/11/10/
    how-swedish-social-democracy-became-neoliberal

—— "Nazi Germany and the Swedes." CounterPunch (website), October 17, 2014. https://www.counterpunch. org/2014/10/17/nazi-germany-and-the-swedes

—— "Sanders, Sweden and Socialism." Louis Proyect, The Unrepentant Marxist (blog), April 6, 2016. https://louisproyect.org/2016/04/06/ sanders-sweden-and-socialism/

—— "Sweden's Children." Louis Proyect, The Unrepentant Marxist (blog), July 15, 2015. https://louisproyect. org/2015/07/15/swedens-children

—— "Swedish colonialism, part 1: the persecution of the Sami." Louis Proyect, The Unrepentant Marxist (blog), July 7, 2015. https://louisproyect.org/2015/07/07/ swedish-colonialism-part-1-the-persecution-of-the-sami

—— "Swedish imperialism in Africa." Louis Proyect, The Unrepentant Marxist (blog), July 9, 2015. https://louisproyect.org/2015/07/09/swedish-imperialism-in-africa

—— "Swedish Social Democracy and the Gotha Programme." Louis Proyect, The Unrepentant Marxist (blog), August 19, 2015. https://louisproyect.org/2015/08/19/swedish-social-democracy-and-the-gotha-programme

—— "Swedish socialism and eugenics." Louis Proyect, The Unrepentant Marxist (blog), July 17, 2015. https://louisproyect.org/2015/07/17/swedish-socialism-and-eugenics

—— "The economic theory and policies of Swedish social democracy." Louis Proyect: The Unrepentant Marxist (blog), September 25, 2015. https://. org/2015/09/25/the-economic-theory-and-policies-of-swedish-social-democracy

—— "The Swedish model (part 1)." Louis Proyect: The Unrepentant Marxist (blog), May 24, 2015. https:// louisproyect.org/2015/05/24/the-swedish-model-part-1

—— "When the Swedish Social Democrats partnered with Nazi Germany in the name of neutrality." Louis Proyect, The Unrepentant Marxist (blog), August 5, 2015. https://louisproyect.org/2015/08/05/when-the-swedish-social-democrats-partnered-with-nazi-germany-in-the-name-of-neutrality

—— "Who rules Sweden?" Louis Proyect, The Unrepentant Marxist (blog), September 3, 2015. https://louisproyect.org/2015/11/10/how-swedish-social-democracy-became-neoliberal

Qiushi, **不断开拓当代中国**马克思主义政治经济学新境界 August 2020. http://www.qstheory.cn/dukan/qs/2020-08/15/c_1126365995.htm

Riddell, John (ed.). *Lenin's Struggle for a Revolutionary International*. New York: Pathfinder, 1984.

Roeber, Joe. *Parallel Markets: Corruption in the International Arms Trade*. London: Campaign Against Arms Trade, 2005.

Romero-Robayo, Carolina, Robert Palacios, Montserrat Pallares-Miralles, and Edward Whitehouse. *World Bank Pension Indicators and Database. Social Protection and Labor*. Washington, DC: World Bank, 2012.

Sahr, Robert. "Individual Year Conversion Factor Tables." Oregon State University, 2019.

Sakai, J. *Settlers: The Mythology of the White Proletariat from Mayflower to Modern*. Montreal & Oakland, CA: Kersplebedeb and PM Press, 2014.

Salih, Mohamed. "Poverty and Human Security in Africa:
    The Liberal Peace Debate." In *Peace and Conflict in
    Africa*, edited by David Francis, 171–84. London: Zed
    Press, 2009.

Sanders, Bernie. "Face the Nation", CBS TV, May 10, 2015.
    https://www.cbsnews.com/news/face-the-nation-
    transcripts-may-10-2015-huckabee-sanders-gingrich

Schmidt, Børge. *80 Louis Pio breve og en bibliografi*. København:
    Fremad, 1950.

Schön, L. "British Competition and Domestic Change:
    Textiles in Sweden 1820–1870." *Economy and History* 23,
    no. 1 (1980): 61–76.

Schoultz, Isabel and Janne Flyghed. "Denials and
    confessions. An analysis of the temporalization of
    neutralizations of corporate crime." *International
    Journal of Law, Crime and Justice* 62 (September 2020).
    https://www.sciencedirect.com/science/article/pii/
    S1756061619303623

Schröm, Oliver and Andrea Röpke. *Stille Hilfe für braune
    Kameraden—Das geheime Netzwerk der Alt- und Neonazis*.
    Berlin: Christoph Links Verlag, 2001.

Schumpeter, Joseph. *Imperialism and Social Classes*. Oxford:
    Blackwell, 1951.

Shahtahmasebi, Darius. "2021 Pentagon Budget Request
    Hints at Russia and China as New Focus of US
    Empire." *Mint Press*, February 24, 2020. https://www.
    mintpressnews.com/2021-pentagon-budget-request-
    russia-china/265124

Short, John Phillip. *Magic Lantern Empire: Colonialism and
    Society in Germany*. New York: Cornell University Press,
    2012.

SIPRI. "Global Arms Trade: USA Increases Dominance; Arms Flows to the Middle East Surge." *SIPRI* March 11, 2019.

Smith, John. "Imperialism & the Globalization of Production." Ph.D. dissertation. Department of Politics, University of Sheffield. thenextrecession.files. wordpress.com

—— *Imperialism in the Twenty First Century.* New York: Monthly Review Press, 2016.

—— "Marx's Capital and the Global Crisis." Paper presented at the conference, Imperialism: Old and New. New Delhi, 2015. https://www.researchgate. net/publication/271442711_Marx's_Capital_and_the_ global_crisis

Söderberg, Johan. "Long-term Trends in Real Wages of Laborers." In *Exchange Rates, Prices, and Wages, 1277– 2008*, edited by Rodney Edvinsson, Tor Jacobson, and Daniel Waldenström. Stockholm: Ekerlids Förlag, 2010.

Statistiska Centralbyrån. *Svenska koncerner med dotterbolag i utlandet 2018.* Östersund: Tillvaxtanalys, 2020. https://www.tillvaxtanalys.se/download/ 18.1235fa2a173481d283c948ea/1598464303883/ Svenska%20koncerner%20med%20dotterbolag%20 i%20utlandet%202018.pdf

Stavrianos, Leften Stavros. *Global Rift. The Third World Come of Age.* New York: William Morrow & Co., 1981.

Strandberg, Pierre. *Sill och Slaveri, C-uppsats,* VT 2020, Historia och kulturarvsstudier.

STV Nyheter. "H&M satsar i Etiopien—med svenska biståndspengar." STV Nyheter, February 18, 2018. svt.se/nyheter/utrikes/h-och-m-satsar-i-etiopien-med-svenska-bistandspengar

Suwandi, Intan and John Bellamy Foster. "Multinational Corporations and the Globalization of Monopoly Capital." *Monthly Review* 68, no. 3 (July–August 2016).

Svenska Freds. "Nya avslojanden om svenska vapen i kriget i Jemen." *Svenska Freds,* August 14, 2019. svenskafreds.se/ upptack/vapenexport/nya-avslojanden-om-svenska-vapen-i-kriget-i-jemen

Svenska Transportarbetareförbundet. *Dags för ett nytt Saltsjöbadsavtal?* (2009). https://da.wikipedia.org/wiki/ Saltsj%C3%B6badsaftalen

Svenskt Näringsliv. "Den svenska modellen har kantrat." April 2005. forsvarastrejkratten.files.wordpress. com/2018/10/den-svenska-modellen-har-kantrat-svenskt-nc3a4ringsliv.pdf

Sveriges Kommunistiska Parti / Uppsala (2016). *De svenska monopolkapitalisterna i Baltikum.* uppsala.skp.se/2016/ 10/27/de-svenska-monopolkapitalisterna-baltikum

Swedish Riksdag. *Rigsdagsprotokoll,* no. 53 (1983). riksdagen. se/sv/riksdagsbiblioteket/litteratur-och-tjanster/ sammanstallning-litteratur-och-tjanster/riksdagstryck

——— *Fred och säkerhet - säkerhetspolitiska utredningen, SOU 2002:108, December 20, 2001.* Stockholm: Statens offentliga utredningar, Utrikesdepartementet, 2002.

Thatcher, Margaret. Interview. *Woman's Own,* September 23, 1987. margaretthatcher.org/document/106689

The Baltic Course. "SEB ranks 1st among Lithuanian banks by assets, loans, Swedbank leads in deposits." *The Baltic Course*, March 9, 2016. http://www.baltic-course.com/eng/finances/?doc=117858

The Economist. "Companies Must Get Ready for a Riskier World," *The Economist*, July 13, 2019. https://www.economist.com/special-report/2019/07/11/companies-must-get-ready-for-a-riskier-world

—— "Back to Making Stuff. Special report: Manufacturing and Innovation." *The Economist*, April 21, 2012.

—— "The Match King." *The Economist*, December 19, 2007. economist.com/christmas-specials/2007/12/19/the-match-king

Tiejun, Wen. *Ten Crises: The Political Economy of China's Development (1949–2020)*. Global University for Sustainability Book Series. London: Palgrave Macmillan, 2021.

Timmer, Marcel P., Erik Dietzenbacher, Bart Los, Robert Stehrer, Gaaitzen J. de Vries. "An Illustrated User Guide to the World Input–Output Database: The Case of Global Automotive Production." *Review of International Economics* 23, no. 3 (August 2015): 575–605.

Togeby, Lisa. *Var de så røde?* København: Fremads Fokusbøger, 1968.

Trading Economics. "Sweden Home Ownership Rate." *Trading Economics*. https://tradingeconomics.com/sweden/home-ownership-rate

Train, John. *Berømte finansfiaskoer*. Oslo: Forlaget Periscopus, 1993.

Tsui, Sit, Erebus Wong, Lau Kin Chi, and Wen Tiejun. "Toward Delinking: An Alternative Chinese Path Amid the New Cold War." *Monthly Review* 72, no. 5 (October 2020): 15–31.

Tudor, H. and J. M. Tudor. *Marxism and Social Democracy: The Revisionist Debate, 1896–1898*. Cambridge: University Press, 1988.

Uchatius, Wolfgang. "Das Welthemd." *Die Zeit*, December 17, 2010. zeit.de/2010/51/Billige-T-Shirts

UNCTAD. *Handbook of Statistics, 2009*. New York & Geneva: United Nations. https://unctad.org/webflyer/unctad-handbook-statistics-2009 https://unctad.org/webflyer/unctad-handbook-statistics-2009

—— *GVCs and Development: Investment and Value Added Trade in the Global Economy*. Summary. Geneva: UNCTAD, 2013. https://unctad.org/system/files/official-document/diae2013d1_en.pdf

Upton, Anthony F. *The Finnish Revolution 1917–1918*. Minnesota: University of Minnesota Press, 1980.

US Department of State. *Growth in the Americas*. 2020. https://www.state.gov/growth-in-the-americas

—— *United States, Australia, India, and Japan Consultations (QUAD)*. 2020. https://www.state.gov/u-s-australia-india-japan-consultations-the-quad-3

Usnews.com. "Patrice Lumumba—Mysteries of History." *Usnews.com.* http://www.usnews.com/usnews/doubleissue/mysteries/patrice.htm

Wall Street Journal. "U.S. Holds Talks Over Economic, Security Arrangements with Greenland." *Wall Street Journal*, October 28, 2020. https://www.wsj.com/articles/u-s-holds-talks-over-economic-security-arrangements-with-greenland-11603927474

Wallerstein, Immanuel. *The Modern World-System: Capitalist Agriculture and the Origins of the European World-Economy in the Sixteenth Century.* New York: Academic Press, 1974.

Warren, Bill. "Myths of Underdevelopment: Imperialism and Capitalist Industrialization." *New Left Review* 81 (September–October, 1973): 3–44.

Weissman, Stephen. "Opening the Secret Files on Lumumba's Murder." *Washington Post*, July 21, 2002.

Widfeldt, Anders. "A Fourth Phase of the Extreme right? Nordic Immigration-critical Parties in a Comparative Context." *NORDEUROPAforum*, no. 1–2 (2010).

Widfeldt, Bo. *The Saab J 29.* Surrey, UK: Profile Publications Ltd., 1966.

Wiinblad, E. and Alsing Andersen. *Det danske socialdemokratis historie fra 1871 til 1921.* København: Forlaget Fremad, 1921.

Willerslev, Rich. "Svenske gæstearbejdere i København 1850–1914." *Fortid og Nutid*, no. 86 (1981).

Wilson, Bill. "Kreuger: The Original Bernard Madoff?" *BBC News*, March 13, 2009. news.bbc.co.uk

WIOD. Socio Economic Accounts (SEA), Release 2013 and 2016.

World Bank. "Arms-Length Trade." In *Global Economic Prospects.* pubdocs.worldbank.org

Xiaotian, Li. "The 996.ICU Movement in China: Changing
    Employment Relations and Labor Agency in the
    Tech Industry." *Made in China Journal* 4, no. 2 (2019).
    madeinchinajournal.com/2019/06/18/the-996-icu-
    movement-in-china-changing-employment-relations-
    and-labor-agency-in-the-tech-industry

Yergin, Daniel and Joseph Stanislaw. *Commanding Heights.*
    New York: Simon & Schuster, 1998.

Young, Crawford. "Ralph Bunche and Patrice Lumumba.
    The Fatal Encounter." In *Trustee for the Human
    Community, Ralph J. Bunche, the United Nations, and the
    Decolonization of Africa,* edited by Robert A. Hill and
    Edmond J. Keller. Ohio: Ohio University Press, 2010.

About the Author

Torkil Lauesen is a longtime anti-imperialist activist and writer living in Denmark. From 1970 to 1989, he was a full-time member of a communist anti-imperialist group, supporting Third World liberation movements by both legal and illegal means. He worked occasionally as a glass factory worker, mail carrier, and laboratory worker, in order to be able to stay on the dole. In connection with support work, he has traveled in Lebanon, Syria, Zimbabwe, South Africa, the Philippines, and Mexico. In the 1990s, while incarcerated, he was involved in prison activism and received a Master's degree in political science. He is currently a member of International Forum, an anti-imperialist organization based in Denmark.

ALL POWER TO THE PEOPLE

ALBERT "NUH" WASHINGTON • 1894820215 • 111 pp. • $10.00

A collection of writings by the late Albert Nuh Washington, a former member of the Black Panther Party and Black Liberation Army. One of the "New York 3", Washington was imprisoned in 1971 as a result of the U.S. government's war against the Black Liberation Movement; he died in prison almost thirty years later, on April 28, 2000, from cancer. (2002)

AMAZON NATION OR ARYAN NATION:
WHITE WOMEN AND THE COMING OF BLACK GENOCIDE

BOTTOMFISH BLUES • 9781894946551 • 160 pp. • $12.95

The massive New Afrikan uprisings of the 1960s were answered by the white ruling class with the destruction of New Afrikan communities coast to coast, the decimation of the New Afrikan working class, the rise of the prison state and an explosion of violence between oppressed people. Taken on their own, in isolation, these blights may seem to be just more "social issues" for NGOs to get grants for, but taken together and in the context of amerikkkan history, they constitute genocide. (2014)

A SOLDIER'S STORY: REVOLUTIONARY WRITINGS
BY A NEW AFRIKAN ANARCHIST, 3RD EDITION

KUWASI BALAGOON • 9781629633770 • 272 pp. • $19.95

Kuwasi Balagoon was a participant in the Black Liberation struggle from the 1960s until his death in prison in 1986. A member of the Black Panther Party and defendant in the infamous Panther 21 case, Balagoon went underground with the Black Liberation Army (BLA). Captured and convicted of various crimes against the State, he spent much of the 1970s in prison, escaping twice. After each escape, he went underground and resumed BLA activity. This is the most complete collection of his writings, poetry, and court statements ever collected, along with recollections from those who knew him, and who have been inspired by him since his passing. (2019)

BASIC POLITICS OF MOVEMENT SECURITY

J. SAKAI & MANDY HISCOCKS • 9781894946520 • 68 pp. • $7.00

Introducing the issues of movement security, and the political ramifications thereof. A transcript of a talk Sakai gave at the Montreal Anarchist Bookfair in 2013, and an interview with Hiscocks about how her political scene and groups she worked with were infiltrated by undercover agents a year before the 2010 G20 summit in Toronto. (2014)

BEGINNER'S KATA:
UNCENSORED STRAY THOUGHTS ON REVOLUTIONARY ORGANIZATION

J. SAKAI • NO ISBN • 15 pp. • $3.00

Plain talk with J. Sakai about what we do and don't know about revolutionary organization, and, indeed, about being revolutionaries. (2018)

CATEGORIES OF REVOLUTIONARY MILITARY POLICY

T. DERBENT • 9781894946438 • 52 pp. • $5.00

An educational survey of the concepts of military doctrine, strategy, tactics, operational art, bases of support, guerilla zones, liberated territories, and more. A study of what has been tried in the past, where different strategies worked, and where they failed, all from a perspective concerned with making revolution. (2013)

KERSPLEBEDEB, CP 63560, CCCP VAN HORNE, MONTREAL, QUEBEC, CANADA H3W 3H8

CHICAN@ POWER AND THE STRUGGLE FOR AZTLAN

CIPACTLI & EHECATL • 9781894946742 • 320 pp. • $22.95

From the Amerikan invasion and theft of Mexican lands, to present-day migrants risking their lives to cross the U.$. border, the Chican@ nation has developed in a cauldron of national oppression and liberation struggles. This book by a MIM(Prisons) Study Group presents the history of the Chican@ movement, exploring the colonialism and semi-colonialism that frames the Chican@ national identity. It also sheds new light on the modern repression and temptation that threaten liberation struggles by simultaneously pushing for submission and assimilation into Amerika. (2015)

THE COMMUNIST NECESSITY, 2ND EDITION

J. MOUFAWAD-PAUL • PREFACE BY DAO-YUAN CHOU • 9781989701003
168 pp. • $13.00

A polemical interrogation of the practice of "social movementism" that has enjoyed a normative status at the centers of capitalism. Aware of his past affinity with social movementism, and with some apprehension of the problem of communist orthodoxy, the author argues that the recognition of communism's necessity "requires a new return to the revolutionary communist theories and experiences won from history." (2020)

CONFRONTING FASCISM: DISCUSSION DOCUMENTS FOR A MILITANT MOVEMENT, 2ND EDITION

XTN, D. HAMERQUIST, J.SAKAI, M. SALOTTE • 9781894946872 • 219 pp. • $14.95

Essays grappling with the class appeal of fascism, its continuities and breaks with the "regular" far right and also even with the Left. First published in 2002, written from the perspective of revolutionaries active in the struggle against the far right. (2017)

THE DANGEROUS CLASS AND REVOLUTIONARY THEORY: THOUGHTS ON THE MAKING OF THE LUMPEN/PROLETARIAT

J. SAKAI • 9781894946902 • 308 pp. • $24.95

This book starts with the paper of that name, on the birth of the modern lumpen/prole-tariat in the 18th and 19th centuries and the storm cloud of revolutionary theory that has always surrounded them. Going back and piecing together both the actual social reality and the analyses primarily of Marx but also Bakunin and Engels, the paper shows how Marx's class theory wasn't something static. His views learned in quick jumps, and then all but reversed themselves in several significant aspects. While at first dismissing them in the Communist Manifesto as "that passively rotting mass" at the obscure lower depths, Marx soon realized that the lumpen could be players at the very center of events in revolutionary civil war. Even at the center in the startling rise of new regimes. This is followed by the detailed paper "Mao Z's Revolutionary Laboratory and the Role of the Lumpen/Proletariat." As Sakai points out, the left's euro-centrism here prevented it from realizing the obvious: that the basic theory from European radicalism about the lumpen/ proletariat was first fully tested not there or here but in the Chinese Revolution of 1921– 1949. Under severely clashing political lines in the left, the class analysis finally used by Mao Z was shaken out of the shipping crate from Europe and then modified to map the organizing of millions over a prolonged generational revolutionary war. One could hardly wish for a larger test tube, and the many lessons to be learned from this mass political experience are finally put on the table. (2017)

KERSPLEBEDEB, CP 63560, CCCP VAN HORNE, MONTREAL, QUEBEC, CANADA H3W 3H8

DARING TO STRUGGLE, FAILING TO WIN:
THE RED ARMY FACTION'S 1977 CAMPAIGN OF DESPERATION
ANDRÉ MONCOURT & J. SMITH • 9781604860283 • 43 pp. • $4.00

Emerging from the West German New Left in the early 1970s, the Red Army Faction was to become the most well-known urban guerilla group in Europe, remaining active into the 1990s. This pamphlet looks at the RAF's activities in the seventies, and how their struggle to free their prisoners culminated in a campaign of assassinations and kidnappings in 1977. (2008)

DEFYING THE TOMB: SELECTED PRISON WRITINGS AND ART OF
KEVIN "RASHID" JOHNSON FEATURING EXCHANGES WITH AN OUTLAW
KEVIN "RASHID" JOHNSON • 9781894946391 • 386 pp. • $20.00

In a series of smuggled prison letters and early essays, follow the author's odyssey from lumpen drug dealer to prisoner, to revolutionary New Afrikan, a teacher and mentor, one of a new generation rising of prison intellectuals. (2010)

DIVIDED WORLD DIVIDED CLASS: GLOBAL POLITICAL ECONOMY AND
THE STRATIFICATION OF LABOUR UNDER CAPITALISM, 2ND ED.
ZAK COPE • 9781894946681 • 460 pp. • $24.95

The history of the "labour aristocracy" in the capitalist world system, from its roots in colonialism to its birth and eventual maturation into a full-fledged middle class in the age of imperialism. Pervasive national, racial, and cultural chauvinism in the core capitalist countries is not primarily attributable to "false class consciousness" or ignorance as much left and liberal thinking assumes. Rather, these and related forms of bigotry are concentrated expressions of the major social strata of the core capitalist nations' shared economic interest in the exploitation and repression of dependent nations. (2012)

ESCAPING THE PRISM ... FADE TO BLACK
JALIL MUNTAQIM • 9781894946629 • 320 pp. • $20.00

Jalil Muntaqim is a former member of the Black Panther Party and the Black Liberation Army. For over forty years, Jalil was a political prisoner, one of the New York Three, in retaliation for his activism. This book contains poetry and essays from behind the bars of Attica prison, combining the personal and the political, affording readers with a rare opportunity to get to know a man who spent most of his life behind bars for his involvement in the Black Liberation Movement. Includes an extensive examination of the U.S. government's war against the Black Liberation Army in general, and Jalil in particular, by Ward Churchill, and an introduction by Walidah Imarisha. (2015)

EUROCENTRISM AND THE COMMUNIST MOVEMENT
ROBERT BIEL • 9781894946711 • 215 pp. • $17.95

A work of intellectual history, exploring the relationship between Eurocentrism, alienation, and racism, while tracing the different ideas about imperialism, colonialism, "progress", and non-European peoples as they were grappled with by revolutionaries in both the colonized and colonizing nations. Teasing out racist errors and anti-racist insights within this history, Biel reveals a century-long struggle to assert the centrality of the most exploited within the struggle against capitalism. The roles of key figures in the Marxist-Leninist canon—Marx, Engels, Lenin, Stalin, Mao—are explored, as are those of others whose work may be less familiar to some readers, such as Sultan Galiev, Lamine Senghor, Lin Biao, R. P. Dutt, Samir Amin, and others. (2015)

KERSPLEBEDEB, CP 63560, CCCP VAN HORNE, MONTREAL, QUEBEC, CANADA H3W 3H8

EXODUS AND RECONSTRUCTION:
WORKING-CLASS WOMEN AT THE HEART OF GLOBALIZATION
BROMMA • 9781894946421 • 37 pp. • $3.00

The position of women at the heart of a transformed global proletariat: "Family-based rural patriarchy was so deeply imbedded within capitalism for so long that abandoning it was nearly unthinkable. A change of such magnitude would require the development of much more advanced global transportation and commodity markets and a tremendous reorganization of labor. It would require a major overhaul of political systems everywhere. It would be a sea-change in capitalism. That sea-change is what's happening now." (2013)

FALSE NATIONALSM FALSE INTERNATIONALISM:
CLASS CONTRADICTIONS IN THE ARMED STRUGGLE
E. TANI AND KAÉ SERA • 9781989701089 • 327 pp. • $26.95

A critical history of revisionism, opportunism, and parasitical relationships between white and Black revolutionary organizations in the United States. Chapters address important aspects of the Russian and Chinese revolutions; different forms of solidarity with the antifascist resistance in Spain and Ethiopia; the racist settlerist machinations of the CPUSA; relationships between revolutionaries in the New Left, including the Weather Underground and the Black Panther Party; and, finally, the tragic experiences of the Revolutionary Armed Task Force. This book first appeared in 1985 as an attempt to evaluate the rise in radical armed activity in the U.S. during the 1960s and 1970s from an activist perspective. (2021)

FULL BODY SCAN: IMPERIALISM TODAY
GABRIEL KUHN & BROMMA • 9781894946957 • 36 pp. • $4.00

Gabriel Kuhn's "Oppressor and Oppressed Nations: Sketching a Taxonomy of Imperialism", with a response from Bromma, debating the nature of nations, nation-states, and countries, and the distribution of privilege and potential in the world today. (2018)

THE GREEN NAZI: AN INVESTIGATION INTO FASCIST ECOLOGY
J. SAKAI • 0968950396 • 34 pp. • $3.00

A critical look at the relationship between social and natural purity, the green movement and the far right, settlerism and genocide. The text jumps off from a review of Blood and Soil, a book by academic Anna Bramwell, disputing her flattering portrayal of Third Reich Imperial Peasant Leader Walther Darre. (2002)

THE HISTORICAL FAILURE OF ANARCHISM:
IMPLICATIONS FOR THE FUTURE OF THE REVOLUTIONARY PROJECT
CHRISTOPHER DAY • 9781894946452 • 26 pp. • $4.00

An exposition of the failure of anarchism to successfully carry out or defend revolution in the 20th century, raising questions for the future. (2009)

INSURGENT SUPREMACISTS:
THE U.S. FAR RIGHT'S CHALLENGE TO STATE AND EMPIRE
MATTHEW LYONS • 9781629635118 • 384 pp. • $24.95

A major study of movements that strive to overthrow the U.S. government, that often claim to be anti-imperialist and sometimes even anti-capitalist yet also consciously promote inequality, hierarchy, and domination, generally along explicitly racist, sexist, and homophobic lines. Revolutionaries of the far right: insurgent supremacists.

Intervening directly in debates within left and anti-fascist movements, Lyons examines both the widespread use and abuse of the term "fascism" and the relationship between federal security forces and the paramilitary right. His final chapter offers a preliminary analysis of the Trump Administration's relationship with far-right politics and the organized far right's shifting responses to it. (2018)

IS CHINA AN IMPERIALIST COUNTRY?
N.B. TURNER ET AL. • 9781894946759 • 173 pp. • $17.00
Whether or not China is now a capitalist-imperialist country is an issue on which there is some considerable disagreement, even within the revolutionary left. This book brings together theoretical, definitional and logical considerations, as well as the extensive empirical evidence that is now available, to demonstrate that China has indeed definitely become a capitalist-imperialist country. (2015)

JAILBREAK OUT OF HISTORY:
THE RE-BIOGRAPHY OF HARRIET TUBMAN, 2ND EDITION
BUTCH LEE • 9781894946704 • 169 pp. • $14.95
Anticolonial struggles of New Afrikan/Black women were central to the unfolding of 19th-century amerika, both during and "after" slavery. "The Re-Biography of Harriet Tubman" recounts the life and politics of Harriet Tubman, who waged and eventually led the war against the capitalist slave system. "The Evil of Female Loaferism" details New Afrikan women's attempts to withdraw from and evade capitalist colonialism, an unofficial but massive labor strike which threw the capitalists North and South into a panic. The ruling class response consisted of the "Black Codes", Jim Crow, re-enslavement through prison labor, mass violence, and ... the establishment of a neocolonial Black patriarchy, whose task was to make New Afrikan women subordinate to New Afrikan men just as New Afrika was supposed to be subordinate to white amerika. (2015)

LEARNING FROM AN UNIMPORTANT MINORITY
J. SAKAI • 9781894946605 • 118 pp. • $10.00
Race is all around us, as one of the main structures of capitalist society. Yet, how we talk about it and even how we think about it is tightly policed. Everything about race is artificially distorted as a white/Black paradigm. Instead, we need to understand the imposed racial reality from many different angles of radical vision. In this talk given at the 2014 Montreal Anarchist Bookfair, J. Sakai shares experiences from his own life as a revolutionary in the united states, exploring what it means to belong to an "unimportant minority." (2015)

LOOKING AT THE U.S. WHITE WORKING CLASS HISTORICALLY
DAVID GILBERT • 9781894946919 • 97 pp. • $10.00
On the one hand, "white working class" includes a class designation that should imply, along with all other workers of the world, a fundamental role in the overthrow of capitalism. On the other hand, there is the identification of being part of a ("white") oppressor nation. Political prisoner David Gilbert seeks to understand the origins of this contradiction, its historical development, as well as possibilities to weaken and ultimately transform the situation. (2017)

LUMPEN: THE AUTOBIOGRAPHY OF ED MEAD

ED MEAD • 9781894946780 • 360 pp. • $20.00

When a thirteen-year-old Ed Mead ends up in the Utah State Industrial School, a prison for boys, it is the first step in a story of oppression and revolt that will ultimately lead to the foundation of the George Jackson Brigade, a Seattle-based urban guerrilla group, and to Mead's re-incarceration as a fully engaged revolutionary, well-placed and prepared to take on both his captors and the predators amongst his fellow prisoners. This is his story, and there is truly nothing like it. (2015)

MEDITATIONS ON FRANTZ FANON'S WRETCHED OF THE EARTH: NEW AFRIKAN REVOLUTIONARY WRITINGS

JAMES YAKI SAYLES • 9781894946322 • 399 pp. • $20.00

One of those who eagerly picked up Fanon in the 60s, who carried out armed expropriations and violence against white settlers, Sayles reveals how behind the image of Fanon as race thinker there is an underlying reality of antiracist communist thought. From the book: "This exercise is about more than our desire to read and understand Wretched (as if it were about some abstract world, and not our own); it's about more than our need to understand (the failures of) the anti-colonial struggles on the African continent. This exercise is also about us, and about some of the things that We need to understand and to change in ourselves and our world." (2010)

THE MILITARY STRATEGY OF WOMEN AND CHILDREN

BUTCH LEE • 0973143231 • 116 pp. • $12.00

Lays out the need for an autonomous and independent women's revolutionary movement, a revolutionary women's culture that involves not only separating oneself from patriarchal imperialism, but also in confronting, opposing, and waging war against it by all means necessary. (2003)

MY ENEMY'S ENEMY: ESSAYS ON GLOBALIZATION, FASCISM AND THE STRUGGLE AGAINST CAPITALISM

ANTI-FASCIST FORUM • 0973143231 • 116 pp. • $10.00

Articles by anti-fascist researchers and political activists from Europe and North America, examining racist and pro-capitalist tendencies within the movement against globalization. (2003)

NIGHT-VISION: ILLUMINATING WAR AND CLASS ON THE NEO-COLONIAL TERRAIN, 2ND EDITION

BUTCH LEE AND RED ROVER • 9781894946889 • 264 pp. • $17.00

A foundational analysis of post-modern capitalism, the decline of u.s. hegemony, and the need for a revolutionary movement of the oppressed to overthrow it all. From Night-Vision: "The transformation to a neo-colonial world has only begun, but it promises to be as drastic, as disorienting a change as was the original european colonial conquest of the human race. Capitalism is again ripping apart & restructuring the world, and nothing will be the same. Not race, not nation, not gender, and certainly not whatever culture you used to have. Now you have outcast groups as diverse as the Aryan Nation and the Queer Nation and the Hip Hop Nation publicly rejecting the right of the u.s. government to rule them. All the building blocks of human culture— race, gender, nation, and especially class—are being transformed under great pressure to embody the spirit of this neo-colonial age." (2009)

KERSPLEBEDEB, CP 63560, CCCP VAN HORNE, MONTREAL, QUEBEC, CANADA H3W 3H8

1978: A NEW STAGE IN THE CLASS WAR?
SELECTED DOCUMENTS ON THE SPRING CAMPAIGN OF THE RED BRIGADES
ED. JOSHUA DEPAOLIS • 9781894946995 • 218 pp. • $19.95

For the first time in English, a selection of the key documents on the strategic logic and conjunctural analysis behind the 1978 offensive of the Red Brigades, the kidnapping and execution of Italy's President Aldo Moro, which brought the BR's strategy of "attack on the heart of the state" to a climax and induced a national political crisis. The book includes: the February 1978 "Resolution of the Strategic Leadership," the nine communiqués issued by the group during Moro's captivity, the editorial "Achtung Banditi" from the June 1978 issue of the Marxist-Leninist journal Corrispondenza Internazionale, and the March 1979 document "The Spring Campaign: Capture, Trial and Execution of the President of the DC, Aldo Moro." (2019)

NOTES TOWARD AN UNDERSTANDING OF CAPITALIST CRISIS & THEORY
J. SAKAI • 1894946316 • 25 pp. • $2.00

An examination of Marx's theories of capitalist crisis, in light of the current economic crisis, asking some tentative questions about what it all might mean in terms of strategy, and things to come. (2009)

ON THE VANGUARD ONCE AGAIN...
KEVIN "RASHID" JOHNSON • 9781894946445 • 23 pp. • $4.00

A response to anarchist criticisms of Marxism-Leninism, defending the concepts of the vanguard party and democratic centralism, from the perspective of the New Afrikan Black Panther Party Prison Chapter. (2013)

OUR COMMITMENT IS TO OUR COMMUNITIES:
MASS INCARCERATION, POLITICAL PRISONERS,
AND BUILDING A MOVEMENT FOR COMMUNITY-BASED JUSTICE
DAVID GILBERT • 9781894946650 • 34 pp. • $5.00

In this pamphlet, interviewed by Bob Feldman, political prisoner David Gilbert discusses the ongoing catastrophe that is mass incarceration, connecting it to the continued imprisonment of political prisoners and the challenges that face our movements today. (2014)

PANTHER VISION: ESSENTIAL PARTY WRITINGS AND ART OF
KEVIN "RASHID" JOHNSON, MINISTER OF DEFENSE,
NEW AFRIKAN BLACK PANTHER PARTY-PRISON CHAPTER
KEVIN "RASHID" JOHNSON • 9781894946766 • 496 pp. • $24.95

Subjects addressed include the differences between anarchism and Marxism-Leninism, the legacy of the Black Panther Party, the timeliness of Huey P. Newton's concept of revolutionary intercommunalism, the science of dialectical and historical materialism, the practice of democratic centralism, as well as current events ranging from u.s. imperialist designs in Africa to national oppression of New Afrikans within u.s. borders. And much more. (2015)

PRISON ROUND TRIP
KLAUS VIEHMANN • PREFACE BY BILL DUNNE • 9781604860825 • 25 pp. • $3.00

First published in German in 2003 as "Einmal Knast und zurück." The essay's author, Klaus Viehmann, had been released from prison ten years earlier, after completing a 15-year sentence for his involvement in urban guerilla activities in Germany in the 1970s. Here he reflects on how to keep one's sanity and political integrity within the hostile and oppressive prison environment; "survival strategies" are its central theme. (2009)

THE RED ARMY FACTION, A DOCUMENTARY HISTORY
VOLUME 1: PROJECTILES FOR THE PEOPLE
ANDRE MONCOURT & J. SMITH EDS. • 9781604860290 • 736 pp. • $34.95

For the first time ever in English, this volume presents all of the manifestos and communiqués issued by the RAF between 1970 and 1977. Providing the background information that readers will require to understand the context in which these events occurred, separate thematic sections deal with the 1976 murder of Ulrike Meinhof in prison, the 1977 Stammheim murders, the extensive use of psychological operations and false-flag attacks to discredit the guerilla, the state's use of sensory deprivation torture and isolation wings, and the prisoners' resistance to this, through which they inspired their own supporters and others on the left to take the plunge into revolutionary action. With introductions by Russell Maroon Shoatz and Bill Dunne. (2009)

THE RED ARMY FACTION, A DOCUMENTARY HISTORY
VOLUME 2: DANCING WITH IMPERIALISM
ANDRE MONCOURT & J. SMITH EDS. • 9781604860306 • 480 pp. • $26.95

This work includes the details of the Red Army Faction's operations, and its communiqués and texts, from 1978 up until its 1984 offensive. This was a period of regrouping and reorientation for the RAF, with its previous focus on freeing its prisoners replaced by an anti-NATO orientation. Subjects examined include: the possibilities and perils of an armed underground organization relating to the broader movement, the contrasting experiences of the Revolutionary Cells and 2nd of June Movement, the emergence of the Autonomen, accusations of the RAF's relationship to the East German Stasi, and the abortive attempt by West Germany's liberal intelligentsia to defuse the armed struggle during Gerhard Baum's tenure as Minister of the Interior. With an introduction by Ward Churchill. (2013)

REMEMBERING THE ARMED STRUGGLE: LIFE WITH THE RED ARMY FACTION
MARGRIT SCHILLER • 9781629638737 • 239 pp. • $19.95

Former Red Army Faction political prisoner Margrit Schiller recounts the process through which she joined her generation's revolt in the 1960s, going from work with drug users to joining the antipsychiatry political organization the Socialist Patients' Collective and then the RAF. She tells of how she met and worked alongside the group's founding members, Ulrike Meinhof, Andreas Baader, Jan-Carl Raspe, Irmgard Möller, and Holger Meins; how she learned the details of the May Offensive and other actions while in her prison cell; about the struggles to defend human dignity in the most degraded of environments, and the relationships she forged with other women in prison. (2021)

SETTLERS: THE MYTHOLOGY OF THE WHITE PROLETARIAT
FROM MAYFLOWER TO MODERN
J. SAKAI • 9781629630373 • 456 pp. • $20.00

America's white citizenry have never supported themselves but have always resorted to exploitation and theft, culminating in acts of genocide to maintain their culture and way of life. As recounted in painful detail by Sakai, the United States has been built on the theft of Indigenous lands and of Afrikan labor, on the robbery of the northern third of Mexico, the colonization of Puerto Rico, and the expropriation of the Asian working class, with each of these crimes being accompanied by violence. This new edition includes "Cash & Genocide: The True Story of Japanese-American Reparations" and an interview with author J. Sakai by Ernesto Aguilar. (2014)

STAND UP STRUGGLE FORWARD: NEW AFRIKAN REVOLUTIONARY WRITINGS ON NATION, CLASS AND PATRIARCHY

SANYIKA SHAKUR • 9781894946469 • 208 pp. • $13.95

Firmly rooted in the New Afrikan Communist tradition, laying bare the deeper connections between racism, sexism, and homophobia and how these mental diseases relate to the ongoing capitalist (neo-)colonial catastrophe we remain trapped within. (2013)

STRIKE ONE TO EDUCATE ONE HUNDRED: THE RISE OF THE RED BRIGADES 1960s-1970s

CHRIS ARONSON BECK, REGGIE EMILIANA, LEE MORRIS, AND OLLIE PATTERSON • 9781894946988 • 296 PP. • $24.95

Today there are many books and countless papers and articles about the Red Brigades' history, but most are from a police and state point of view. Strike One is a unique and practically useful work, because it tells the other side, of innovative anti-capitalism. It details how the spectre of urban guerrilla warfare grew at last out of the industrial centers of modern Italy, showing how this was a political project of a young working class layer that was fed up with reformism's lies. The authors, who were varied supporters who chose to remain anonymous due to Italy and NATO's draconian "anti-terrorist" laws, tell much of this story in the militants' own words: in translations of key political documents, news reports, and communiqués. Indispensable. (2019)

THE STRUGGLE WITHIN: PRISONS, POLITICAL PRISONERS, AND MASS MOVEMENTS IN THE UNITED STATES

DAN BERGER • 9781604869552 • 128 pp. • $12.95

An accessible, wide-ranging historical primer about how mass imprisonment has been a tool of repression deployed against diverse left-wing social movements over the last fifty years. Berger examines some of the most dynamic social movements across half a century: Black liberation, Puerto Rican independence, Native American sovereignty, Chicano radicalism, white antiracist and working-class mobilizations, pacifist and antinuclear campaigns, and earth liberation and animal rights. (2014)

WHEN RACE BURNS CLASS: SETTLERS REVISITED

J. SAKAI • 9781894820264 • 32 pp. • $4.00

An interview with author J. Sakai about his groundbreaking work Settlers: Mythology of the White Proletariat, accompanied by Kuwasi Balagoon's essay "The Continuing Appeal of Imperialism." Sakai discusses how he came to write Settlers, the relationship of settlerism to racism and between race and class, the prospects for organizing within the white working class, and the rise of the far right. (2011)

THE WORKER ELITE: NOTES ON THE "LABOR ARISTOCRACY"

BROMMA • 9781894946575 • 88 pp. • $10.00

Revolutionaries often say that the working class holds the key to overthrowing capitalism. But "working class" is a very broad category—so broad that it can be used to justify a whole range of political agendas. Bromma breaks it all down, criticizing opportunists who minimize the role of privilege within the working class, while also challenging simplistic Third Worldist analyses. (2014)

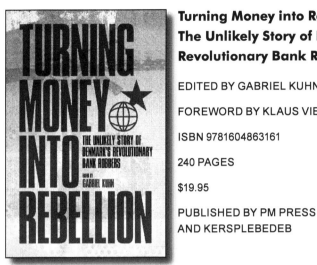

Turning Money into Rebellion: The Unlikely Story of Denmark's Revolutionary Bank Robbers

EDITED BY GABRIEL KUHN

FOREWORD BY KLAUS VIEHMANN

ISBN 9781604863161

240 PAGES

$19.95

PUBLISHED BY PM PRESS
AND KERSPLEBEDEB

Blekingegade is a quiet street in Copenhagen. It is also where, in May 1989, the police discovered an apartment that had served Denmark's most notorious twentieth-century bank robbers as a hideaway for years.

One of the most captivating chapters from the European anti-imperialist milieu of the 1970s and '80s; the Blekingegade Group had emerged from a communist organization whose analysis of the metropolitan labor aristocracy led them to develop an illegal Third Worldist practice. While members lived modest lives, over a period of almost two decades they sent millions of dollars acquired in spectacular heists to Third World liberation movements.

Turning Money into Rebellion includes historical documents, illustrations, and an exclusive interview with Torkil Lauesen and Jan Weimann, two of the group's longest-standing members. It is a compelling tale of turning radical theory into action and concerns analysis and strategy as much as morality and political practice. Perhaps most importantly, it revolves around the cardinal question of revolutionary politics: What to do, and how to do it?

KERSPLEBEDEB, CP 63560, CCCP VAN HORNE, MONTREAL, QUEBEC, CANADA H3W 3H8

**Marx & Engels
On Colonies,
Industrial Monopoly and
the Working Class Movement**

INTRODUCTION BY ZAK COPE
AND TORKIL LAUESEN

ISBN 9781894946797

160 PAGES • $10.00

Excerpts from the corpus of Marx and Engels, showing the evolution of their ideas on the nascent labor aristocracy and the complicating factors of colonialism and chauvinism, with a focus on the British Empire of their time. In their introduction, Cope and Lauesen show how Marx and Engels's initial belief that capitalism would extend seamlessly around the globe in the same form was proven wrong by events, as instead worldwide imperialism spread capitalism as a polarizing process, not only between the bourgeoisie and the working class, but also as a division between an imperialist center and an exploited periphery.

KERSPLEBEDEB, CP 63560, CCCP VAN HORNE, MONTREAL, QUEBEC, CANADA H3W 3H8

V.I. Lenin
On Imperialism
& Opportunism

INTRODUCTION BY
TORKIL LAUESEN

ISBN 9781894946940

191 PAGES • $13.00

This collection of texts by V.I. Lenin was originally compiled by the Communist Working Circle, a Danish anti-imperialist group. In the late 1960s, the CWC developed the "parasite state" theory linking the imperialist exploitation and oppression of the proletariat in the Global South with the establishment of states in the Global North in which the working class lives in relative prosperity. In connection with studies of this division of the world, CWC published these texts by Lenin with the title "On Imperialism and Opportunism."

What is the relevance of these texts today? Firstly, the connection that Lenin posits between imperialism and opportunism—that is, the sacrifice of long--term socialist goals for short-term or sectional gains—is more pronounced than ever. Second, imperialism may, in many respects, have changed its economic mechanisms and its political form, but its content is fundamentally the same, namely, a transfer of value from the Global South to the Global North.

With an introduction by former CWC member Torkil Lauesen.

KERSPLEBEDEB, CP 63560, CCCP VAN HORNE, MONTREAL, QUEBEC, CANADA H3W 3H8

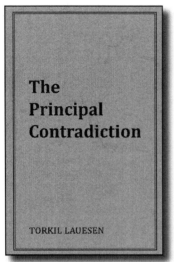

The Principal Contradiction

BY TORKIL LAUESEN

ISBN 9781989701034

157 PAGES

$14.95

Dialectical materialism allows us to understand the dynamics of world history, the concept of contradiction building a bridge between theory and practice, with the principal contradiction telling us where to start.

Drawing on his own decades of experience as an anti-imperialist, Lauesen shows how dialectical materialism can be employed as a method to understand the past five hundred years of capitalist history, how contradictions internal to European capitalism led to colonialism and genocide in Asia, Africa, and the Americas, as all humanity was brought into a single exploitative world system. The globalized capitalist system has developed through successive and changing principal contradictions, decisively impacting regional, national, and local contradictions. This has in turn given rise to new reactions, interacting with and modifying the principal contradiction. Identifying the principal contradiction is indispensable for developing a global perspective on capitalism. This methodology is not just a valuable tool with which to analyze complex relationships: it also tells us how to intervene.

KERSPLEBEDEB, CP 63560, CCCP VAN HORNE, MONTREAL, QUEBEC, CANADA H3W 3H8

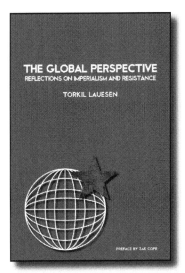

The Global Perspective: Reflections on Imperialism and Resistance

BY TORKIL LAUESEN

ISBN 9781894946933

544 PAGES

$24.95

We today live in a world of massive and unprecedented inequality. Never before has humanity been so starkly divided between the "haves" and the "have nots." Never before has the global situation been accelerating so quickly. The Third World national liberation movements of the 20th century very much triggered the liberatory movements that did manage to emerge in the First World, and seemed for an all-too-brief moment to point to an escape hatch from history's downward spiral ... but for many today that all seems like ancient history.

The Global Perspective bridges the gap between Third Worldist theory and the question of "What Is To Be Done?" in a First World context. As Lauesen explains, "It is a book written by an activist, for activists. Global capitalism is heading into a deep structural crisis in the coming decades, so the objective conditions for radical change will be present, for better or for worse. The outcome will depend on us, the subjective forces."

KERSPLEBEDEB, CP 63560, CCCP VAN HORNE, MONTREAL, QUEBEC, CANADA H3W 3H8

KER
SPL
EBE
DEB

Since 1998 Kersplebedeb has been an important source of radical literature and agit prop materials.

The project has a non-exclusive focus on anti-patriarchal and anti-imperialist politics, framed within an anticapitalist perspective. A special priority is given to writings regarding armed struggle in the metropole, the continuing struggles of political prisoners and prisoners of war, and the political economy of imperialism.

The Kersplebedeb website presents historical and contemporary writings by revolutionary thinkers from the anarchist and communist traditions.

Kersplebedeb can be contacted at:

Kersplebedeb
CP 63560
CCCP Van Horne
Montreal, Quebec
Canada
H3W 3H8

email: info@kersplebedeb.com
web: www.kersplebedeb.com
www.leftwingbooks.net

Kersplebedeb